Collins

English GCSE for AQA

English Language
Targeting Grade C
Student Book

Keith Brindle
and Mike Gould

Published by Collins Education
An imprint of HarperCollins Publishers
77-85 Fulham Palace Road
Hammersmith
London
W6 8JB

Browse the complete Collins catalogue at
www.collinseducation.com

© HarperCollins Publishers Limited 2010

10 9 8 7 6 5 4 3 2 1

ISBN 978 0 00 734211 2

Keith Brindle and Mike Gould assert their █████ rights to be identified as the authors of this work.

British Library Cataloguing in Publication Data.
A Catalogue record for this publication is available from the British Library.

Editor: Catherine Martin
Design and typesetting by EMC Design
Cover Design by Angela English
Printed and bound by L.E.G.O. SpA, Lavis, Italy

With particular thanks to Lucy Hobbs, Caroline Green and Jill Thraves.

Contents

What's it all about?

Being able to analyse the different kinds of non-fiction texts that we meet every day is an important life skill. It helps you understand how writers try to influence their readers. For the exam, you need to be able to move beyond describing what a text is about into explaining how effects are achieved and analysing why particular features are effective. The ability to compare texts will also help you to cope well with the demands of the exam.

How will I be assessed?

- You will get **20% of your English Language marks** for your ability to deal with close-reading questions in the exam.
- You will have to answer questions based on your reading of **three** non-fiction texts. You will not have seen these texts before the exam.
- The questions will carry a total of **40 marks**.

- This forms Section A of the exam paper and you will have **one hour** to complete it.

What is being tested?

You are being examined on your ability to

- read and respond to the texts, focusing on the questions
- select facts, details and quotations from the texts to answer the questions
- interpret the texts
- use evidence from the texts to support your answers
- compare the language used in the texts
- explain and evaluate how writers use language, grammar, structure and presentational features to achieve effects and engage and influence the reader.

Above all, it's important to understand the kinds of questions you are likely to be asked in the exam. This chapter will develop your close-reading and offer you practice in the necessary skills.

Understanding Non-fiction Texts and Writers' Choices

Introduction

This section of Chapter 1 helps you to

- explore a range of non-fiction texts and their features
- prepare to analyse texts in the exam.

Why is the close reading of different texts important?

- In everyday life, we are surrounded by texts which attempt to influence us, so knowledge of how they work is vital.
- You will be tested on your understanding of non-fiction texts in the exam.

A **Grade E** candidate will

- show some understanding of the texts and use some relevant quotation to support their ideas
- attempt to interpret features of the texts and offer some explanations.

E

A **Grade D** candidate will

- show understanding of the texts and use appropriate quotations to support their ideas
- interpret features of the texts and offer explanations that show understanding.

D

A **Grade C** candidate will

- show a clear understanding of the texts and use relevant quotations to demonstrate understanding
- offer clear explanations and will make personal and analytical responses, referring to specific aspects of language, grammar, structure and presentational features to justify their views.

C

Prior learning

Before you begin this unit, think about

- the many kinds of non-fiction texts you read in a day, and how they are different

  Can you list them all? What are the main features of each one?

- the different purposes of those texts

  Are they informing you, persuading you, entertaining you?

- what you learnt about non-fiction texts at Key Stage 3.

  How many technical terms for features can you use: headline, caption, pull-quote?

What are non-fiction texts?

Learning objectives

- *To consider a range of non-fiction texts.*
- *To begin to identify what makes them different.*

What does the term non-fiction mean?

Non-fiction texts are about reality, for example:

- **journalistic text** – an article, a report, a leader from a newspaper
- **informative text** – a leaflet, a set of instructions, rules, a guide
- **biographical writing**, when someone writes about the life of someone else, or **autobiographical writing**, when they write about their own experiences
- **travel writing**
- an extract from a **diary** or a **blog**
- a **letter**, perhaps of a personal kind or for publication
- an **advertisement**
- a **webpage**.

In the exam, you will have to respond to three short non-fiction texts of different kinds. They will not be from a novel, short story or play and there will not be any poetry.

Checklist for success

- If you read a different kind of non-fiction text every day, you will become more used to their different purposes and styles.
- You need to read texts for more than just their meaning: ask yourself what the writer wants you to think and how the words and pictures influence you.

ACTIVITY

Make a log of the different non-fiction texts you have read today. For each kind of text, say why you read it.

Continue to keep your log of non-fiction texts for the next week.

Remember to include posters, notices and web texts in your list.

Focus for development:
Analysing textual features

Each form of non-fiction text has its own typical features that help you recognise what kind of text you are reading.

The exam will ask you about the language and presentational features of texts.

ACTIVITY

Take a careful look at the following four texts with a partner.

Discuss these questions:

- What kinds of text are they? What features tell you this? (Think about language and presentation, how the text looks and is laid out.)
- Where has each one been taken from? How do you know?
- Who would be interested in reading each one and why?
- Why do you think each of the features you have identified have been used? (For example, 'Nobody's safe!' grabs the reader's attention; the photo of 'glossy' women helps the reader picture who the show is about.)

dramatic caption

exciting language: 'murder mystery', 'tested', 'exposed', 'terrifying struggle for survival'

NOBODY'S SAFE!
This glossy murder mystery follows a group of family and friends who travel to a secluded island to attend a wedding – and find their lives in danger. As the festivities begin, friendships are tested and secrets are exposed as a murderer claims victims one by one – transforming the week of celebration into a terrifying struggle for survival. Followed by the second episode.

Harper's Island, 9pm and 9.40pm, BBC3, Sunday 6 September

Friendships get tested as a murderer preys on wedding guests

'glossy' women to go with text

clearly tells you when to watch

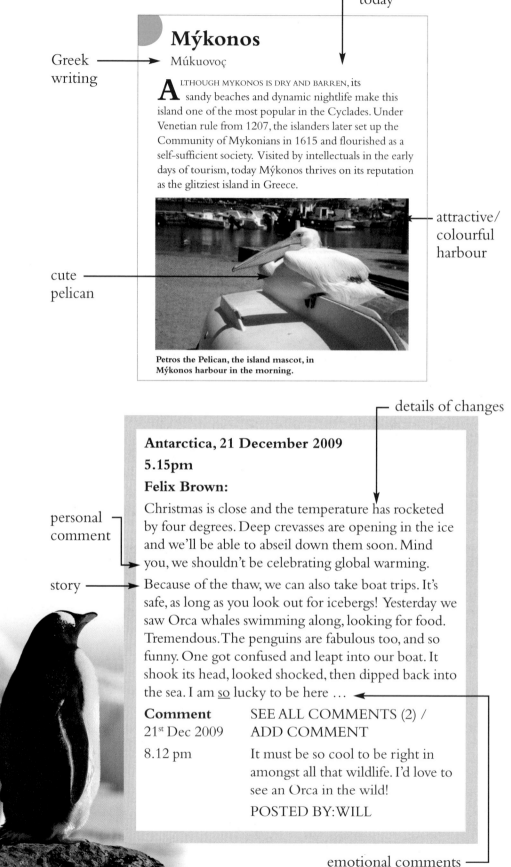

geographical/historical information and tells how island is regarded today

Greek writing

Mýkonos

Μúκuovος

ALTHOUGH MYKONOS IS DRY AND BARREN, its sandy beaches and dynamic nightlife make this island one of the most popular in the Cyclades. Under Venetian rule from 1207, the islanders later set up the Community of Mykonians in 1615 and flourished as a self-sufficient society. Visited by intellectuals in the early days of tourism, today Mýkonos thrives on its reputation as the glitziest island in Greece.

attractive/ colourful harbour

cute pelican

Petros the Pelican, the island mascot, in Mýkonos harbour in the morning.

details of changes

Antarctica, 21 December 2009

5.15pm

Felix Brown:

personal comment

Christmas is close and the temperature has rocketed by four degrees. Deep crevasses are opening in the ice and we'll be able to abseil down them soon. Mind you, we shouldn't be celebrating global warming.

story

Because of the thaw, we can also take boat trips. It's safe, as long as you look out for icebergs! Yesterday we saw Orca whales swimming along, looking for food. Tremendous. The penguins are fabulous too, and so funny. One got confused and leapt into our boat. It shook its head, looked shocked, then dipped back into the sea. I am <u>so</u> lucky to be here …

Comment	SEE ALL COMMENTS (2) /
21ˢᵗ Dec 2009	ADD COMMENT
8.12 pm	It must be so cool to be right in amongst all that wildlife. I'd love to see an Orca in the wild!
	POSTED BY: WILL

emotional comments

AFTER THE RAIN, HERE COMES THE Sun

Headline includes *Sun* logo and a pun

inset photo – reminds us of flood damage

caption for photo

Drenched . . clear-up in Cockermouth yesterday

THE Sun joined the Cumbrian relief effort yesterday by helping people cut off by the devastating floods.

We took food to residents stranded when a raging river smashed the only bridge linking hundreds of locals with Workington.

The vulnerable and elderly like Agnes Bell have been particularly hard hit, so she was thrilled when we arrived with goodies from Asda. Great-gran Agnes, 84, said: "I am so pleased The Sun is helping us. When I heard that the bridge had gone I felt so alone.

"So many kind people have offered help. It makes you realise we have a great community."

Five hundred homes in Northside were cut off when the bridge over the Derwent collapsed on Friday, killing cop Bill Barker, 44.

It has turned a two-minute trip to town into a 20-mile detour.

Locals can collect food and toiletries from a supermarket-supported emergency aid station in the community centre.

Council officials have set up a Job Centre, GPs' surgery and a creche upstairs. Housing

By ROBIN PERRIE

officer Estelle Kent, 44, said: "People have been cut off, so we're bringing services to them."

Engineers fear the town's sinking Calva Bridge may collapse. If it goes, 1,000 homes will lose their phoneline.

Tory leader David Cameron described the damage as "biblical" yesterday on a visit to flood-ravaged Cockermouth.

Warnings

Asked if his party would help people in the county if elected next year, he said: "Of course we will. They're going to need help."

Residents and business owners, meanwhile, continued to return. Alison Watson, 37, of Al's Toys, said: "This couldn't have come at a worse time."

Locals were hoping the floods would not return after up to **FOUR INCHES** of rain in Cumbria yesterday. Eight roads and 21 bridges remained closed.

Across Britain, there were 15 flood warnings in place last night – ten in North West England, three in Wales and one each in the Midlands and the North East.
r.perrie@the-sun.co.uk
The Sun Says — Page Eight

Visit . . . Cameron in Cockermouth

Supplies . . The Sun's Perrie with Agnes Bell

main photo – large and colourful

pull-quote

subheading

Focusing on purpose

Learning objectives

- *To explore writers' purposes.*
- *To read and analyse different kinds of texts.*

What does purpose mean?

Whenever anyone writes a text, they have an **aim** or **purpose**. For example, they could be writing to

- persuade the reader to buy a particular product
- entertain the reader
- inform the reader about an important issue.

Checklist for success

You need to identify

- the purpose of every text you read (why it has been written)
- which features make the text appropriate for that purpose
- why the writer includes each feature.

For all to see: Sarah laps up the glory next to her time display

Bolt 100m record is beaten by a cheetah

WORLD record 100m sprinter Usain Bolt may have thought he was pretty fast – until a cheetah lopped more than three seconds off his time. The Jamaican athlete ran 9.58sec last month but eight-year-old Sarah has managed the feat in just 6.13sec – meaning she is now officially the fastest land animal in the world. She was so quick around the track at Cincinatti Zoo in Ohio on Wednesday that she caught up with the lure encouraging her to run.

'I'm proud of Sarah every day of her life – she's a wonderful animal with a wonderful spirit,' said Cathryn Hilker, founder of the Cat Ambassador Program, which runs a cheetah exhibit at the zoo. But the record may soon fall – cheetah Zaza from South Africa is limbering up for an attempt in the next few weeks.

Blur: Usain Bolt broke his own 100m record last month

ACTIVITY

Read this short text from *The Metro News*.

Then discuss with a partner:

- which features are typically included in a newspaper report (see the example on page 9 for a reminder)
- which of these features appear in this report
- why this report has been written.

Here is part of one **Grade C** response focusing on the purpose of this text:

> The text is obviously meant to inform and interest us by using pictures of a beautiful cheetah and the fastest man on earth and telling us about the cheetah's new record. It's also supposed to make us laugh, with the cheetah sitting next to its record. We are also supposed to smile at the idea that Sarah has a rival who wants to be faster, just like a proper runner.

Notice how the student

- identifies the purpose clearly
- refers to the effect
- extends the comments
- gives evidence for each of her ideas.

Focus for development:
How adverts work

ACTIVITY

With a partner, read the advert below and decide what its purpose is. What does it want the reader to do?

Now take a closer look at each of its features. How does the advert appeal in order to achieve its purpose?

Complete a grid like this one.

Feature	Description of feature	Effect on the reader
Picture	It shows a bald man who looks like a potato!	The picture makes us laugh, and read further. The man is smiling and looks friendly so we are more likely to listen to his advice.
Layout (how it is organised)		
Fonts		
Colours		
Voice (how it speaks directly to 'you')		
Language		

POTATO LOVERS
hate waste

I love spuds. So I store mine in a cool dark place to make them last longer. If they've gone sprouty, after a proper peel they're ready to mash. And I always like freezing any leftovers in bags for a quick and easy shepherd's pie topping. Lovely jubbly.

lovefoodhatewaste.com has more tips and recipes to help you waste less food and save up to £50 a month.

LOVE FOOD hate waste

ASSESSMENT FOCUS

Write up your points, explaining the advert's **purpose** and how it tries to achieve this.

The purpose of this advertisement is...

The advertisement makes us think of potatoes from first glance because...

The man is...

The whole use of colour is supposed to make us think...

The heading focuses on...

The main text reads as if... One sentence that is memorable is... This is good because...

Overall, I think the text works well/does not work well) because...

Remember

- Work out what the purpose is; it will always help you to interpret the text.
- Look closely at the language and the presentational features; these will have been chosen to support the purpose.

Audience

Learning objective

- To understand how texts are designed to attract a particular target audience.

Examiner's tip

Be aware of the fact that texts can have more than one specific audience. Peter Kaye's autobiography, for instance, would hope to appeal to fans, lovers of comedy or people who enjoy a 'light read' – perhaps while on holiday.

Why is it important to think about the audience?

Writers always keep their **audience** in mind, and write in an appropriate style for their readers. It could be a general readership, perhaps of a daily newspaper, or a specific readership, such as readers of *Bee-Keeper's Monthly*.

Being aware of the target audience helps you read texts more effectively.

Checklist for success

You need to

- think about how the words and the presentational features, such as pictures, have been used to appeal to the target audience.

Advertisers are particularly aware of their target audience and produce adverts specifically for that group. So, television adverts for toys might feature happy children to attract parents to buy.

ACTIVITY

This webpage below is from the Club 18–30 website.

Why do you think this might attract 18–30 year-olds to take one of these holidays?

repetition and list intended to make it sound exciting for 18–30s

adjectives to make it sound wonderful

attractive young people

nightclub colours

what 18–30s might like to do

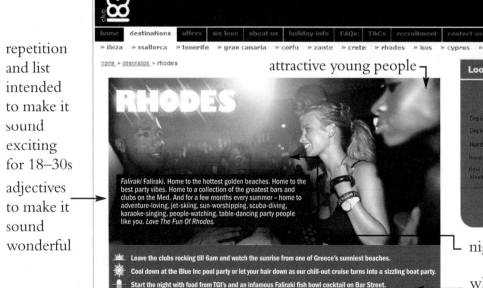

Here are three brief extracts from student responses.

With a partner, decide why the E extract is weakest and what the others do better.

Grade E

> The picture has happy young people to make the audience interested.

Grade C

> The young adults in the picture look happy, which suggests to the reader that an 18–30 holiday might be just what they need too – it would be a good reason for going.

Grade D

> The young adults in the picture look happy, so the readers think they might be like that with 18–30.

ACTIVITY

Now look at this leaflet. It is aimed at a different tourist audience.

Working with a group, decide:

Autumn & Winter 2009/2010

Best Western
WROXTON HOUSE HOTEL
Wroxton, Nr Banbury

Do you enjoy the finer things in life?

Excellent service
Award winning food
Cosy elegant lounges
Log burning fire
Superb location for exploring the Cotswolds

.....then visit Banbury's best kept secret!

- What do the pictures tell us about the hotel? (What they suggest as well as what they show.)
- Why has the gold colour been used?
- How is the text set out and why?
- What can you say about the language used?
- What is the target audience for the text? Give your reasons.

ASSESSMENT FOCUS

Write your own response to this question:

> *What is the target audience for the Wroxton House Hotel leaflet and how successful will it be in attracting those visitors?*

Try to include the details from your group discussion.

Remember

- Always think about what audience the writer had in mind.
- Be prepared to write about both the presentational features and the language.

13

Exploring the effects of language

What do we mean by language?

You will be writing about the writer's **choice of words**. You might also comment on different sentence lengths or language techniques such as similes, metaphors and alliteration.

The language will be suited to the **purpose and audience**: it might be emotive or humorous or grimly factual.

In this piece of travel writing about 1920s Mexico, D H Lawrence captures the excitement as a crowd gathers to watch men dangling snakes from their mouths.

> …three thousand people had massed in the little *plaza*, secured themselves places on the roof and in the window-spaces, everywhere, till the small pueblo seemed built of people instead of stones. All sorts of people, hundreds and hundreds of white women, all in breeches like half-men, hundreds and hundreds of men who had been driving motor-cars, then many Navajos, the women in their full, long skirts and tight velvet bodices, the men rather lanky, long-waisted, real nomads. In the hot sun and the wind which blows the sand every day, every day in volumes round the corners, the three thousand tourists sat for hours, waiting for the show.

ACTIVITY

Which words give this description a flavour of Mexico?

Decide what effect is created by the long sentences. Do they make it sound slow and boring or busy and excited?

Which words or phrases emphasise how many people were there and what it was like? Select three and say what picture they paint for the reader.

Read this opening to a **Grade D** response which analyses how language is used in the extract.

> Lawrence is in a very busy place, because there are thousands of people. To give the impression, he uses words like 'hundreds and hundreds', which sounds as if there are lots. He also uses Mexican words like 'Navajos'.
>
> He gives you a picture of what is happening by giving a clear image: 'the small pueblo seemed built of people instead of stones'. There is also a simile, because the women were 'like half-men'.

For a better grade, this response would need to include more interpretation of **how** the language features are used to gain a certain reaction from the reader, thinking about

- the Mexican words
- images and metaphors
- vocabulary designed to give an impression of crushing
- repetition of 'every day'
- different sentence lengths.

ASSESSMENT FOCUS

Write your response to this question about the extract below.

> **How does the writer, Henry Winter, use language in this extract to affect our feelings about these football fans?**

Consider

- descriptive vocabulary
- the uses of metaphor
- emotive phrases.

ACTIVITY

Write your own answer to this question.

> **How does D H Lawrence bring to life the excitement of the event?**

Use this frame to help you.

- Start by saying briefly what happened.
- Explain the impressions created and how they were created.
- Use precise detail from the text to support your points.

For more on how to use quotations in your writing see pages 38–31.

As Burnley's magnificent fans made their way out of Turf Moor, muttering about how lucky Spurs had been and how proud they were of their claret-and-blue idols, a father tried to console his son. The lad's hair was damp from the rain and his face moist from the tears. 'Their legs went,' the father kept saying to the boy, 'they'd given everything.'

The lad was heart-broken, his mind too confused to take in the reasons for Burnley's late collapse…

from *The Telegraph*, 21 January 2009

Remember

- Interpret what the writer says to show how he/she wants the reader to react.
- Focus on the words, descriptive language and sentence lengths.
- Support what you say with close reference to the text.

15

Exploring presentational features

What are presentational features?

Presentational features are the visual elements of a text: colours, pictures and text boxes. Their arrangement on the page is the **layout**.

When writing about them, you need to say how they are used.

Colours are usually chosen carefully to match the text and its message. For example, yellow might represent happiness or green might be used if dealing with environmental matters.

Pictures or illustrations will set a mood or appeal specifically to the audience.

The **layout** will hope to focus the reader's attention on the most important elements.

Checklist for success

When reading any media text, you need to do the following.

- Consider layout. (What do I notice first and why? Where do my eyes go next? How have these features been arranged?)
- Decide if the use of colour is significant. (Is there more of one colour? For example: Does the yellow represent sunshine? Is there red to suggest excitement?)
- Notice how pictures represent or add to what the text is saying.
- Think about how any other presentational features are intended to affect the reader.

Leaflets generally have to catch the reader's attention quickly, and be simple but effective. Design and presentation is therefore very important.

⭐ **Examiner's tip**

Generally, pictures support the text. They will either

- *add to what we are told*
- *or reflect what we are told.*

ACTIVITY

Look at the leaflet on the following page. Then discuss these questions with a partner.

- Who is the leaflet designed to target? Explain.
- What mood does the use of blue suggest?
- How would you describe the two women pictured? Why have they been used on the leaflet?
- What can you say about the choice of text fonts?
- Which language would you identify as being most noticeable?
- How successful do you think the leaflet will be? Give reasons.

FREE eye test and £50* off glasses

From Dollond & Aitchison

Book your FREE eye test and take advantage of your special offers today

It's not every day something of real value drops through the letterbox. At Dollond & Aitchison, we're committed to the highest level of eyecare and we'd like you to find out for yourself with this exclusive offer – a FREE eye test worth £27.50, as long as you visit us before 31st December 2009.

Not only that, we'd also like to offer you £30 cash back when you join our Contact Lenses By Post Scheme** and a FREE Contact Lens Assessment & Trial.

If you've never visited us before, you'll discover customer service built up over 250 years. We can offer extraordinary value on quality glasses and more, we'd also like to take this opportunity to give you £50 off a complete pair of new glasses* with the vouchers attached.

Combined with the FREE eye test, that's an incredible saving of over £100 on the health and look of your eyes.

Why have an eye test?

Looking after your eyes is our highest priority at D&A and an eye test is the best way to confirm they're in good condition.

An eye test can help pinpoint any health issues such as glaucoma and diabetes, so you'll have peace of mind.

Try contact lenses at D&A today

ACUVUE
BRAND CONTACT LENSES
Johnson&Johnson

ACTIVITY

Read this opening to a **Grade D** response to the following question.

> *How are presentational features used in the optician's leaflet?*

When you look at the leaflet, the first thing you notice is the woman. She looks rich and superior. Maybe that is how the glasses make you feel. The other woman is normal and must be wearing contact lenses. She is pretty though, so the lenses might be for pretty people. Every time you look at the leaflet, you notice FREE in block capitals, so it seems to be saying you won't spend any money, but then when you read the text...

Complete a table like this to evaluate the student's answer.

What has the student done well?	• *looked closely at the pictures* • • •
What can be improved?	• *no mention yet of colour* • •
What needs to be added?	• *purpose and audience* • *mention of particular language such as...* • •

ASSESSMENT FOCUS

Write a full analysis of how presentational features are used in the optician's leaflet.

- Decide on the purpose and audience.
- Say how each presentational feature contributes to the purpose and is designed to affect the target audience.

Remember

- **Link your comments about presentational features to the text's purpose(s).**
- **Consider the effects of layout, colour, pictures or font choices and how these appeal to the audience.**

Perspective and point of view

Learning objective

- To learn how to identify and analyse the writer's perspective.

What does perspective mean?

A text will usually have a **point of view**, a perspective or 'angle' on its subject. This influences how we react to the content.

Checklist for success

- Read as many different kinds of non-fiction texts as you can.
- For each text, ask yourself what the writer thinks about the subject and how they want you to react.

The following extracts are taken from the book *Don'ts for Husbands*, published in 1913 and written by a woman.

Don't drop, while alone with your wife, the little courtesies you would offer to other women. For instance, always get up to open a door for her, as you would for a lady guest.

Don't refuse to play tennis or croquet or billiards with your wife because it is 'not worth while' to play games with a woman. If she plays badly, show her how to improve. She certainly won't play better by being left out of the game altogether.

Don't insist on giving holidays to the servants during *your* holiday on the ground that your wife can 'manage' at the seaside. You are not the only person to be considered, and it's no holiday for her to be tied to the children day in and day out while you go golfing or fishing. Probably *she* would like to golf or fish as well if she got the chance.

ACTIVITY

Discuss these questions with a partner:

- What sort of life does the writer lead? How can you tell?
- What is her view of how a husband should treat his wife? Give examples from each paragraph.
- What attitudes is she arguing against?

Focus for development:
Understanding different perspectives

The perspective of the text can make the same subject seem very different. A writer can be for something, against it, or can offer a balanced viewpoint.

Read this view on smacking children, from actress Linda Robson. Then discuss the following with a partner:

- Find three points that show Linda Robson's view on smacking.
- How far do you agree with her view?

> They say you should pick on someone your own size – and smacking a child is picking on someone smaller. In fact, it's a form of bullying.
>
> I've got three kids aged 13, 17 and 26, and I've never smacked any of them. I've always found other, more effective ways of disciplining them.
>
> For younger children, I think tone of voice can be enough…

Now read another mother's response to Linda's view. Does it present a more balanced view? Why/Why not?

> I have never set out to hurt my children. I love them and would never hit them without due cause. No one should ever want to harm a child. There are times, though, when a little tap shows them something is wrong, and they won't do it again. For example, they must be stopped from running with scissors. They need that discipline. After all, it's less traumatic for them than being screamed at by a parent: that is much more violent…

ASSESSMENT FOCUS

Write about the perspective in the mother's response about smacking.

Explain her viewpoint, supporting what you say with evidence from the text.

A student writes…

I usually just ask myself, 'Is this written from a first person perspective?'; 'Is it biased or balanced?'; Am I taking the right approach?

Answer…

If you can decide what viewpoint the writer is adopting, that is a good beginning.

Remember

- Identify the writer's point of view first. Then find evidence to support your choice. The perspective affects how the reader responds to the subject.
- Practise analysing perspective in texts and you will learn to spot viewpoints more easily in the exam.

Analysing structure

Learning objective

- To learn about how texts are constructed.

Glossary
anecdote: a short story that illustrates a point

What does analysing structure mean?

Structure is the way texts have been put together: how they start, develop and end, and how the different parts contribute to the overall purpose.

Checklist for success

You need to

- decide on the purpose of the text, then how the writing is structured to fulfil that purpose
- pay particular attention to how texts begin, develop and end
- focus on the techniques writers use to develop their points – for example, including quotations, anecdotes, facts, opinions and figures or contrasts.

Structure and purpose

Texts are structured in different ways depending on their purpose. Some writers of newspaper articles create a balanced argument, offering different viewpoints and ideas. Others might focus on just one argument or idea, as in the short report below.

gives summary of findings ⟶

ARCTIC GETS HOTTER

summarises ⟶ main argument

presents overview ⟶ of problem

presents evidence ⟶ to support main argument

GREENHOUSE gases are being blamed for soaring Arctic temperatures – they are higher than at any time in the past 2,000 years.

US scientists examined ice cores, tree rings and lake sediments at 23 sites across the region to form a decade-by-decade picture of temperatures. And 1998 to 2008 stands out as the warmest decade in the entire series.

Darrell Kaufman of Northern Arizona University said: "The last half-century was the warmest of the 2,000-year record, and the last 10 years have been especially dramatic."

It backs up other reports, including NASA satellite measurements, which show Arctic sea ice is both shrinking in size and thinning.

The study's co-author David Schneider said: "Greenhouse gases from human activities are overwhelming the Arctic's climate system."

links back to ⟶ the opening

offers more supporting evidence

ACTIVITY

Discuss these questions about the article with a partner.

- What techniques does the writer use to support his argument (look back at the checklist above)?
- How effective are the opening and ending?
- What might have been added in a more detailed text?

Focus for development:
Organising a text

Below are details from an article about Radio 1 DJ, Chris Moyles.

- Decide what description of Chris Moyles you could create from the details. Put the details into the best order to create this 'picture'.
- Be ready to explain your decisions.

1. Moyles' success is the result of professionalism for which he is rarely given credit.
2. His job appeared under threat recently but, whilst other presenters were sacked, he remained to rule the airwaves.
3. He first worked at a radio station as a schoolboy doing work experience.
4. 'I find his continued presence on Radio 1 unacceptable' said Oxford University's professor of broadcast media.
5. His programmes appear to 'just happen' but that cleverly disguises Moyles' real attention to detail.
6. He has been criticised for being racist, disliking gay people, and 'laddish'.
7. He is Radio 1's longest serving breakfast DJ.

ASSESSMENT FOCUS

Here is part of a formal letter to a newspaper. Write an analysis of the text explaining

- the writer's viewpoint
- how the writer uses facts and opinions in their argument
- how the structure supports that viewpoint.

You could use a writing frame like this:

- The writer wants to...
- The letter starts with the writer explaining...
- In the second paragraph, the main point is developed by...
- To conclude, the writer...

Sir,

I am tired of reading about young people running wild and terrorising their neighbourhoods. It is true that teenagers are not all angels but, similarly, they are not all bad, either.

Young people collect for charity, live as part of communities and are just as civilised as many older people. It is criminal to keep picking fault because of the behaviour of the few. Every year, British jails are filled with murderers, burglars and drug addicts: that does not make the entire adult population a set of criminals. In the same way, you should not generalise about the young.

We have our rights too: please remember that when you are reporting.

Remember

- Always identify how the structure of the text supports its purpose.
- Analyse the structure stage-by-stage for the best results.

Grade Booster

Extended Exam Task

Choose a lead story or article from a newspaper to use with this question.

> *What features can you find in the text that are typical of newspaper text's? How successfully have they been used?*

Focus on

- the headline
- any pictures or illustrations
- other presentational features
- the structure
- the story and/or argument
- the language used
- the writer's point of view.

Evaluation: what have you learned?

With a partner, use the Grade checklist list below to evaluate your work on the Extended Exam Task.

C
- I can say why texts have been produced and can identify the target audience.
- I can identify and explain why the language and presentational features of the text have been used.
- I can comment on the effects created.
- I can understand and explain clearly the writers viewpoints.
- I can include appropriate supporting quotations for the points I make.

D
- I can understand texts and am aware of their purposes.
- I can identify the text's language and presentational features and make comments on them.
- I can comment on writers' viewpoints.
- I can include some evidence for the points I make.

E
- I can make some points and attempt to interpret the text, using some relevant evidence.

F
- I can make a few points about the text, with limited explanation.

You may need to go back and look at the relevant pages from this section again.

Close Reading in the Exam

Introduction

This section of Chapter 1 helps you to

- focus on the reading skills you will have to show in the exam
- develop and practise these skills by analysing different non-fiction texts in detail.

What will close reading mean in the exam?

You will have to select the right material to answer the questions on the exam paper. These will require the following skills:

- Finding information in the text
- Dealing with inference – what the text is suggesting
- Analysing the language and presentational features.

A Grade E candidate will

- show some understanding of the texts and use some relevant quotations to support their ideas
- attempt to interpret features of the texts, offer some explanations and attempt to compare the texts when asked.

E

A Grade D candidate will

- show that they understand the texts and use some relevant quotations to support their ideas
- interpret features of the texts, offer explanations which show understanding and compare the texts when asked.

D

A Grade C candidate will

- show clearly that they understand the texts and use relevant quotations to show their understanding
- show that they engage with the content of texts and interpret them through the writer's choice of language, presentational features and structure
- offer clear explanations and make clear and appropriate comparisons when asked.

C

Prior learning

Before you begin this unit, think about

- what you have already learnt in school about language, structure and presentational features in non-fiction texts (look back at pages 14–15, 16–17 and 20–21 if you need to)
- what features you are likely to consider when comparing texts
- the different kinds of texts you read every day.

Have you thought about the use of colour or font size and why a particular picture or headline has been used?

Think about the 'story', the message, the writer's viewpoint, the purpose, audience, language and presentation.

As you read newspapers, letters, leaflets and notices, focus on **how** they have been written.

Selecting and putting together information

What does selecting and putting together information mean?

To respond to questions with authority, you first need to be able to **select** the details from the text that are most relevant to answering the question.

You then link these details logically as you comment. For example, you might put together three relevant related points or develop a point using more than one piece of evidence.

Checklist for success

Whenever you write about texts, you need to make sure

- the information you select answers the question
- any quotation or reference to the text actually supports the point you are making.

ACTIVITY

Look at the advertisement on the opposite page. With a partner, answer the following question.

- What do we learn from the advertisement about Herta Frankfurter sausages? List your points.

Now, look back at the information you have written down. Have you included information from

- the text at the top
- the text in red and black under the picture
- the details on the right hand side.

If necessary, add more points.

ACTIVITY

Looking back at the information you selected, write a response to this question.

- What reasons does the advertisement give for buying Herta Frankfurters? Think about how this information is presented. Consider the effect of

- images
- headlines
- colour.

Try to develop your points, putting different pieces of information together to explain them.

Focus for development: Putting ideas together

In the exam, one question is likely to ask you to write about information you find, rather than just listing points.

Notice how the annotations around this text pick out details to answer the question:

How does Shaq try to attract viewers to his television series?

Shaq tells Becks that the football's in his court

Jeered by ungrateful LA Galaxy fans, David Beckham has now fallen foul of a true American sporting icon.

Shaquille O'Neal, the NBA basketball legend, has challenged Beckham to a game of "soccerball" in a new all-star reality TV series, *Shaq Vs*, in which the hoop king takes on his sporting peers at their own game. Shaq will swim against Michael Phelps, the Olympic champion, fight the former world boxing champion Oscar De La Hoya and challenge Serena Williams to a set of tennis in the Disney series.

But will the England star play ball? Negotiations are under way through the traditional medium of Twitter.

"Dear david beckham," tweets Shaq. "I kno u heard about my *Shaq Vs* show, anyway u will never score a goal on me, I challenge you lil man."

With no reply forthcoming, O'Neal upped the ante. "David beckham I kno u hear me, dnt be scared, dnt make me call u out, u will never score a goal on me." And finally: "Dnt make me tweet to 2 million people that yur scared of shaq, u betta respnd, if u scared get a dog."

With Shaq on his back, as well as the Galaxy boo boys, perhaps Becks should invest in a rottweiler.

The Times 29 July 2009

— issues challenges to other famous sporting figures

— some he will compete against

— using Internet to generate interest

— challenging David Beckham

This is how two students responded to the question.

Grade D response

Shaq does a lot of things to attract viewers. He has challenged David Beckham to play him at soccer. He has challenged other sporting people as well for his Disney series. He is also insulting Beckham which might appeal to some people and make them interested in him.

Grade C response

Shaquille O'Neal wants to attract viewers to his television show so he has challenged a number of sporting figures, who are well-known. He will swim against Michael Phelps, box the ex-world champion Oscar De La Hoya and play tennis against Serena Williams. Finally, he generates interest by trying to get David Beckham on the programme and by pretending to threaten him on Twitter: 'if you scared, get a dog'.

ACTIVITY

Decide exactly why the second answer is better.
Think about:
- the precise details used
- the way the ideas are organised and put together
- how the Grade C response starts
- how the first sentence is explained
- how the student deals with the points related to David Beckham.

ASSESSMENT FOCUS

Re-read the report about Shaq and Becks.
How does Shaq try to persuade David Beckham to come on to his show?

Examiner's tip ⭐

Start with a general statement then put in as many details as you can to explain it.

Remember

- Make sure you select evidence that is appropriate to the question or to the point you are making.
- Put material together with care, so that relevant points are linked together.

Using quotations and examples effectively

Learning objective

- To learn how to use evidence to support the points you make.

★ Examiner's tip

Always use the Point, Evidence, Explanation technique (P.E.E.) in your answers. If you do, the marker knows where you got the idea from and that you can explain the effect of each detail in the text.

What are the essential features of evidence?

When you write about non-fiction texts in the exam, you will need to use evidence from the text to support your points.

What this **evidence** is depends on the question being asked but you are most likely to be using a direct quotation from the text or picking out details about the text's layout or presentational features.

Checklist for success

You need to

- remember that any analytical points you make require proof from the text
- select **brief** quotations – usually no longer than two lines
- refer to detail and make your examples precise, rather than offering generalised thoughts. For example, 'We know the rescue has been successful because the woman in the picture is smiling. This makes us think…'

ACTIVITY

Here are two examples of evidence. What does the second example include that the first one does not?

The family looks silly and happy.

The family looks silly because they are wearing cat costumes and we know they are happy because the parents are smiling and the boy is playing.

The second example is better, because of the evidence and explanation supporting the points being made.

Focus for development: Using evidence well

It's important to select the best quotations to be convincing in your exam answers.

Read this letter which was sent to a local newspaper, in which the writer makes a series of points about his disappointment when trying to find peace on a day of remembrance in his local churches.

NO PEACE TO BE FOUND IN THE HOUSE OF GOD

September 11th is a date we all know – the anniversary of the attack on the Twin Towers in New York. Over three hundred firefighters died that day – and as a firefighter myself, it is not a moment I will ever forget.

Each year, when not working, I try to find some peace to remember the fallen. I live in the country, so my local church is always open and I use that as my sanctuary.

However, this year, I was visiting your city and was saddened to find all the churches locked. I can understand why, with all the vandalism that takes place, but I was upset that there was apparently nowhere for me to go.

When I e-mailed the church nearest to my mother's house, I got a short, sharp reply saying that the church would not be open. The message was not even signed.

I drove around the district in the morning, but it was the same everywhere. Since all places of worship were closed, my wife and I headed for the Cathedral. We knew that would be open every day.

How foolish we were! The noise inside was unbelievable. We hoped for peace and meditation – what we got was chatter and laughter from those working inside and loud comments from other visitors who were viewing an exhibition inside. With the busy bustle from the shopping area, we might just as well have been in the city's market.

We moved as far as we could from the disturbances and sat in the front pew, only to have a female cleric arrive with a visitor in a suit: they stood beside us and discussed the planned visit by the mayor the next day, where he should sit and what he needed to do. They had no manners and no respect for us or the building.

When we crossed to sit at the other side, a man came in and sat beside us and repacked his chocolate bars and crisps in his Morrison's bag. Unbelievable!

I know the church is trying to attract new worshippers by encouraging all kinds of people to enter, not just the old and committed. But I for one will never set foot in the Cathedral again.

Where there should have been peace, there was noise and disturbance. Heaven alone knows what the builders of such a beautiful shrine to the almighty would think, when worshippers are treated so badly.

ACTIVITY

Copy and complete this table, which focuses on what the man's feelings were and the evidence for this in the letter.

Point	Evidence	Explanation of effect
He struggled to find a peaceful place	•	•
Several unfortunate and noisy incidents upset him in the cathedral	• 'We hoped for ... what we got was chatter and laughter from those working inside' • •	• Contrast between first part and second part of sentence – what they wanted and what they got... • •
He is very unhappy about the changes to the Cathedral	•	•
He uses powerful language to emphasise his feelings	• •	• •
The ending sums up his emotions	•	•

A good answer will use this P.E.E. technique.
For example:

> He uses powerful language to emphasise his feelings:
> 'Heaven alone knows...' He sounds upset and we can
> imagine the emotion as he says those words.

However, if you can move beyond a relatively
simple explanation (P.E.E.) into **analysis**, with
extended thoughts about the evidence (P.E.**A.**),
you will gain better marks. For example, by adding
extra thoughts to the example above:

> ... we can imagine the emotion as he says those words.
> They are particularly appropriate with his call to 'heaven',
> for he is in a cathedral and it is to heaven that he is
> looking, for its peace. Whereas many people might say
> casually 'Heaven knows...', he is writing what he really
> means.

Notice how the student has explored the meaning
of one word in detail.

ASSESSMENT FOCUS

Write a response to this question, trying
to use the P.E.A. approach.

> **Why does the writer of 'No peace to be
> found in the house of God' feel so
> strongly about what happened that he
> had to write the letter?**

- Explain why the writer was in the
  Cathedral.
- Work through what happened and
  his feelings.
- Support each point you make with
  evidence – in most cases, a quotation
  – and explanation or analysis.

Examiner's tip ★

*Looking closely at individual
words can lead to higher
marks. Where possible, try to
think about a word's
connotations. This means what
it suggests or any associations
it has. For example, the word
'red' literally means the colour
red, but its connotations are
passion, romance, anger or
sometimes warning.*

Remember

- **Find evidence for each point, then explain or analyse it.**
- **Good answers are usually sprinkled with short quotations.**

Drawing inferences

Learning
objective

- *To understand
  what inference
  means and to
  practise using it.*

What does inference mean?

When you make an inference, you look beyond the obvious thing someone has said or written, and think about what they are suggesting. You read 'between the lines'.

So, if someone writes, 'her hairstyle is really quite interesting', you might wonder what 'interesting' really suggests and conclude that the writer was less than impressed.

ACTIVITY

What might be being suggested in each of these examples?

- 'Anyone who sees your paintings can tell that you try really hard.'
- 'Don't worry: every grey hair you grow makes me love you more.'
- 'No one will be losing their job today.'

ACTIVITY

What can you work out about this family, from the picture?
A few things are obvious, but you will need to **infer** others.

Focus for development:
How texts make suggestions

Sometimes, we gain an impression from a whole text; at other times, we respond to particular words or phrases.

ACTIVITY

On your own, read the newspaper report below. Then answer these questions, which focus on what the text suggests.

- Which words or phrases suggest the gardener's actions are not normal?
- Explain what each one makes the reader think.
- How does the picture add to this impression of the gardener?
- What is the attitude of the writer to what has happened? Is he amazed, shocked or amused, for example? Find evidence to support your view and comment on how the writer's viewpoint affects the reader.

MADNESS ON A RIDE-ON MOWER

Are you off yer hedge?

By RICHARD WHITE

A POTTY gardener trims his hedge — using a sit-on lawnmower and a CRANE.

Drivers screeched to a halt as they watched the grinning man slice through the foliage after getting a pal to hoist him skywards.

He spent 20 minutes balancing precariously on top of the 6½ft high bush in Cambridge, New Zealand.

One passer-by said: "His wife was horrified, he's lucky he wasn't killed."

Sun gardener Peter Seabrook said: "This certainly isn't a method I'd recommend. Apart from the obvious danger, he probably didn't get the even cut he wanted." *r.white@the-sun.co.uk*

Here are two students' responses and the marker's comments on how they wrote.

> The writer is amused because at the end he says 'he didn't get the even cut he wanted'. At the start, he calls him 'potty' too...

This is from a **Grade D** response – it has well-chosen support and shows understanding, though the quotation is not explained. The student understands the writer is amused but fails to add detail and clarify the point.

> The writer is telling us the story with tongue-in-cheek because he quotes a gardening expert at the end 'he didn't get the even cut he wanted'. He is making a joke of the fact that after all the gardener's efforts, he did not make a success of trimming the hedge.

This is from a **Grade C** response. The point is proven and explained. The student also makes an inference about the writer's attitude which is explained appropriately.

As we read **biography** and **autobiography**, we enjoy finding out about a particular person and the events in their life, but we also make inferences about them and their character. We interpret them through the words the writer chooses.

This is an **autobiographical** extract, in which the writer meets a bookseller in Afghanistan.

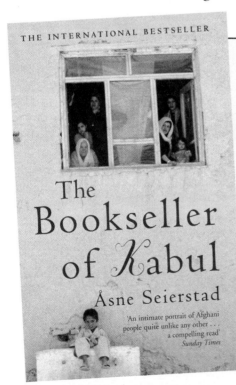

THE INTERNATIONAL BESTSELLER

The Bookseller of Kabul

Åsne Seierstad

'An intimate portrait of Afghani people quite unlike any other . . . a compelling read'
Sunday Times

One day he invited me home for an evening meal. His family – one of his wives, his sons, sisters, brother, mother, a few cousins – was seated on the floor round a sumptuous feast.

Sultan recounted stories, the sons laughed and joked. The atmosphere was unrestrained. […] But I soon noticed that the women said little. Sultan's beautiful teenage wife sat quietly by the door with the baby in her arms. His first wife was not present that evening. The other women answered questions put to them, accepted praise about the meal, but never initiated any conversation […]

On a foggy day in February I moved in with the family. […] I was given a mattress on the floor next to Leila, Sultan's youngest sister, who had been assigned the task of looking after my well-being.

'You are my little baby,' the nineteen-year-old said the first evening. 'I will look after you,' she assured me and jumped to her feet every time I got up.

Sultan had ordered the family to supply me with whatever I wanted. I was later told that whoever did not comply with this demand would be punished.

The Bookseller of Kabul, Asne Seierstad

ACTIVITY

Produce two lists of points in answer to these questions, with quotations to prove them.

- What do we know about life in Sultan's home?
- What is the writer's view of it all? (For example, what might she be thinking when she writes, 'The other women ... never started any conversation'?)

ASSESSMENT FOCUS

Turn your lists of points about the extract into a full answer to this question:

What sort of life does the writer find in Sultan's home and what does she seem to think about it?

Make sure you identify details in the text and comment on
- the effect they have on the reader
- the writer's view (make inferences about what she is suggesting).

Remember

- Focus on events but also make inferences and comment on what is being suggested.
- Look for what you can say about people's attitudes or views.

Writing about presentational features and language

Learning objective

■ To learn how to write effectively about presentational features and language in the exam.

What does writing about presentational features and language involve?

Presentational features are usually the first things we notice in a text – the pictures, headings and text boxes. They are there to create an effect: to make the reader react or think in a certain way.

You will need to answer a question about these features in the exam and show you understand how they **link to the purpose** of the text.

There will also be a question in the exam on exploring the writer's **choice of language** and the effects this creates.

Checklist for success

• You need to decide how the presentational features are used and explain **how** the language affects the reader.

When writing about the presentational features of a text, you might find it useful to follow these three steps:

• Decide on the purpose and audience.
• Identify the writer's point of view.
• Work though the features, commenting on how each one is intended to affect the audience – what it makes them think or feel – and linking them to the text's purpose.

ACTIVITY

Read this section from a longer text.

Working in a group, discuss these questions:

• What is the purpose and audience of the text? How do you know?
• Which presentational features would you comment on?
• What would you say about how each one is used?
• How do the features link to the language used in the text?

HAVE YOU GOT money flu?

Here's how to fight off the spending bug

Whether it's keeping up with the constant string of parties or your inability to resist the 'bargain' sales, affluenza (living beyond your means) is highly contagious at this time of year. Luckily for you, after a quick consultation with our experts, you can boost your immunity *and* your bank balance.

SYMPTOM YOU CAN'T SEPARATE 'WANT' FROM 'NEED'

OK, it's winter and of course a nice wool coat is essential, but do you *really* need a brand new one? We're all guilty of spending on the non-essentials, but if you regularly put off paying the gas bill because you've convinced yourself you 'need' something else, it's a problem. *CURE:* "Work out how much cash you have left *after* paying off your bills," says Katie Edwards, from debt experts Ladies In The Red (www.ladiesinthered. com). "If all you have left is money on your credit card, that's *not* spare cash. Prevent irrational spending by locking your credit card in a box, hiding it and giving the key to a trusted friend. Then sew some new buttons on your old coat."

SYMPTOM YOU CAN'T RESIST TREATING YOURSELF

SYMPTOM YOU STRUGGLE TO KEEP UP WITH YOUR FRIENDS

SYMPTOM YOU CAN'T RESIST THE SALES

Woman cannot live on shoes alone

When asked how presentational features were used in this text, two students responded like this:

Grade D response

We know that the woman is obsessed with her shoes because she is staring at one of them and there are other shoes all around her. Her fridge is full of shoes but she cannot eat them because women cannot live on shoes alone. We can see that there must be something wrong with her and so it links with the headline – 'Have you got money flu?' We know she must have a kind of illness, especially because 'money flu' is in red and stands out …

Examiner's comment: Understanding is shown throughout, and the beginnings of explanation ('because she is staring' and 'we can see that there must be something wrong with her'). However, there is no clear sense of why the features are there or how they are being used – or of the purpose and audience for the text.

Grade C response

— identifies purpose and audience

The writer wants to stop women spending money unnecessarily. The picture is of a typical young woman (with painted toenails and make-up) who is clearly unhappy, and gazing at a golden shoe, like Cinderella. She will not go to the ball, because she has got 'flu'. The word is highlighted in red, like her T-shirt and nail varnish, and like the subheadings. This links to the idea of being 'in the red' or in debt, as in the name of the expert's website 'www.ladiesinthered.com'.

— provides evidence

— links red features in text and picture

— offers extended explanation

Examiner's comment: This is a Grade C response. The purpose and audience are set out in the first sentence and, rather than being written about individually, the effects of the presentational features are linked as the notes above show.

Read through the examiner comments on the Grade C answer, then complete your own response

- using ideas from your group discussion and evidence from the text
- linking presentational features to purpose and audience.

Focus for development: Language features

Language features will be present in any text analysis. The important thing is not to try and write about them all. Instead, focus on the ones that are most relevant to the question. To write about the language, you might follow these three steps:

- Identify what the text is saying and the writer's viewpoint.
- Decide on the writer's attitude – whether he/she is amused, excited, being coldly analytical or whatever.
- Find at least four words, phrases or sentences that are typical of the text and which you could analyse: for example
  - a simile
  - a metaphor
  - a short sentence
  - a gripping opening.

★ Examiner's tip

Focus on trying to find language which is 'typical' of the text. It is then easier to say why it has been used – it will be appropriate for the writer's purpose and will fit with his point of view.

ACTIVITY

Re-read the 'Money flu' text on page 37 again and make notes on the first two steps above.

Then copy and complete this grid, adding any extra language features you wish to comment on.

Language feature	Link to purpose	How it is used
Women cannot live on shoes alone	Text is saying some women waste too much money on non-essentials	• Variation of 'cannot live on bread alone' • Paying the bills is more important than shoes • To amuse • Link to picture – shoes like food • 'alone': she looks alone!
how to fight off the spending bug		
affluenza		

On your own, read the text below carefully.
Then write your response to these questions.

- How are the presentational features used in this article?
- How has the writer used language to interest the reader?

SHOPTALK

HIGH STREET BUYER'S GUIDE

ruki.sayid@mirror.co.uk

Glamazon? I think not

THE huge warehouse could be just another faceless building nestling in the shadow of a motorway.

Yet this grotty location off the M1 in Bedfordshire is a real life Santa's Grotto.

The warehouse, which is the size of eight football pitches, is run by one of Britain's busiest online stores – amazon.co.uk.

Tens of thousands of boxes are piled high, while row upon row of metal shelves house countless racks of books, CDs, DVDs, video games and toys.

The interior not only looks like the world's biggest library, it has the same air of silent toil.

At times the only sound is the stamp of the machine that scans parcels and puts on an address label.

This was a rare glimpse behind the scenes at Amazon which expects to process at least a million orders a day at Christmas.

Allan Lyall, the firm's vice-president of European operations, says: "We are

on to an order within four hours of a customer placing it online. At their click of a mouse, we swing into action as the product is picked from the shelf, packed, scanned, labelled and out."

There are 1,000 staff at the Marston Gate warehouse near Milton Keynes – and Amazon has 3,000 more in four other areas

With Brits expected to spend £7billion on Christmas and almost nine out of 10 adults buying online, the company has to be slick. Which is why I was told off for moving an item several feet from its original location.

It's a rigid system with no room for frivolity.

The pickers methodically go about their business, electric scanners in hand, piling goodies into boxes.

The boxes are then transported on conveyor belts to the packers who encase them in cardboard, stick a barcode on and pop them

on another moving belt to be machine weighed, addressed and stamped before being sorted into areas for next-day delivery.

The 24-hour business may not have the fairytale Disney feel of Santa's work-

shop but for millions of armchair shoppers looking for a merry click-mas, Amazon does the job.

Allan says: "We can even take an order at 8.30am on Christmas Eve and guarantee same-day delivery in London and Birmingham."

Savvy online shoppers can cash in on the e-tailers' free delivery for orders that can wait three to five days. This will leave a little extra cash to spend on carrots for the reindeer.

BOOK BEHIND THE SCENES Ruki in the massive warehouse

PICTURES: IAN VOGLER

WIN SUPERHERO BEN10'S JACKET

SUPERHERO Ben10 is starring in a new film which had its world premiere in London and airs on Cartoon Network on Saturday.

Ten fans who attended the screening of Ben10: Alien Swarm, won one of his trademark leather jackets. And we have the 11th to give

away after being worn by Perri Kiely, pictured with Alesha Dixon, who performed at the bash with Diversity.

Send your entries to: Daily Mirror, Shoptalk, Ben 10 Jacket, PO Box 6867, London E14 5AN, to arrive by Friday,

December 4. Include your name, address and daytime phone number.

The Editor's decision is final and usual Daily Mirror rules apply.

Who performed at the Ben10: Alien Swarm world premier?
A) Jedward.
B) Diversity.
C) JLS.

Remember

- By linking presentational feature and language to purpose and audience, you will make it easier to say how they are used.
- Approach your analysis methodically, using the 'three step' approach on page 38.

Comparing texts

Learning objective

- To understand how language comparison questions work in the exam.

Examiner's tip

It is vital to compare things that are actually comparable, for example how sentence length or particular words are used in the texts. 'Comparing' metaphors with alliteration, for example, is unlikely to earn the best marks.

Will there definitely be a comparison question in the exam?

You will always have to compare two texts. At Foundation tier, you will need to compare the **presentational features** of the texts. At Higher tier, you will need to compare the **language** in the texts.

Checklist for success

Here are two different ways of comparing for you to consider. You might

- make a general statement of comparison, then work though features, comparing them as you go:

  picture in Text 1 / picture in Text 2

  colour in Text 1 / colour in Text 2

- work through Text 1, writing about its features – for example, a simile, use of alliteration, pun – then work through the features of Text 2 in a similar way, but mentioning how these differ from Text 1.

Comparing presentational features

Here are two football products: a matchday programme and a sports magazine cover. Take a careful look at their presentational features.

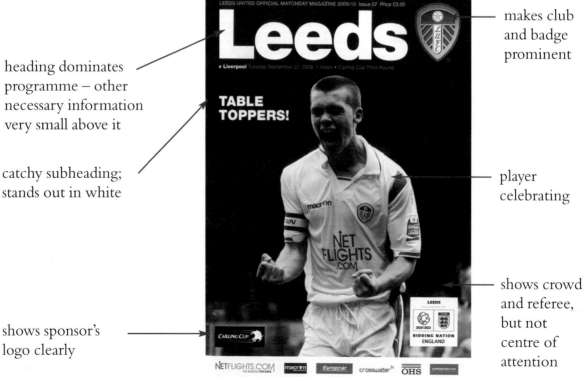

heading dominates programme – other necessary information very small above it

catchy subheading; stands out in white

shows sponsor's logo clearly

makes club and badge prominent

player celebrating

shows crowd and referee, but not centre of attention

puts title behind head –
Michael Owen is more
important than name of
magazine

focuses on famous player to
attract readers – looks like a man
worthy of respect

makes
people want
to read lead
article (can't
read it
elsewhere)

attracts
readers with
different
sporting
interests

uses red as
main colour
for whole
cover,
matching the
shirt colour

quotation to
grab attention

big names
to attract
football fans

sense of fans
watching
but Owen is
the focus

shows variety of
material on offer inside

ACTIVITY

Make lists of
- the presentational features that are similar
- what is different about the presentation of
  the two texts.

Examiner's tip ★

At home, practise comparing whenever you can, by reading
- *magazine covers – deciding why they are different*
- *adverts – looking at how they are designed*
- *newspaper reports and articles – comparing the
  language and pictures.*

Here is the opening of a **Grade C** response comparing the presentational features of both front covers:

Because a programme is produced mainly for the home fans, buyers would know the player. By having the young player looking excited in the Leeds programme, it would attract the home fans. It helps if readers know a footballer on a magazine cover, so the picture of Michael Owen, who plays for England, must have been chosen to get football fans generally to buy the magazine.

The texts obviously have things in common. In each case, the focus is on the player and the crowd is fuzzy in the background because they don't matter. The first thing you notice is the difference in attitude of the two players. Michael Owen looks cool and serious, as if we should have respect for him. The Leeds player looks younger and much more excited, as if he has just become a 'Table Topper.' He seems to be screaming, which shows his happiness. His white kit stands out against the darker background to make it seem bright and attractive. That headline says that Leeds are at the top of the league – in white again, to match with the kit – whereas the other cover has mostly red showing because that is the colour of Owen's shirt...

ACTIVITY

Work with a partner to analyse the **Grade C** response.

- At the start, locate the comparisons and the mention of purposes and audience.
- Find all the points of comparison.
- Find all the explanations of why things are there and how they are used.
- Identify any ideas that are developed beyond just a simple point.

On your own, complete the comparison of the two football texts.

Comparing language

This is the start of an article from a national newspaper:

Let's think the unthinkable: is anything in life more boring than football? It seems more important than any other element of life in modern Britain, but in reality it is about as exciting as queuing at Sainsbury's. A typical afternoon? Ninety minutes of watching distant figures running around chasing a lump of leather; one goal – a scrambled effort as twenty-two athletes throw themselves into a heaving, muddy melee; thirty pounds paid and nothing to show for it but a soaking pair of trousers and a sore throat.

Dull, dull, dull. Who cares about the FA Cup? Even the World Cup? The British are better at cycling and swimming – that's what we should be getting excited about, if anything, not the League Cup or the Egg Cup…

ACTIVITY

You are going to compare the language used in this newspaper article with the language used on the cover of *Sky Sports Magazine* (on page 41). Start by

- noting down some initial points of comparison
- listing four or five language features of each text to write about.

In this case, you are going to use this three-step structure to compare them:

- First, offer general comparative statements.
- Next, write in detail about the language on the magazine cover.
- Then, writing about the article's language, make any comparisons you can.

A student writes…

Do we have to make a comparison using four or five features? That sounds a lot.

Answer…

In any comparison, you will have to decide how many points you are able to make, and how many direct comparisons you can find.

ASSESSMENT FOCUS

Write your own comparison of the way language is used on the cover of *Sky Sports Magazine* and in the newspaper article.

Use the notes you made on the two texts and follow the three steps provided above.

Remember

- **Decide how you are going to organise your comparison.**
- **Link ideas clearly when comparing the texts.**
- **Do not just make general statements – make sure you explain or analyse details of the texts' features.**

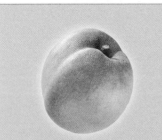

Nature perfected
the fruit.

We perfected the pack.

SPC Nature's Finest fruit is picked when perfect and
then packed in juice with no added colours or
artificial flavours. Find it in the packaged fruit aisle.

Fuss free fruit.

www.surprisingfruityfacts.co.uk
'SPC Nature's Finest' is a Registered trademark of SPC Ardmona Operations Ltd

Extended Exam Task

How does this advert attempt to tempt the reader?

Write about the

- purpose and likely audience
- colours and the two sections
- pictures
- main messages in the text
- language used.

Evaluation: what have you learned?

With a partner, use the grade checklist below to evaluate your work on the Extended Exam Task.

C
- I can write appropriately about purpose and audience, presentation, language and the writers' viewpoints.
- I can link what I say to the texts' purposes.
- I can support my ideas with relevant evidence from the texts.

D
- I can understand texts' purposes and audiences.
- I can write about presentation, language and viewpoints in texts.
- I can use some appropriate evidence for my ideas.

E
- I can comment on the purpose and audience, presentation and language of the text, using some evidence.

F
- I can comment on some things about the text that are relevant, mentioning purpose and audience, colours, pictures and the language.

You may need to go back and look at the relevant pages from this section again.

Exam Preparation
Unit 1A: Reading non-fiction texts

Introduction

In this section you will

- find out the exact facts about, and requirements of, Unit 1A, the Reading section of the exam
- read, analyse and respond to the sorts of texts you will face in the exam
- answer the sorts of questions you will face in the exam
- assess the quality of sample answers by different candidates
- evaluate and assess your answers and the progress you have made.

Why is exam preparation like this important?

- If you know exactly what you need to do, you will feel more confident when you sit the real exam.
- You need to be able to work under timed conditions: in the sample tasks you can learn what is required of you in an hour.
- Answering the questions yourself, then judging your answers against answers written by others will help you see what you need to do to improve your own work.

Key Information

Unit 1 is Understanding and Producing Non-Fiction Texts.

- It has an exam of **2 hours**, worth **80 marks.**
- It is worth **40%** of your overall English Language GCSE mark.
- Section A of the exam is on Reading.
- Section B of the exam is on Writing.

Section A Reading

- The reading part of the exam is **1 hour** long, and is worth **40 marks**.
- It is worth **20%** of your overall English Language mark.

The reading exam

You will have to read three non-fiction texts.

- The **Foundation Tier paper** will have **five** questions:
  - **Question 1:** finding relevant information in a text **(4 marks)**
  - **Question 2:** explaining what is suggested in a text **(4 marks)**
  - **Question 3:** explaining what is suggested in a text **(8 marks)**
  - **Question 4:** analysing how language is used in a text **(12 marks)**
  - **Question 5:** comparing how presentational features are used in two texts.

    (12 marks)

- The **Higher Tier paper** will have **four** questions:
  - **Question 1**: finding information in a text **(8 marks)**
  - **Question 2**: analysing the presentational features of a text **(8 marks)**
  - **Question 3**: explaining what is suggested in a text **(8 marks)**
  - **Question 4**: comparing the language used in two texts **(16 marks)**

The Assessment

The assessment objective for reading (AO4) states that you must be able to do the following:

- Read and understand texts, selecting material appropriate to purpose, collating from different sources and making comparisons and cross-references as appropriate.
- Develop and sustain interpretations of writers' ideas and perspectives.
- Explain and evaluate how writers use linguistic, grammatical, structural and presentational features to achieve effects and engage and influence the reader.

Targeting Grade C

Some of the key differences between a Grade D and a Grade C are as follows:

Grade D candidates	*See examples on pages 52, 53 and 54*
• show some understanding of texts • use evidence to support what they say • are able to interpret the text • can compare texts and make connections between them.	D

Grade C candidates	*See examples on pages 51, 53 and 55*
• show clearly that the texts are understood • use appropriate evidence to support their views • offer relevant interpretations of the texts • make clear connections and comparisons • leave the reader in no doubt that they know why and how particular features have been used.	C

Item 1

Marathon runner Ron Hill tells of when he was a boy and his dog fell though some frozen ice.

The dog that nearly drowned

I called and called and Bruce began to make his way back, but after a couple of feet the ice became too thick and Bruce couldn't make any further progress. He tried to climb on to the ice but his paws just kept slipping off. After three or four minutes his efforts began to get weaker and weaker and he began to whine. I just couldn't leave him like that, he was loved like one of the family. I'd got him in, so it was up to me to get him out again. I looked around; but there was no one about and I slipped off my clothes until I had on only a pair of swimming trunks, which I was going to wear under my shorts in the afternoon.

I kneeled on to the ice and began to crawl out towards the dog. As I edged closer I could feel the ice beginning to bend, so I stretched out flat trying to reach as far forward as I could for his paws. I slithered slowly out and was just reaching for his collar when the ice gave way and in I went. The shock was terrific! It took my breath away, and all I could gasp was, 'Aagh!' My first thought was of getting my legs caught in weeds or submerged branches, but then I had to think of getting out. I trod water and tried in vain to slide on to the ice myself. I couldn't do it. I tried to push Bruce on to the ice. Again, no success, so I began to smash the ice with my fists. It was slow progress as I was out of my depth and Bruce had his paws on my shoulders for support.

Eventually I reached the trunk of an overhanging willow tree and, with one hand grasping this, yanked Bruce by his collar on to solid ice, then pulled myself up on to the bank.

The Long Hard Road, Ron Hill

By **James Parry**

VENTURE out today on a wildlife ramble and you'd be lucky to see anything much bigger than a rabbit or squirrel. Perhaps a fox (although only if you live in a town). Yet moves are afoot to plot the return of bigger animals long-vanished from our landscape. Yes, we're talking wolf. Possibly lynx. Maybe even bears and bison. It's hard to imagine how this might work but the process of bringing back some of our lost wildlife has already begun.

Although Britain has a good record on wildlife conservation our countryside is a tame old affair. Our ancestors did a great job of cutting down British wildwood and hounding to extinction the animals that lived there.

The last native brown bears were probably wiped out during Roman times, although bears were imported regularly thereafter for the so-called sport of bear-baiting, a favourite entertainment of Queen Elizabeth I. Good Queen Bess was so keen on watching bears fights with dogs that her favourite nobles competed with each other to obtain as many bears as possible for when Her Majesty came to stay. Thankfully she wasn't as extreme as one European count who used to fire live bears out of cannons and then try to shoot the hapless beasts as they hurled through the air.

'Red Kites are busy scavenging road-kill off the M40'

Meanwhile in Britain there were hardly any big animals left to hunt. Once the larger carnivorous mammals and birds of prey had been exterminated attention turned to smaller fry such as wild cats, martens, polecats, hawks, falcons

Daily Express Thursday October 1 2009

WALK ON THE WILD SIDE

NICE TO SEE YOU: Beasts set to return to the UK include, clockwise from left, wolf, elk, lynx and white-tailed eagle

Britain is being 'rewilded' as large animals that once roamed our country are introduced again

and owls. […] Only with the advent of the First World War, when most young estate workers and keepers were sent off to the trenches, did the pressure let up and give surviving predators a chance to bounce back.

Some species haven't needed asking twice. Buzzards and marsh harriers are now more plentiful than for at least 150 years. Polecats are appearing in places where they have not been seen for decades. Red kites, given a helping hand with young birds imported from Sweden and Spain, are busy scavenging road-kill off the M40. […]

NOW the stakes are being upped. In May this year a group of wild beavers were reintroduced to Scotland to the Knapdale Forest in Argyll and immediately set about felling trees and building a dam. It was as if they'd never been away.

But even bolder plans are afoot elsewhere. Paul Lister, the owner of 23,000-acre Alladale Estate in Sutherland, has already released wild boar and elk on to his land and hopes to introduce wolves, lynx and brown bears over the next few years. […]

BUT wolves need space. With the population of Britain spiralling towards 70million it is difficult to see how they could ever "fit" in a densely-populated country like ours. Wolves can probably never really roam free here again. The most we can expect is a huge enclosure in which they live wild but in a controlled environment.

Is it worth the effort or should we just accept that the spirit of the wilderness has no place in Britain any more?

Item 3

DESTRUCTION OF THE RAINFORESTS CAN BE FELT ALL OVER THE WORLD.
HELP STOP IT.

The clearing and burning of rainforests is responsible for 17% of the world's CO2 emissions and contributes directly to the melting of the polar ice-caps.

**Tell the world to stop tropical deforestation by sending a Rainforest SOS.
Visit www.rainforestSOS.org or text SOS and your full name to 60777***

THE PRINCE'S RAINFORESTS PROJECT

RAINFOREST SOS

Targeting Grade C in the Foundation tier exam

Foundation tier questions

Answer these questions.

Read **Item 1,** 'The dog that nearly drowned' by Ron Hill.

1. What four things did Ron Hill do to try to rescue his dog?

1	
2	
3	
4	

4 marks

2. What do we learn about the sort of person Ron Hill was?

Find details from the text and say what they tell us about him.

4 marks

Now read **Item 2,** 'Walk on the wild side'.

3. To what extent does the writer feel that wildlife has a place in modern Britain?

Answer in two sections, beginning:

- 'The writer suggests that wildlife has a place in modern Britain by saying…'
- 'The writer is less positive about the place of wildlife in modern Britain when he says …'

8 marks

4. How does the writer use language to make the article informative and interesting for the reader?

Answer in two sections:

- Language to make it informative.
- Language to make it interesting.

12 marks

Now look again at **Item 2,** 'Walk on the wild side' and look at **Item 3,** 'Destruction of the rainforests can be felt all over the world'.

5. Compare the ways in which these items have been presented in an effective and attractive way.

Compare them using these headings:

- pictures and colours
- headings, subheadings and captions.

12 marks

Total: 40 marks

Targeting Grade C in the Higher tier exam

Higher tier questions

Answer these questions. (Refer back to the three texts on pages 47–49.)

Read **Item 2,** 'Walk on the wild side'.

1. What do we learn about the way wildlife has been treated in Britain?   **8 marks**

Now read **Item 3,** 'Destruction of the rainforests can be felt all over the world'.

2. How have presentational features been used to make the text effective?   **8 marks**

Now read **Item 1,** 'The dog that nearly drowned'.

3. What do we learn about the relationship between Ron Hill and his dog?   **8 marks**

Now you need to refer to **Item 1,** 'The dog that nearly drowned', and to **either Item 2 or Item 3.** You are going to compare two texts, one of which you have chosen.

4. Compare the ways in which language is used in the two texts. Give some examples and explain what the effects are.   **16 marks**

Total: 40 marks

Exploring Sample Responses
Foundation tier

Targeting Grade C in the Foundation tier exam

1. What four things did Ron Hill do to try to rescue his dog?

Example 1

1	He took off his clothes and went on to the ice because he felt it was his fault and there was no other choice if the dog was to be saved.
2	He crawled across the ice to try to be as safe as possible until it broke under him.
3	He smashed the ice with his fists because there was no other way of getting to the side.
4	He allowed the dog to rest its paws on his shoulders because it was worn out from trying to escape.

Examiner feedback

The candidate selects four sensible and separate things, all of which are relevant. He also includes detail with his choices – for example, giving two very accurate reasons for his first choice. He resists the temptation to simply copy out sections of the text.   **Suggested Grade: C**

2. What do we learn about the sort of person Ron Hill was?
   Find details from the text and say what they tell us about him.

Example 2

Ron Hill loves his dog. He says, 'he was loved like one of the family'. He felt he was responsible for the dog being in the water, so he has to try to get him out. He took off his clothes.
   He is brave because he goes out on to the ice to help his pet. We know he can swim but also he is tough because he smashed the ice with his fists. He even manages to get the dog out at the end and also to get out himself so he must have been quite fit but he must have been very cold and obviously wet.

Examiner feedback

This response has some valid points (we know he loved his dog and the point is supported; he is brave because he risks the ice; he must have been fit because he got both of them out) but other points tell us nothing about him ('He took off his clothes'). We get some retelling of the story rather than appropriate selection of detail with comment.   **Suggested Grade: D**

Read the following responses to Questions 3 and 4 and judge how well you have done against the quality of these answers, bearing in mind the Examiner feedback.

3. To what extent does the writer feel that wildlife has a place in modern Britain?
   Answer in two sections, beginning:
- *'The writer suggests that wildlife has a place in modern Britain by saying…'*
- *'The writer is less positive about the place of wildlife in modern Britain when he says…'*

Example 3

focuses on the positive → | offers effective detail | gives opposite viewpoint | provides detail in support →

The writer suggests that wildlife has a place in modern Britain by saying that 'the country is being 'rewilded' as large animals that once roamed our country are introduced again'. This is presented as a fact.
        In the article, he mentions lynx, bears and maybe bisons could be brought here. He tells us that buzzards and marsh harriers are more common than before, and there are polecats and red kites. In Scotland, there are now beavers and might soon even be wolves. All these things suggest there is a place for wildlife in Britain. ◄
        The writer is less positive about the place of wildlife in modern Britain when he says at the end that there will be no room for wildlife because of all the people. Not only that, he has already told us that the British are horrible to animals, like using bear baiting and hunting and shooting birds and animals like wild cats. Anyway, he does not think that wolves will ever be able to roam free.

← gives a quotation for support | sums up and relates back to start | ends strongly

Examiner feedback

This answer deals with both sides of the argument and offers supporting detail for what is said, which is well selected. There is insight into the writer's ideas, which are clearly understood. This also moves way beyond copying from the text, organising the material and summing up the writer's viewpoint with phrases such as 'there will be no room for wildlife because of all the people' and 'All these things suggest…'

Suggested grade: C

4. **How does the writer use language to make the article informative and interesting for the reader?**

    Answer in two sections:
- **Language to make it informative**
- **Language to make it interesting.**

Example 4

<u>Language to make it informative</u>
Ron Hill uses lots of facts to make it clear what is happening, like 'the ice became too thick'. There is also repetition to make it all come to life: 'weaker and weaker'. We also know he loved his dog because he uses a simile: 'like one of the family'. He uses short sentences sometimes and that shows exactly what was happening and how he was feeling: 'I couldn't do it'. He also uses some good verbs which tell us things, like 'yanked' which was when he pulled the dog suddenly out of the water.

<u>Language to make it interesting</u>
Some of the language makes it quite interesting. It starts with 'I called and called' which is repeated like he was repeating himself when he called. And later, he shouts 'Aagh' and we know he is in trouble. He sounds a bit like a snake too when it says 'I slithered slowly out' and then the ice breaks and he says 'The shock was terrific!' which doesn't mean it was good – it means he was really upset. That is why it ends with an exclamation mark.

Examiner feedback

This answer responds to both headings, offering relevant details on which to comment, but often falls short of real clarity in what is said. For example, 'yanked' and 'Aagh' are mentioned, but not the effect they have on the reader. When we read 'There is repetition to make it all come to life', we think that is a comment that could easily apply to any language, in any text. The mention of sounding like a snake is better, though the alliteration and the effect of the 's's is not really dealt with. The fact that the student knows about the effect of the exclamation mark deserves credit.

Suggested grade: D

ACTIVITY

Read the following response to Question 5 and judge how well you have done against the quality of this answer, bearing in mind the Examiner feedback.

5. **Compare the ways in which Items 2 and 3 have been presented in an interesting and attractive way.**

Compare them using these headings:
- **pictures and colours**
- **headings, subheadings and captions.**

Example 5

opens with comparison →

explains why features are used →

gives reason for colour choice →

appropriate vocabulary →

highlights the effect →

explained →

> <u>Pictures and colours</u>
> 'Walk on the wild side' has animals, and the one that stands out is the snarling wolf. On the other hand, 'Destruction of the rainforests' is very peaceful, and the polar bear and frog seem happy together, to show the world could be happier.
>
> Although the 'Walk' pictures are in black and white, they show the sort of animals being talked about in the article. The elk and lynx look beautiful, and the wolf and eagle fit well with the heading. The teeth of the wolf look wild. There is also a map, perhaps showing where the wild animals can be found in Britain.
>
> 'Destruction of the rainforests' is different. It's about global warming and it makes it look as if nature is getting together to say 'please stop', because you would not expect a frog and bear to be together. The blue sea behind them looks dirty, which fits with destruction, and the 'Help stop it', help address and number are in green at the bottom, because this is about try to be greener to save the planet. SOS is the warning in red.
>
> It attracts you, but in a different way to 'Walk on the wild side'.
>
> <u>Headings, subheadings and captions</u>
> 'Walk on the wild side' has alliteration in the title, to make the idea of a wild walk stand out. The pull-quotes are to attract the reader to certain ideas, and the best one is 'Red kites are scavenging road kill off the M40', which makes it seem like the wild life is dangerous. The caption under the picture says what is coming back, but also makes a joke ('Nice to see you') because they may not be very nice.
>
> 'Destruction of the Rainforests' is more serious. 'Help stop it' is short and seems to be shouting at us. The detail about the rainforests at the top is in small font, because they think we will read it after the big heading. At the bottom it is again telling us what to do, and the white writing on the black makes it serious. 'Rainforest SOS' is really noticeable and looks like an emergency is happening. It is not like 'Walk on the wild side' because it is softer and sadder but also demanding things.

← gives some interpretation of features

← more explanation needed

← partly explains pull-quote

← carries on comparison

← ends with sensitive comparison

Examiner feedback

This is a good answer which covers everything that has been asked, gives some clear and quite sensitive comparisons between the texts and backs up everything it says with detail. The black and white terror of 'Walk on the wild side' is set against the much more dreadful situation that is arising through global warming. We feel the candidate knows what the texts are about and ties the impressions created back to the texts' main messages.

Suggested grade: C

Exploring Sample Responses
Higher tier

ACTIVITY

Read the following responses to Questions 1 and 2 and judge how well you have done against the quality of the answers, bearing in mind the examiner feedback.

1. *What do we learn about the way wildlife has been treated in Britain?*
Example 1

opens with a summary →

The writer points out that wildlife has been treated badly in Britain in the past but has been 'making a comeback' more recently.

includes relevant details →

He points out that in the past we lost bears during Roman times, though there was bear baiting later. Then the British hunted 'carnivorous mammals and birds of prey', then the smaller animals and hawks, falcons and owls. However, since the First World War, polecats are back and red kites have been re-introduced from Sweden and Spain which means that the British seem to care more about them.

← gives some interpretation of features

not just copying but selecting information →

Wild beavers have been brought back to Scotland and a man in Sutherland has got wild boar and elk on his land and wants to also have wolves, lynx and brown bears.

However, there is not much land free in Britain, so wolves might have to live in enclosures. This means we are caring but can't do any more for them.

← concludes

Examiner feedback

This response has most of the important details, and they are used to make clear points. There is an appropriate first statement, setting out the basic situations, then and now, and then the response includes information about what was lost and what has been re-introduced. Crucially, the candidate selects what is relevant and the facts are blended with an overview – for example, in the last two sentences.

Suggested grade: C

2. How have presentational features been used to make the text effective?
Example 2

The text shows a polar bear and a frog together, with the frog on the bear's back, so this attracts the reader and makes us think they are together. Actually, the advertisement is trying to get people to help stop rainforest deforestation so it wants us to think about these animals and all the others like them. It has blue at the back, which makes it a bit summery. The title is in white but then 'Help stop it' is in green, because this is about green things. There is green writing at the bottom as well, to remind us of the message at the top and 'SOS' is in red because it also attracts our attention and it is as if the letters are burning.

Examiner feedback

This response identifies many relevant features and says things about them (such as 'it makes us think they are together') but it does not ever make clear comments about their effects. For example, it would have been helpful to say **why** the writer wants us to see the bear and the frog together (perhaps the reader sees different elements of nature sticking together as man destroys the planet). Similarly, towards at the end it shows understanding when pointing out that the letters 'SOS' appear to be on fire, but it would have been useful to say **why** the writer wanted to give that impression; and what is the advantage in creating a depressing impression overall. A better response would have said **how** these things affect the reader and what they make us think – linking all this to the purpose of the advertisement.

Suggested grade: D

ACTIVITY

Produce a better response by examining each of the presentational features and saying how it is intended to affect the reader.

Write about
- how the features help support the text's purpose
- each feature in turn, including mention of the picture, the colours, the headings, information in the text boxes and the overall layout.

ACTIVITY

Read the following responses to Questions 3 and 4 and judge how well you have done against the quality of the answers, bearing in mind the Examiner feedback.

3. *What do we learn about the relationship between Ron Hill and his dog?*

Example 3

begins with a summary that will be developed →

Ron Hill loved his dog, saying it was 'like one of the family'. This is why he could not leave the dog to drown, even if it meant getting into the water himself. He also feels responsible because he says he was the one who caused the dog to be in the water in the first place.

← adds to our understanding of why the writer responded as he did

makes point, supports and explains →

We know how fond he must be. When he has taken off almost all his clothes in the freezing conditions, he risks a real disaster by keeping going even though the ice was 'beginning to bend'. When he actually falls in himself though, he does not just get out. First he still has to rescue his dog. He pushes him and even lets Bruce have his paws on his shoulders, which must have made it very tricky to break the ice with his fists.

← retains focus on question

ends with conclusive idea →

It is also significant that he gets Bruce out first, then follows himself. This proves that they were very close.

← clear points throughout

Examiner feedback

This is a very thorough answer which makes clear points about the relationship and backs up what is being said with quotation or detail from the text. Everything is relevant and each detail is presented in a logical order. Even in the final sentence, the response focuses back on the question. There is never the sense that the story is just being re-told.

Suggested grade: C

4. *Compare the ways in which language is used in the two texts. Give some examples and explain what the effects are.*

Example 4

Ron Hill uses repetition in his story, like 'I called and called' and 'weaker and weaker', which lets us know exactly what was happening. He also uses a simile to describe his dog ('like one of the family'), so Bruce was like a brother to him. He uses alliteration to describe what it was like on the ice: 'I slithered slowly out'. This makes it sound slippy. He also uses some exclamation marks so we know what a shock he had ('Aagh!'). There are a lot of short sentences, such as 'I couldn't do it' and this makes it more descriptive of what was happening. The last sentence though is quite long and that is as he escapes. He uses a verb – 'yanked' – to show how he pulled Bruce out.

The language in 'Walk on the wild side' is not telling a story, it is talking about animals and how they have disappeared. Unlike Ron Hill, it uses some old-fashioned words like 'Venture' and talks about 'Good Queen Bess'. It can be like someone is talking to us because some of the sentences aren't proper sentences, like 'Possibly lynx'. This is chatty, and it isn't like Ron Hill either. He also mentions 'hapless beasts' and calls the smaller animals 'smaller fry'. There are lots more difficult words, such as 'carnivorous' and 'predators' so you would have to be quite bright to read this. It is not as much fun as the Ron Hill text.

Examiner feedback

This response is sensibly organised so that it makes points about the first text and then makes comparisons as it moves through the second text. Some points are almost clear ('This makes it sound slippy') but the comments always fall just short of real relevance (for example, **how** the alliteration gives the sense of slippiness). The response compares the style, noting how the second text has chatty features and also compares the kind of vocabulary used. However, while the student shows some understanding, there is always more to say and they do not provide real insight into how the language affects the reader.

Suggested grade: D

ACTIVITY

Write an improved response to Question 4, remembering to
* compare the language used in both texts
* make clear how the language affects the reader and why
* comment on a selection of language features in each text.

If you only do five things…

1 Try to read at least one non-fiction text each day, always deciding on its purpose and audience.
2 Work out what the writer wants us to think and spot the techniques the writer uses to convince us.
3 Focus on how the writer uses presentational features and explain the effect of these in detail.
4 Select elements of the language you could comment on, such as alliteration or similes.
5 Make comparisons between non-fiction texts, for example comparing how they use pictures and colour. Structure your ideas so that they link and develop.

What's it all about?

Writing non-fiction texts means you have a chance to write a fantastic variety of texts, many of which will be very useful for life after school. What's more, a good letter, exciting news article or a snappy web text can be just as creative as a story or a poem.

What is required?

You will get **20% of your English Language marks** for your ability to write non-fiction texts. You will have to complete **two** written tasks in an exam lasting **one hour**. You will be marked on your writing of **two responses** – one **short**, one **long** – to two set tasks.

What is being tested?

You are being examined on your ability to

- write for specific audiences and purposes
- communicate clearly, effectively and imaginatively
- organise information in a structured way using a range of paragraphs
- use a variety of sentence structures and styles
- use a range of linguistic features for impact and effect
- write with accuracy in punctuation, spelling and grammar.

Purposeful Writing

Introduction

This section of Chapter 2 will help you to

- understand what a question in the written paper is asking you
- understand the meaning of the words, 'purpose, audience, and form'
- come up with good ideas and plan your writing.

Why is planning for purpose important?

- You need to **understand what you have to do** and, once you have done that, to **focus on how you get there**.
- The **plan** helps you stay focused and stick to what you want to write.

A **Grade E** candidate will

- plan with some idea of purpose in mind
- include several points and ideas, but possibly leave out several others
- not include all the correct layout or structure (such as the correct way to close a letter).

E

A **Grade D** candidate will

- plan with the purpose in mind, but without always thinking about the audience or form
- use paragraphs but not link them well, so the structure is not really clear
- include some, but not all, of the relevant features for the chosen form of writing.

D

A **Grade C** candidate will

- plan so that the organisation of his/her writing is effective, for example using clear paragraphing to sequence ideas
- use appropriate features and language to interest the reader.

C

Prior learning

Before you begin this unit, think about:

- what you already know about **purpose**, **audience** and **form**

- previous occasions when you have had to **come up with ideas** for a written task

- how well you structure your written work

- how easy it is to read your handwriting.

Could you jot down what you understand by these terms?

What did you do?
What techniques did you use?

Can others follow your ideas easily?
Why? Why not?

Understanding task, purpose, audience and form

What do these terms mean?

The **purpose** is the **reason for writing** or the **job** it has to do: for example, to persuade or to explain.
The **audience** means the reader or readers, the person or people you are writing **for**.
The **form** is the type or **genre** of writing: letter, article, report.

Checklist for success

- You need to correctly identify the purpose, audience and form in the writing task when you read your examination paper.
- You need to think about all three things when you write your plan.
- You need to make sure your piece of writing is in the right form, does the right job and is suitable for the named audience.

ACTIVITY

Here is a sample task. Look at what the purpose, audience and form are.

Sample title: Write a letter to the manager of your local football club persuading him or her to come to your school to give a talk on leadership.

Form (the type of text) = *letter*
Audience (the reader) = the *football club manager*
Purpose = to *persuade him* or *her* to come to your school to give a talk on leadership

In pairs, note down the **purpose**, **audience** and **form** in the following three tasks.

1 Write a leaflet for householders explaining some of the different ways in which people can save energy in their homes.
2 Write an article for a website called 'Great days out', informing families of your favourite place to visit.
3 Write a letter to your local supermarket manager advising him or her about how the shop could be made more appealing to teenagers.

Focus for development: Matching your writing style to your audience

When you have identified the purpose, audience and form, you need to choose the right style for the task.

Try to picture the audience in your mind's eye. Imagine how you might speak to that person and this will help you to decide how formal or informal your writing should be.

Exploring the terms formal and informal

You have been sent the two invitations below. Discuss with a partner:

- At which party would you dress formally? What does formal mean?
- At which party would you dress informally? What does informal mean?

Year 11 Prom *At The Palace Hotel* *Saturday 6th June* *Dinner and Disco* *Evening Dress*	*Hiya Guys! I'm having a barbeque* *to celebrate the end of exams (hooray!)* *Thursday 4th June* *My back garden – 6ish* *Love Keisha xx*

Now think about writing. What are the features of our language 'wardrobe'?

Gather ideas in a grid like the one below.

Features of formal writing	Features of informal writing
Using standard English *Being polite*	*Using more chatty phrases*

Look again at the sample task on the previous page.

Write the first three or four sentences of your response. You could begin

> *Dear Sir,*
> *We are writing in the hope that you may be able to find some time in your busy schedule to visit our school.*

Make sure

- you don't use slang or chatty language
- your grammar and spelling are correct
- you write in complete sentences.

Glossary

Standard English: the form of English that is generally thought to be grammatically correct and appropriate for polite, formal or professional situations.

Examiner's tip ⭐

Remember the standard way of beginning and ending formal letters.
Dear Sir/Madam ends… Yours faithfully
Dear Mr/Mrs ends… Yours sincerely.

Remember

- **Identifying the purpose, audience and form in the task will help you write in the correct style.**

Planning an answer

What does it mean to plan an answer?

When you plan an answer you are thinking ahead. You note down what you are going to do in a series of easy-to-follow steps.

Checklist for success

- To write a successful plan, you need to
  - answer the **main purpose** of the task
  - cover the **main points** you want to make.
- It is recommended that you spend **five minutes** planning each answer in the exam, then 20 minutes writing the short answer and 30 minutes the longer one. First, though, you need to come up with some **ideas**.

⭐ Examiner's tip

You don't have to use a spider diagram. Try a list, a flowchart, or whatever works for you. The main thing is to get ideas down on paper!

ACTIVITY

Generating ideas

The task is:

form   audience   purpose

> Write a **letter to** your **headteacher advising** him or her about **whether it would be a good idea to make the school day** longer by an hour and a half.

A student has started **generating ideas** using a spider diagram. With a partner, see if you can add any other ideas of your own.

letter of advice – longer school day, good or bad?

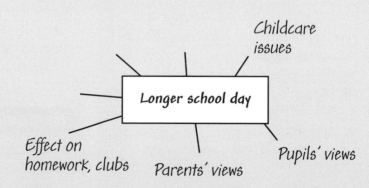

Longer school day

Childcare issues

Effect on homework, clubs

Parents' views

Pupils' views

Focus for development: What makes a good plan

ACTIVITY

Read this plan based on the spider diagram.

Look at the plan with a friend and discuss the following.

- Would you be able to write an answer based on this plan?
- Is there anything else you could add which would help?
- Could it have been organised in a different way? For example, could the 'bad points' come first?

Plan
1. Formal start – Dear Headteacher, Thank you for asking me to advise ...
2. Good points:
– less childcare for parents
– homework done in school, so gets it out of way
3. Bad points:
– some pupils don't like school, so may be problems
– buses, train times?
4. End/conclusion: Overall, a good idea if parents are kept informed

ASSESSMENT FOCUS

Now look at this task.

First, take two minutes to generate ideas, using a spider diagram.

> A website called 'Classic Films' has asked users to review their favourite film, saying why they like it so much. Write about your film.

Now write a plan for six paragraphs. Take no more than four minutes. The first two have been done for you.

1.	Introducing my film – what it's called
2.	Basic story ...
3.	(your ideas/notes)
4.	(your ideas/notes)
5.	(your ideas/notes)
6.	End/conclusion

Examiner's tip ★

As you plan, it's a good idea to jot down some good words or phrases you could use, for example, 'thrill-a-minute film', 'completely hilarious'. Jot them down beside your plan.

Remember

- A good plan will help you write a clear and relevant response.
- Your plan will keep you calm and focused as you write your answer.

Structuring your text

What does structure mean?

The **structure** of the text is the way it is **organised**: how it begins, develops and ends.

Checklist for success

To have a successful structure, you need to

- put your content in a suitable **order** (deciding whether to put your main point right at the start, for example)
- **organise** content effectively (deciding whether to group certain ideas together, or keep them separate, for example)
- make sure the structure **fits the form**.

ACTIVITY

Read this email sent to an employer to ask if they have any job vacancies. The student has forgotten that ideas need to be clear and meet the needs of the reader. His ideas are in completely the wrong order.

- Can you move the sentences around so that the ideas are in a more logical order? What should come first, for example?
- Then, rewrite or change any parts that don't work any more.

To: Brown Buildings Ltd

From: D Samuels

I've got 7 GCSEs (5 with grade Cs) and I have worked in a café for six months. So, if you have any vacancies can you let me know. Oh, by the way, I go to Peters Street High School. Plus, I'm 16. I work really hard too and I'm reliable.

I'm writing because I saw your advert in the paper.

Yours

D Samuels

Focus for development: Finding a logical order

Read this response to the task on page 64 about lengthening the school day. If it were longer, it would be a Grade D response.

> Dear Mr Robson
>
> We should make the school day longer. It's a great idea, and I thoroughly recommend that you go ahead with the change. Yes, there are some negatives, but they are not many.
>
> The good points are that kids get to do their homework, that parents don't have to pick them up til later and this frees them up to do shopping or stay at work. A bad point, though, is that kids will probably get bored at school if they stay too long and they'll miss buses and trains.
>
> More good points could be that kids will spend more time with their friends and this will help friendships.
>
> I hope this helps you make a decision.
>
> Yours sincerely,
>
> David

Talk about these questions with a partner.

- What is the structure here?
- Where does David's 'decision' (what he thinks) come?
- Where does David talk about the good points and where about the bad points?

As this is a formal letter, it needs

- a polite opening
- clear paragraphs in which the ideas are separated out
- connectives to help link, explain or develop ideas, such as 'so', 'therefore', 'In addition' etc.
- a conclusion in the right place – after the different sides of the issue have been put across.

Improve the letter by reorganising the paragraphs and following the plan on page 65.

Give each paragraph a key point and make sure the tone is formal enough.

Develop your ideas fully. For instance, could you offer a solution to how the 'bad points' could be overcome?

A student writes…

What is wrong with giving the conclusion first?

Answer…

It can be done, but if you choose to start by saying what your opinion is, then you will need to do it far more politely than David did. Beginning like this may put off the reader.

Write your own email to an employer, introducing yourself, explaining what you have to offer and asking about job vacancies.
Decide what kind of job you are applying for.
Make sure your tone is suitably formal.

Remember

- Put your ideas in a logical order.
- Make sure the structure suits the purpose and form of the task.

Grade Booster

Extended Exam Task

Now generate ideas, write a plan and decide on a structure/sequence for this question:

> *Write an article to go on the school website in which you persuade your year group to volunteer to work for local charities.*

Remember to follow this process:

Generate ideas ➡ Plan ➡ Decide on structure

Then, if you feel ready, write the opening two paragraphs of your article.

Evaluation – What have you learned?

With a partner, use the grade checklist below to evaluate your work on the Extended Exam Task.

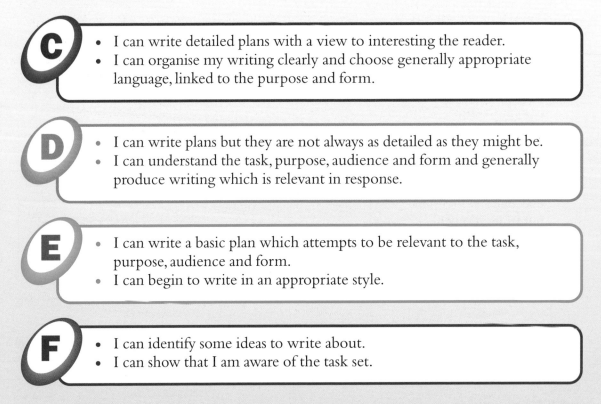

C
- I can write detailed plans with a view to interesting the reader.
- I can organise my writing clearly and choose generally appropriate language, linked to the purpose and form.

D
- I can write plans but they are not always as detailed as they might be.
- I can understand the task, purpose, audience and form and generally produce writing which is relevant in response.

E
- I can write a basic plan which attempts to be relevant to the task, purpose, audience and form.
- I can begin to write in an appropriate style.

F
- I can identify some ideas to write about.
- I can show that I am aware of the task set.

You may need to go back and look at the relevant pages from this section again.

Communicating Clearly, Effectively and Imaginatively

Introduction

This section of Chapter 2 will help you to

- communicate clearly
- select vocabulary for its effect on the reader
- use a variety of sentences accurately
- structure and organise paragraphs
- use a range of accurate punctuation
- begin to engage the reader.

Why is communicating clearly and accurately important?

- Your ideas may be wonderful, but you need to make sure what you have in your head is clear to the reader.
- You also need to make the reader interested in what you have to say.

A **Grade E** candidate will	A **Grade D** candidate will	A **Grade C** candidate will
▪ attempt a range of sentences and use some accurate punctuation ▪ use fairly simple vocabulary, with some attempt made at choosing words for effect ▪ use some paragraphs but without much sense of overall structure.	▪ attempt a range of sentences, though not always chosen for their effect on the reader ▪ use mostly accurate basic punctuation ▪ select a wider vocabulary, but not always appropriately ▪ use paragraphs but not always link them effectively.	▪ use a wider range of sentences, thinking about their effect on the reader ▪ use a generally accurate range of punctuation and a varied and sometimes imaginative vocabulary ▪ use clear, logical and linked paragraphs to structure his/her writing ▪ produce writing that interests the reader.
E	**D**	**C**

Prior learning

Before you begin this unit:

- Make a quick list of any ideas you have about how and when to use paragraphs.
- Note down the different sorts of punctuation marks you can use in writing (for example, full-stops, capital letters and commas) and, if you can, say when and why you use them.
- Look over your past work and pick out any particular difficulties you had with paragraphing or punctuation.

Structuring paragraphs

What does structuring paragraphs mean?

Paragraphs are generally made up of **several sentences**. Deciding how you start your paragraph and what you include in it affects the meaning.

Checklist for success

- You need to use a **topic sentence** to state the main point or idea of your paragraph.
- You need to make sure the sentences in the paragraph are **linked by connectives** where appropriate.

Glossary

Connectives are words or phrases used to link ideas. There are several different types:

To show time or sequence: 'firstly', 'later', 'finally'.

For contrast: 'however', 'on the other hand'.

To show logical order: 'as a result', 'consequently'.

For developing ideas: 'moreover', 'in addition'.

ACTIVITY

This paragraph comes from a task in which the student was asked to advise a younger pupil how to cope with everyday life in school.

Topic sentence introduces first point of advice in response

Second sentence clearly linked to the first by use of the pronoun 'it' (the bell)

> My first piece of advice would be to make sure you arrive well before the bell goes. When it does, there will be a stampede of students into the front hall. As a result, any small Year 7 who is hanging around by the office will be crushed!

Third sentence is linked to the others by a connective and develops the point.

Now write a second paragraph about doing Games or PE.
Advice could be about PE kit, getting changed – whatever.

- Start your second paragraph with a **topic sentence** that makes it clear what your next bit of advice is about in this paragraph. You should refer to Games or PE directly.
- Use at least two further sentences which provide **more detail, or explain the first**.
- If you need to, use **connectives** such as 'because' or 'however'.

Focus for development: Your first paragraph

Although topic sentences are excellent for introducing the main idea in a paragraph, you might like to start your very first paragraph in a more exciting way. Here is the opening paragraph to the advice text for Year 7s.

> 'Can you help me please? I've lost my bag, my best friend and my form room!' These were my first words to a teacher on my first day at secondary school. They sum up everything that can go wrong for a new pupil, and for that reason I am going to give you the benefit of five years' experience in big school. Most importantly, I am going to give you advice on surviving that first day.

Discuss these questions with a partner.
- What technique has the writer used to **grab the reader's attention?**
- How does it make the text **more interesting?**
- At what point do you find out the **main subject** of the text?

There are other ways you can write your first paragraph. For example, you could use a vivid description, an anecdote, a conversation, or even a question.

ASSESSMENT FOCUS

Write the first two paragraphs in response to the following task.

> Your Headteacher has asked for suggestions for someone you know to visit the school and talk to your year group. Write a letter to him or her suggesting someone and persuading the Head why this person would be suitable.

- Make sure the first paragraph grabs the reader's attention.
- The second paragraph should deal with the first main point you want to make.

Remember
- Opening paragraphs should grab the reader's attention.
- Paragraphs usually have a topic sentence that introduces the main idea.

Varying paragraphs

Learning objective

- *To understand how to vary your paragraphs for effect.*

What does varying paragraphs mean?

Paragraphs are usually made up of several sentences. If your paragraphs are all the same length they may not be as interesting to read.

The order of paragraphs in a text affects how the reader follows your point of view.

Checklist for success

- You need to make sure the order of your paragraphs is **logical** and **clear** and that the paragraphs are **linked**.
- Generally, you need to introduce the subject in your first paragraph and sum up in your final one.
- You need to use a variety of paragraphs, some longer and some shorter. Don't just deal with topics in a mechanical and dull way.

⭐ Examiner's tip

It's important to start a new paragraph when you begin to write about a new point. The change of paragraph shows your reader you have something new to say.

ACTIVITY

Read these paragraphs from a Grade D review of a school production.

> This is a review of the school's production of West Side Story. It was really great. It had everything you could wish for. It had good acting and great dancing. It was definitely worth coming to see. Tickets sold out in minutes and we were quite lucky to get in.
>
> Amy Fisher did really well as Maria. She sang beautifully and acted well too. David Wellings in the part of Tony also made an impact. His acting was excellent and we all cried our eyes out when he was killed.
>
> The production design was very effective. The design really reminded me of the streets of New York. The art department did a great job. Miss Harris even got a special bunch of flowers at the end.

Discuss with a partner how the paragraphs could be improved.

Think about

- the opening paragraph's impact
- the content of each paragraph (vocabulary and sentences)
- the length and variety of the paragraphs.

Examiner's tip

Even a simple connective such as 'then' can create an effect. In this example, it brings the writer back to reality – in the school hall.

Here is the ending from a higher grade response.

> The production design was very effective. The art department had created a look that made you feel you were actually walking the streets of New York, and the lighting was moody and romantic. For a moment, you were taken out of the school and over the Atlantic. It was simply wonderful – like a dream.
>
> Then the play ended and the house lights came on. We cheered and cheered but reality had returned. We were in the school hall and it was a rainy Friday night. So much for romance!

What is effective about the second paragraph?

ASSESSMENT FOCUS

You have been asked to write a review of any event at school – sporting, theatrical, musical, or a competition.

Write a plan of five paragraphs in response.

Paragraph 1: say what I'm reviewing and when it happened (grab the attention!)

Paragraph 2: first main point or area discussed

Paragraph 3: next point/development

Paragraph 4: final point/development

Paragraph 5: conclusion.

Remember

- Begin impressively.
- Make each paragraph create an impact through a range of sentences and good vocabulary.
- Use a variety of paragraph lengths for effect.

Exploring sentence types

Learning objective

- To learn how to use sentences accurately and effectively.

What are sentence types?

The way your sentences are constructed can affect your meaning.

Checklist for success

- You need to know that sentences should usually contain at least one main **verb** and a **subject**, and should make complete sense.
- You need to use a variety of sentences (**simple**, **compound** and **complex**) and to use punctuation and capital letters correctly.

ACTIVITY

Read these two extracts written by students to persuade readers that their favourite beach is the best.

This is a **Grade D response**.

> Combe Warren is always sunny. There are sunbeds and there are cafes everywhere and they have hot showers nearby. There are quad bikes to hire. You can see lots of private boats, plus there are also private flats you can hire.

This is a **Grade C response**.

> Combe Warren is always sunny, with sunbeds available whenever you want them. Hot showers are nearby, and there are quad-bikes for hire for those who have the energy. If you have the money, there are private boats for rent, with on-board satellite televisions, mini-bars and, most important of all, luxury ensuite bedrooms. There are also exclusive private flats alongside the beach.

Discuss the two responses with a partner. Try to be precise about why the Grade C response is better.

- What do you notice about the length of sentences in each response?
- What do you notice about the way sentences begin in each response?
- Which response provides more interesting details?
- What do you notice about the punctuation in each response?

Glossary
Verb: a 'doing' or 'being' word
I *am*
She *went*

Focus for development: Three types of sentence

Using a variety of sentences and punctuating them to make the meaning clear is essential for a Grade C and higher. The three main sentence types are: **simple, compound** and **complex**.

A **simple sentence** has a **subject** and **verb**. It must 'make sense' on its own:

subject   verb

Combe Warren is always sunny.

A **compound sentence** links two simple sentences (or clauses) together with 'and', 'or' or 'but':

*Combe Warren is always sunny **and** it has sunbeds and cafés.*

*Combe Warren is popular with holidaymakers **but** it is not as popular as Portland Bay.*

A **complex sentence** adds extra detail to a simple sentence (the main clause):

extra detail   main clause

*When it rains, **you can shelter in the cafés**.*

The **main clause** will make sense on its own but the extra detail (or **subordinate clause**), 'When it rains', does not.

If all your sentences were the same length they would be dull and repetitive, especially if they all began in the same way:

__There are__ luxurious sunbeds. __There are__ lively bars along the beach.

It would be better to combine the sentences, adding extra detail:

__All along the beach__, there are lively bars and luxurious sunbeds, which I love.

Placing the phrase 'All along the beach' at the start, emphasises the beach.

Varying sentence length for effect

What does varying sentence length for effect mean?

Different lengths of sentence can produce different effects.

A **simple** sentence can express an idea simply or clearly, while a series of short simple sentences can create a sense of excitement and pace.

Longer, **complex sentences** can be used to explain or develop ideas, adding extra detail for the reader to think about.

Questions or **command** sentences allow you to address your audience directly.

Sometimes writers use **minor sentences** for impact and emphasis. These are sentences without a verb (*Christmas Day. A time of happiness.*). They force us to read slowly and pay attention to what they say.

Checklist for success

- You need to select the right form and length of sentence.
- Read your writing out loud to hear how your sentences sound.

ACTIVITY

Look at the different sentences used in these charity leaflets.

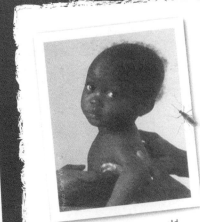

Temba, nearly two years old

EVERY MORNING CHILDREN LIKE TEMBA WAKE UP WITH MALARIA.

MANY OF THEM WILL DIE.

A goodnight kiss. A hug. Then, as they sleep, you hope that tonight your child won't be bitten by the mosquito that will take their life.

Temba was bitten by a mosquito carrying malaria, a disease which is the main killer of children under 5 in Africa.

Copy and complete the table below.

Discuss with a partner the effect of each sentence, thinking about the message and purpose of the leaflet.

ARE YOU ALONE?

DRAW THE CURTAINS. SIT IN A COLD ROOM. **SPEAK TO NO ONE.**

That's Christmas for 1 million older people in the UK.

[...] With your help we can change all this. Even a small donation could transform Christmas for lonely older people, enabling us to provide them with Christmas Lunch at a community centre, bringing them warmth, entertainment, and much-needed relief from their loneliness.

Sentence	What type of sentence is it (simple, complex, question, command, minor)?	Possible effect on the reader
Many of them will die.		
Temba was bitten by a mosquito carrying malaria, a disease which is the main killer of children under 5 in Africa.		
A goodnight kiss.		
Are you alone?		
Speak to no one.		
Even a small donation could transform Christmas for lonely older people…		

ASSESSMENT FOCUS

Work in teams to write the text for a leaflet for a charity of your choice.
- write a dramatic simple sentence for the slogan
- provide information using a range of simple, compound and complex sentences
- use rhetorical questions, or questions and answers, and command sentences to engage the reader.

Remember

- Vary sentence length to create effects.
- Use questions and commands to involve your audience.

Using punctuation accurately

Learning objective

- *To understand that punctuation must be accurate.*

What does accurate punctuation mean?

It means you are using the main punctuation marks correctly and in the right contexts, so that your writing is clear and effective.

Checklist for success

For a Grade C you should
- use punctuation marks accurately
- try to use as full a range as possible (see pages 80 to 81).

ACTIVITY

Read this student's response to a task about raising the school leaving age to 19. What has he done well? What needs to improve?

> It is clearly crazy to raise the school leaving age to 19. Everyone needs a break from education its a fact that many children would like to leave school when theyre 9 let alone 19. As my friend Jake puts it, more school. No way.

Focus for development: Basic sentence punctuation

Full stops and capital letters

Full stops exist to mark the end of a unit of sense.

Capital letters indicate the start of a new unit. They are also used to highlight names of people and places, days, months and titles.

> *Schooldays are the best days of your life.*
>
> *I'm not sure I agree with that statement and my friend Jake doesn't either.*
>
> *Now it's nearly June, the pressure is on at Bilton High School, where they expect good results.*

Commas

You use **commas** to

- separate items in a list (except the final two items which are joined by 'and' or 'or'):

  School has many facilities such as **a cosy canteen, great playing fields, brilliant IT facilities and a theatre space**.

- separate extra detail (subordinate phrases and clauses) from the main part of the sentence:

  Despite my best efforts, the team were absolutely useless, **so we were thrashed 10–0!**

  Lucy, **a really true friend**, lent me the money.

- separate connectives that begin a sentence:

  Finally, we were ready to go.

  A day later, the painting was finished.

Apostrophes

Apostrophes put in the wrong place – or left out altogether – can lose you valuable marks. Remember, they are used to

- show **possession**. If the owner is **singular** (just one), it goes before the 's':

  Bilton High's Principal; my friend's schoolbag

  *If the owner is **plural (more than one)**, it goes after the 's':*

  pupils' coats; students' coursework

- show **omission** (when a letter or letters have been removed). The new word that is created is called a contraction and sounds more informal.

  you have not – you haven't

  you are winning – you're winning

ACTIVITY

Decide where commas should be added to make these sentences clearer.

> It's true that school has lots of qualities such as seeing friends teaching you new stuff and preparing you for life.
> However there's a limit to what school can do.
> Although school's brilliant it is only one part of your life, despite what teachers say.
> Life for all its faults is the best education.

ACTIVITY

Here are the final sentences from the same student. Rewrite them, adding or removing apostrophes to make it correct.

> Its clear to me that youll get the best quality of life if you leave at 16 or 18. Pupil's lives will be better if school ends sooner rather than later.

Examiner's Tip ★

Watch out for its/it's and your/you're.
it's = shortening of it is or it has
its = belonging to it
you're = shortening of you are
your = belonging to you

Remember

- **Check your sentences carefully for accurate punctuation.**

Using a range of punctuation

What does the full range of punctuation mean?

There are many punctuation marks that can help your writing other than full stops, commas and apostrophes. To target Grade C, try using exclamation marks, question marks, speech marks, brackets, dashes and colons.

Checklist for success

- You need to use a range of punctuation.
- You need to make sure it is accurate and appropriate.
- If you can, try to use it for effect.

ACTIVITY

Exclamation marks add impact and are used to show humour or emotion such as anger or surprise.

Shopping in the sales is possibly the worst experience I have had in a long time!

When the doors to the centre opened it was like someone had fired a starting pistol!

Add one exclamation mark and one set of brackets to make this text 'come alive'.

I absolutely adore shopping in the sales. The sight of those red banners and half-price stickers is enough to drive me crazy. I empty my pocket-money tin which is usually full of 20 pence pieces, persuade my dad to advance me a fiver for washing the car and then head off to town.

★ Examiner's tip

Don't over-use exclamation marks or your text will seem to 'shout out' from the page. It is best not to use them in a formal text.

ACTIVITY

Discuss with a partner how this writer uses the following two types of punctuation.

Brackets

Having children is one of the most wonderful (and most expensive!) experiences of your life.

Dashes

Babies demand a lot of time, energy and love – not to mention sleep – but are well worth it.

Now try it yourself. Add brackets to this sentence to highlight a particular part of it.

Shopping in the sales is an expensive and physically dangerous experience.

Focus for development: Adding information

Colons can

- introduce a list, after a statement:

  Shopping is hard work: the queues, the long walks, the grumpy shop assistants and the despair of not finding what you want.

- introduce a clause that develops or leads on from another clause:

  The store closed: at last it was silent.

ASSESSMENT FOCUS

Now use the full range of punctuation marks you have learned about to write the opening two paragraphs to this exam task.

> *Write a light-hearted article for a magazine in which you argue that snowballing is not a fun activity.*

Remember

- Accuracy is vital for a Grade C.
- Use the full range of punctuation marks (brackets, dashes, colons and exclamation marks) to create effects – but don't over-use them.

Selecting vocabulary

What does selecting vocabulary mean?

Vocabulary is your **particular choice** of **individual words** and **phrases**. For example, you might select the word 'thrilling' rather than 'good' to describe an album in a review.

Checklist for success

In order to use vocabulary successfully, you need to choose words or phrases that

- **accurately describe** what you have in your mind
- **create** the **effect** you want by painting pictures in the reader's mind
- **fit** what you are writing about and are **appropriate** to your audience.

For Grade C, you need to choose vocabulary that will have an effect on the reader.

EXAMPLE

Read this extract from a **Grade D response**. The student has been asked to persuade a large business to open a new shop in her town.

> You should open a shop in our town because it's really dead. There's nothing for young people and they reckon it's dead, too, so come to our town and help us out. There are lots of shops we could have, I don't care, as long as what comes is for young people.

This is a fair response because it

- **answers the task** (it is trying to persuade the business to come to her town)
- is written in **sentences** with mostly accurate **punctuation**.

However, the vocabulary is rather dull and repetitive. It also sounds informal and unprofessional. More detail could have been added to develop the student's description of the town and her suggestion for what would improve it.

ACTIVITY

- With a partner, look for the words that are repeated. (Ignore words like 'for'.)
- Where might the student have added more detail?
- Which parts sound a bit too informal?
- How could you improve it?

Focus for development: Building vocabulary

You can improve your vocabulary in lots of ways, as this table shows.

Feature	Example before improvement	Example after improvement
Use more precise, professional language.	*If you **look at** our town, you'll **get** what I'm saying.*	*If you **visit** our town, you'll **understand / recognise / empathise with** what I mean.*
Use specific, not general, terms.	*We could **put** lots of **trees** down the **roads** all over town.*	*We could **plant** **willows / beeches / cypresses** along the **high street** and **residential roads**.*
Add detail.	*New shops are needed which are attractive.*	*New, **customer-friendly** and **chic** shops are needed, which are **attractive, welcoming** and offer **good value**.*
Use more powerful verbs, adverbs, adjectives and nouns.	*Our town needs help.*	*Our **suffering** town **desperately needs** of a **boost**.*
Use imagery.	*The streets are empty.*	*The **dusty, grey** streets are **as empty as an abandoned film-set**.*

ACTIVITY

The same student has now had a go at rewriting the first two sentences. What is better than in the original version?

> I would definitely recommend that you open a shop or other retail outlet in our poor old town's concrete-jungle of a centre because it's incredibly quiet. It is in desperate need of a shot in the arm from your company.

The same student has also written about where the new shop could go.

> The new shop could go at the end of the high street. This is a good location because lots of people would come. It's near a nice park bit and you could put seating there. People would like sitting there. In the summer there's a street market which is really fun. You would get people who shop there popping in.

Rewrite this, improving it to Grade C or better:

* Strengthen words or phrases (for example, 'good location', 'really fun').
* Be more precise or specific. (What types of 'people'?)
* Give more detail. (What about the 'park-bit'? Is 'nice' all that she could say?)
* Find alternatives for repeated words.

Alternatively, write your own response to the tasks from scratch.

Read this question.

> A tourist magazine has a section called 'Visit this beach'. Write an article for it in which you persuade readers to visit a beach you have chosen. You will need to describe the beach and what makes it so great.

Start by planning what you are going to include. Use this table to find interesting vocabulary to describe the different aspects of the beach. Try to use **specific nouns**, rather than general ones like 'buildings' or 'people'.

Feature	Examples	Others?
Buildings, places	café, beach-hut, bar, sailing-club, harbour	
People	tourists, visitors, shopkeepers, lifesavers	
Beach/landscape	pebbles, stones, dunes	
Weather	sky, clouds, storm, sun, shade	

Once you have your nouns, you can build up your descriptions with adjectives, to create a picture in your reader's mind. For example:

*a **stylish** bar with **polished wood** decking which looks over the **glamorous, white** yachts in the **little** harbour*

***tanned, muscle-bound** lifesavers checking me out!*

Glossary

Noun: a word for a thing, person, place or idea – *grass*

Adjective: a word which adds detail to a noun – ***green, smooth** grass'*.

A student writes…

I get all the stuff about making vocabulary better but I don't know how to get started.

Answer…

For a piece like this, it can be good to start by thinking of places or things you can picture in your mind (for example, 'the promenade' or 'a luxury hotel with a pool').

ASSESSMENT FOCUS

Either: | Write the first two paragraphs of your own response to the task on page 84.

Or: | Use the response below as a starting point and add two more paragraphs of your own in a similar style.

> The best beach you could possibly wish for is Rolliwell Bay. You couldn't find a more relaxing, more refreshing or more beautiful place. With fluffy sand, calm clear water, and exceptional views,...

Remember

- Build ideas using vocabulary, choosing specific nouns and adding detail with adjectives.
- Try to keep your writing lively and interesting – come up with a variety of words and phrases.
- Engage your reader by painting a picture with your choice of words.
- Get the tone right (formal or informal) for your audience.

Grade Booster

Extended Exam Task

Now write at least three paragraphs in response to this task.

> *Is there an everyday activity which you hate doing?*
> *Write an article for a magazine explaining what it is*
> *and why you dislike it so much.*

Make sure your focus is on communicating two or three ideas clearly and imaginatively through

- varied sentences
- appropriate, well-chosen vocabulary
- accurate and effective punctuation
- clear and logical paragraphing.

Evaluation – What have you learned?

With a partner, use the grade checklist below to evaluate your work on the Extended Exam Task.

C
- I can use an increasing variety of sentence forms, accurately punctuated.
- I can use logical paragraphs and clearly present main ideas.
- I can communicate my viewpoint and support it with some good ideas.
- I can use well chosen, but not especially varied, vocabulary.

D
- I can use simple sentences, and occasionally complex ones.
- I can sometimes use more varied vocabulary, but it is still rather limited.
- I can use paragraphs but they lack thought and variety.
- I can create a point of view but it is not well developed.

E
- I can use simple sentences, and attempt longer ones but often with inaccurate punctuation.
- I can use paragraphs mostly correctly but with little or no sense of their effect.

F
- I can use simple sentences and vocabulary.
- I can use paragraphs sometimes but not always properly or set out as they should be.

You may need to go back and look at the relevant pages from this section again.

Writing to Engage the Reader

Introduction

This section of Chapter 2

- looks at how you can interest your readers in your work
- explores how you can adapt form and style to your readers' needs
- develops your use of some particular language features.

Why is it important to engage your reader's interest?

- No one wants to read a text that is dull or does not provide what the reader wants.
- You will be more persuasive, appear knowledgeable, and be better understood if your writing creates impact.
- The higher grades at GCSE are given when the writing is not just clear but also makes the reader really take notice.

A **Grade E** candidate will

- have a sense of purpose and audience
- communicate his or her main ideas reasonably clearly
- choose some appropriate features to meet the audience's needs
- attempt to sustain and/or develop ideas.

E

A **Grade D** candidate will

- have a sense of purpose and audience
- develop and communicate his or her main ideas
- use some appropriate, if limited, language techniques to meet the audience's needs but the tone and ideas will not always be sustained.

D

A **Grade C** candidate will

- have a very clear sense of purpose and audience
- communicate his or her ideas clearly and appropriately
- clearly attempt to engage the reader using particular language techniques for effect
- clearly attempt to sustain and develop ideas.

C

Prior learning

Before you begin this unit, think about

- any particularly impressive texts, or parts of texts (maybe an opening to a story, or an end to a report?) you have written when your writing has really 'shone' and made an impact your teacher
- what keeps **you** interested in texts or engaged in what the writer has to say
- what techniques or approaches you already know that help your writing create an impact on the reader, or sustain their attention.

Adapting texts to purpose

What does adaapting texts to purpose mean?

Often, you need to change your approach according to the purpose of a text (for example, an absence note wouldn't work as a 100 page novel!).

Checklist for success

- Use the common features for a specific text: for example, a headline for a newspaper article.
- Change the language to fit the situation: use serious language for a serious issue.

ACTIVITY

Look at the following front page of a two-page leaflet.

Playing sport is great for your health. In my opinion you really should give it a go, 'cos it's great fun and you will feel the benefit to your body. I used to be really unfit and a bit lonely but doing sport has made me fit and now I also meet lots of people which is great. I don't feel out of breath and my body is kinda toned now, which is also great. So, play sport and feel great!

It makes some good points:

- Sport can help you get fit.
- Your body can become more toned – and look good.
- It can help with general breathing.
- Sport is great fun – you meet people.

However, it could be improved.

Discuss with a partner what is *wrong* with it as a leaflet.

Think about

- what the purpose of a leaflet usually is
- the presentational features you would expect to see
- how the language might need to change
- what other features might be vital.

Note down:

- What might be the leaflet's purpose (or purposes)?
- How has the writer tried to engage the reader with his/her use of language?
- What point of view emerges?
- How does the sequence of the sentences lead the reader into the detailed discussion?

Focus for development:
Improving the layout

Here is the same leaflet, with some improvements.

THINK SPORT'S A WASTE OF TIME? THINK AGAIN!

Playing sport:

★ Enhances and maintains fitness
★ Allows for better respiration
★ Exercises the muscles you never use
★ Is fun, friendly and sociable.

For more info visit sport4health.com or talk to your local doctor about opportunities to get fit locally. More info overleaf.

ASSESSMENT FOCUS

Draft a leaflet to warn people about the dangers of only eating 'fast-food' and 'takeaways'.

- Try to include a catchy heading – for example, notice how the sport leaflet repeats 'Think' and uses a question and command sentence to address the reader directly.
- Consider using bullet points and simple, clear and professional-sounding words and phrases.

Remember

- Make the language you choose fit the form.
- Consider basic features of layout.

Adapting language to purpose

Learning objective

- To understand how to write in different ways on the same subject.

What does adapting language to purpose mean?

In the exam, you will be told clearly what your purpose is: for example, whether to explain, argue or persuade. This will mak a difference to how you write and what you say.

Checklist for success

- Choose your language carefully according to the task, purpose and audience.

ACTIVITY

Read these two articles on the same topic – CCTV surveillance.

EXAMPLE 1

> I passionately believe that CCTV cameras are an invasion of our privacy. Nowadays they are on every street corner, in every shop and even in many schools. They are silent, secretive and scary. Do we really want every aspect of our lives watched? Certainly not!

EXAMPLE 2

> So what are CCTV cameras and why are there so many on our streets? The CCTV camera is a device, often owned by an organisation or business, which records on computer or tape the movements of people. The answer to why there are so many probably lies in rising levels of crime and the fact that some are concerned that there are not enough police on the beat. Others feel differently, saying that...

Discuss with a partner:
- Which text is arguing a particular point of view?
- How do you know which text is arguing a point of view? (Think about the language and how it is written.)

Focus for development:
Writing to argue a personal point of view

Example 1 on page 90 uses some language features that are often used when you write to argue a personal viewpoint:

- the first person ('I')
- rhetorical questions ('Do we really want …?')
- emotive, powerful language ('passionately')
- lists, or repeated words ('every')
- patterns of three ('silent, secretive and scary').

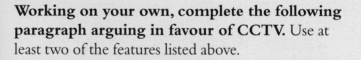

ACTIVITY

Working on your own, complete the following paragraph arguing in favour of CCTV. Use at least two of the features listed above.

CCTV is needed in every city. Can we really allow …

Now compare your paragraph with a partner's. Identify the 'argue' features you used.

⭐ Examiner's tip

For questions like this, it is generally best to use quite a formal tone even if you think a chatty, conversational style might connect with some readers. Remember: you must sustain this tone throughout.

ASSESSMENT FOCUS

Write one or two more paragraphs of the text arguing in favour of CCTV. Try to use further features from the list.

Remember

- Subjects can be the same, but the way you approach them (to analyse, explain or argue for/against them) will affect the language you choose.

Using imagery for effect

What does using imagery for effect mean?

Imagery is the use of language techniques, such as similes and metaphors, to 'paint pictures' in the reader's mind.

Checklist for success

You need to make sure that when you are writing to describe something you create a clear picture for the reader in their mind's eye.

ACTIVITY

Here, Kathy Lette describes putting on fake tan in preparation for a holiday.

It said 'rich Mediterranean' on the bottle, but I was beginning to look more tandoori than tanning salon. My so-called 'tan' pulsated. It radiated. I looked as if I was wearing a tangerine wet suit, with darker elbow patches and kneepads. I was like a distress flare. People could employ me at the scene of a boating accident.

Good Housekeeping

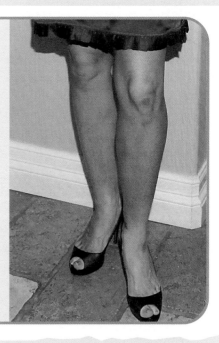

Discuss with a partner two ways in which Kathy Lette has used imagery.

- Think about her use of **similes**.
- Think about her use of **powerful verbs** to describe how her tan looked and felt.

Glossary

Simile: a simile compares one thing to another thing using the words 'as' or 'like'.

Verb: a 'doing' or 'being' word.

I *was*

It *radiated*.

Kathy Lette used these techniques to make her writing come to life – and make us laugh. She has used description **related to the senses** to help us imagine how she felt.

Focus for development:
Describing the look and feel

Look at this task.

> *Describe the strangest outfit you ever had to wear and how it made you look and feel.*

Now create a simile that you could use in a response. You can develop one of the similes below or write one of your own. Try adding some extra adjectives to make it funny.

> *The huge, fluffy, white woolly coat my gran gave me made me look like ...*

> *The hat was grey, round and enormous; it looked like I was wearing a ...*

Now use **metaphors** to describe what it was like to wear the outfit. Try to include **powerful verbs**, too. For example:

> *The trousers strangled my legs they were so tight. My muscles throbbed and ached for a whole week.*

A student writes...

Similes are easy, but I don't get metaphors.

Answer...

Metaphors are when you compare one thing to another by saying it actually is something else, for example: 'In my pink, long, skin-tight trousers I was an overgrown flamingo'. It's a more powerful way of expressing an idea.

Examiner's tip ★

You need to judge when to use imagery. For example, in more logical texts, like explanations, imagery would not be so suitable.

Write an article advising students in Year 7 about what they should wear and bring to school.

Make the article lively – this is a 'survival guide' for your audience!

You could write about

uniform:

- how to wear the tie/uniform
- what your hair should look like

other matters:

- what sort of bag or pencil-case they should bring
- what coat to wear – or not!

Write at least two paragraphs, and use some amusing similes or metaphors to get your points across.

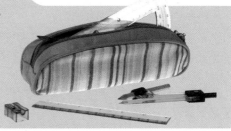

Remember

- Imagery can help readers to picture your ideas.
- Choose carefully when to use imagery; don't over-use similes.
- Powerful verbs can be as effective as long similes.

Sustaining your ideas and tone

What does sustaining your ideas mean?

It means keeping to the task, following what you set out to say, and using the right language from start to finish.

Checklist for success

- Be clear about your outcome – if you stated your aim at the beginning, have you kept to it at the end?
- Keep to the style you start with. For example, don't suddenly become informal (unless for deliberate effect) in a formal text.
- Try to engage and hold the reader's attention throughout.

ACTIVITY

Read the opening to the Grade C response to this task.

> It is often said that we are a nation of animal lovers. If that is true, why does the RSPCA report rising numbers of abandoned animals every year? Write an article in which you argue either for or against the idea that people should only be allowed a maximum of one pet at home.

> Do people really deserve to have pets? The RSPCA reports rising numbers of abandoned animals, and I would like to consider in this article whether one solution would be to simply limit how many pets a person can have. Perhaps there could even be a test to make sure people are fit to keep a pet in the first place. Animals are really important and I feel we should care for them properly.

Discuss with a partner:

- Has the student said what his intention is in writing the article?
- Is he actually answering the task?
- Does the style – so far – seem appropriate to the task?

Focus for development:
Planning to sustain your ideas

To be successful, you need to be writing in the same way at the end as you were are the start. Your ideas and tone need to be consistent.

ACTIVITY

Now read the final paragraph from the student's article about pet ownership.

> I love animals and I think most people do. Pets become part of the family, and deserve to be cared for properly. Although some people want lots of pets, maybe it would be best if they just had one each and gave that animal all their love. If they deserve a pet, the pet deserves affection.

With your partner, discuss these questions, finding evidence to back up your opinion.

- Does the ending sustain the ideas from the opening?
- Is the same style maintained? Is it still addressing the same audience?

ASSESSMENT FOCUS

Write your own article in response to the pet ownership task. Give yourself 35 minutes to plan and write it in – no more!

If you need a reminder of planning techniques, turn to page 64.

Remember

- **Your text must be consistent. Take a 'step back' to check your style, viewpoint and tone have been sustained throughout.**

Writing to persuade and advise

Learning objectives

- *To learn how to persuade and advise effectively.*
- *To be aware of techniques which can be used to persuade and advise.*

What is the difference between persuading and advising?

When you **persuade**, you try to make someone accept your point of view, or do what you want.

Advising is similar but the focus is usually on trying to help someone, which is not always the case when you are persuading (you may want someone to give *you* money, for example).

Checklist for success

- When writing to persuade, you need to ask yourself: will this convince the reader?
- For any piece of advice, you need to ask if it is detailed enough, so someone will accept your advice.

Focus for development: Convincing the reader

Persuading

You need to organise your ideas sensibly and use techniques to help persuade your reader that yours is the right point of view. You might

- simply focus on one viewpoint
- balance your view against the opposite point of view, as in an argument, but show that yours is better!
- use **emotive language** to convince the reader
- include examples and **anecdotes** to illustrate your ideas
- use rhetorical questions to hammer home what you say.

Notice how this **Grade C** response uses persuasive techniques.

> **Glossary**
> **emotive language** is language which touches the emotions: 'Tiny starving babies, crying out for food'
> **anecdote**: an extended example; a very short story

definite; allows no challenge →

list of three to impress →

extra ideas →

rhetorical question →

> Stratford is a great place to live. It's got <u>the theatre, Shakespeare's</u> <u>birthplace and where he's buried,</u> but that's not why most people like living there. You don't have to worry about lots of heavy traffic (well, apart from the visitors going to see plays!) and you've got countryside all round, which can be fun, even if lots of people don't believe it. Most people would like to live with lovely clean air all around and being able to hear birds singing if they could, wouldn't they?

← a touch of emotive language

Write the opening paragraph of an article to persuade the reader that a city of your choice is the most beautiful in the world. Use persuasive techniques.

Advising

Here are the main techniques you could use:

- setting out a problem, then giving a solution
- dealing with each part of the problem in turn
- using imperative verbs ('Remember', 'Do this')
- using a more sensitive approach ('Have you ever considered...?')
- using logic and evidence to support what you say.

ACTIVITY

Discuss with a partner how this Grade D advice might be improved by

- adding detail
- varying sentence length
- using a more sensitive approach.

You must find yourself a new boyfriend, and quickly. Things aren't going to improve. You need to tell him straight that it's all over. Don't be nice to him. He won't listen then. The important thing is to do it sooner rather than later.

ASSESSMENT FOCUS

Write a letter to a friend to advise them to work harder for their exams and to persuade them they will be glad later if they do.

Use effective persuasive and advice writing techniques.

Remember

- **People usually respond better if your advice and persuasion is sensitive rather than heavy-handed.**
- **Using suitable techniques will make your writing more convincing.**

Writing to inform and explain

Learning objectives

- To learn how to inform and explain effectively.

- To understand the differences between the two types of writing.

What is the difference between informing and explaining?

The difference between these two types of text is important.

Information writing involves presenting facts and perhaps offering a personal interpretation of them.

Explanation writing involves going behind a set of facts and explaining why things have happened or how they can be improved. It means interpreting the information.

Checklist for success

- You can improve your writing to inform by adding facts and details. Think about how newspaper reports try to engage their readers.
- Writing to explain is best when it moves logically from information to explanation. For example, you might write:
  - what the situation is (information)
  - how it came about (information and explanation)
  - how we might resolve it (explanation).

EXAMPLE

This extract from a **Grade C** response **informs** about having to move home and **explains** the problems involved.

gives information about the change and begins to explain the problem →

more details →

> I moved from my dad's house in Barnsley to live with my mum in Eastbourne and everything was different. Barnsley is where I had always lived and I knew what it was like. Eastbourne made me feel scared at first.
>
> My mum was renting this sort of apartment, in North Harbour. It was really posh. I had to get used to all sorts of new things. People spoke differently and couldn't understand me some of the time. Not only that, they made fun of me and that's really hard to get used to.

← personal slant on the change

introduces the main problem

develops explanation and shows feelings

Focus for development:
Clarity and effectiveness

Informing

Writing to inform usually contains facts and sometimes interprets them too. Research the facts when you can but be ready to invent them in an exam.

Explaining

When you give reasons for some facts, you might be explaining

- why something happened and the effect it had
- how someone feels about something.

ACTIVITY

Write a paragraph to inform your reader about what life is like where you live.

Include facts or statistics and interpret them (for example, 'So, we must do more to help the pensioners…')

ACTIVITY

Complete a table like this about where you live.

Problem with area	Explanation: how it came about	Explanation: how it could be solved
Vandalism	Not enough to do	More youth centres/evening activities

ACTIVITY

Read this Grade C piece by a student explaining what his area is like.

With a partner, identify the **information** and then the **explanations**.

My town is not the sort of place anyone would choose to live. There is nothing for young people to do because the council is not prepared to spend any money on what we need. At the same time, older people have to sit indoors and just watch television because since the college closed there aren't even night classes for them to go to …

ASSESSMENT FOCUS

Write a letter to a shop to
- inform them about the present you bought from them
- explain what went wrong with it.

Remember

- **Use detail whenever you can to make your ideas more believable.**
- **When you are explaining, give reasons.**

Writing to review

What does reviewing mean?

A review looks back at something and examines it critically. It offers opinions. Good reviews look beyond the obvious and pick out different parts for comment.

Checklist for success

Learn from reviews in newspapers and magazines. See how they review television programmes, films, plays and music.

Reviews

Look at this **Grade C** review. It looks back on an event and criticises, with detail not just comment.

overview of event ⟶ *Everyone had been looking forward to our big day. We all thought we would raise hundreds of pounds for Macmillan nurses, but it went pear-shaped and everyone was really disappointed.*

details of what happened and begins to comment ⟶ *It started well enough, and even though the mayor did the opening, she wasn't as boring as we expected. Everyone rushed off to the stalls and started hooking ducks and things, but then the rain came down and we weren't prepared for it...*

ACTIVITY

Think about the last TV drama you watched. What would you say about it if you were asked to review it? Think about its strengths and weaknesses.

Strengths/weaknesses	Comments to make

Focus for development:
Sustaining an approach

This means

- structuring your ideas into an effective order
- using the same style throughout
- linking your opening and ending, so that you return to the ideas you began with.

ACTIVITY

Read the start of this Grade E review.

> I went round to my mate Alfie's last week. We were going to the park but in the end we stayed in. The TV programme we watched instead was rubbish. I've seen better things on kids' programmes. It was all aliens and strange things and some man who pretended to be Scottish. What's that all about? It just wasn't real. Nobody would have believed it. The special effects were awful. I hated the music. The best thing was the coke and pizza we rang up for afterwards.

With a partner, discuss what needs to be improved.

- Break down the ideas, so that each one could form a paragraph. Add anything extra that is needed, including opinions. For example:

  1 *When/where saw the programme: name of TV drama, who was in it, etc.*

  2 *Main character: Scottish. Not convincing. Clearly using a false accent.*

- Use the student's thoughts about the film to decide what sort of ending the review might have. Write the ending, making up the details you need.

ASSESSMENT FOCUS

Write the review of your chosen TV drama, making sure you

- use an effective opening and ending
- analyse what happened
- include relevant detail
- give your opinions.

Remember

- For reviews, you need to include details to support your opinions.
- Readers will be more interested if you include detail.
- Sustain your style and link your opening and ending.

Grade Booster

Extended Exam Task

Draw on what you have learned about engaging the reader's interest to respond to this task.

> *Write an article for a cycle magazine offering advice to cyclists on how to deal with aggressive car and van drivers.*

Think about how you can

- create an impact with some powerful language and examples
- use a personal style which fits the text (an article for a magazine)
- make sure you develop your points.

Evaluation – What have you learned?

With a partner, use the grade checklist below to evaluate your work on the Extended Exam Task.

C
- I can offer a clear response to the purpose and audience and write with some success so that the audience is interested.
- I can use language for effect and can sustain an appropriate tone.
- I can develop my ideas and structure my writing effectively.

D
- I can write suitably for the purpose and audience.
- I can begin to develop ideas.
- I can [sometimes] use interesting language but occasionally my tone is not sustained.
- I can organise my writing but don't always link ideas well.

E
- I can communicate with some success and attempt to write a convincing response.
- I can use some features that are appropriate, so that at some points it reads like a suitable article.
- I can attempt to develop my ideas.

F
- I can write about the subject and offer a few relevant ideas, though the style is not convincing.

You may need to go back and look at the relevant pages from this section again.

Exam Preparation

Introduction

In this section you will

- find out the exact facts about, and requirements of, the written element of Unit 1B of the exam
- read, analyse and respond to two sample answers by different candidates
- plan and write your own answer to a sample question
- evaluate and assess your answer and the progress you have made.

Why is exam preparation like this important?

- If you know exactly what you need to do, you will feel more confident when you sit the real exam.
- Looking at sample answers by other students will help you see what you need to do to improve your own work.
- Planning and writing a full sample response after you have completed the chapter will give you a clear sense of what you have learned so far.

Key Information

Unit 1 is Understanding and Producing Non-Fiction Texts.

- It has an exam of **2 hours**, worth **80 marks**.
- It is worth **40%** of your overall English Language GCSE mark.
- Section A of the exam is on Reading.
- Section B of the exam is on Writing.

Section B Writing

- The writing part of the exam is **1 hour** long, and is worth **40 marks**.
- It is worth **20%** of your overall English Language mark.
- You will be asked to write **two pieces** of writing.
- One of the writing tasks is a **shorter task,** worth **16 marks**. You should spend about **25 minutes** on this task, including reading and planning time.
- One of the writing tasks is **slightly longer**, worth **24 marks**. You should spend about **35 minutes** on this task, including reading and planning time.

The Assessment

The Assessment Objectives for Writing (AO4) states that you must:

- Write to communicate clearly, effectively and imaginatively, using and adapting forms and selecting vocabulary appropriate to task and purpose in ways that engage the reader.
- Organise information and ideas into structured and sequenced sentences, paragraphs and whole texts, using a variety of linguistic and structural features to support cohesion and overall coherence.
- Use a range of sentence structures for clarity, purpose and effect, with accurate punctuation and spelling.

Targeting Grade C

Some of the key differences between a Grade D and a Grade C are as follows:

Grade D candidates	See example on page 106 and 110
<ul><li>develop some points, attempting to match their style to the audience, but not always successfully</li><li>use paragraphs which are correct but not always well structured</li><li>begin to use a range of sentences, but do not always think about their effect on the reader</li><li>mostly use basic punctuation accurately</li><li>begin to use a wider vocabulary, but not always appropriately</li><li>spell simple words correctly and most attempts at more complex words will be recognisable if sometimes wrong.</li></ul>	D

Grade C candidates	See example on page 107 and 111
<ul><li>develop subject matter in more detail than those writing at the lower grades, showing a clearer understanding of form and genre</li><li>paragraph effectively to give structure to their responses and make their meaning clear</li><li>use a variety of sentence forms (short and long) for deliberate effect, although sometimes the effect is not always thought through</li><li>use generally accurate punctuation</li><li>occasionally make original choices of sentence type or vocabulary</li><li>spell more complex words with increasing accuracy.</li></ul>	C

Targeting C in the Foundation Tier Exam

The Two Writing Tasks

- You will have to respond to two writing tasks in your Foundation Tier exam.
- The most obvious difference between the two tasks will be in how much you might write in response. The first, shorter task is likely to be more straightforward, perhaps a letter to a friend, or something in which the format is short and more easily controlled. Whatever you do, don't spend more time on this than the longer second task.
- The second, longer task in the Foundation Tier exam may ask you to consider different viewpoints or develop your ideas a little more.
- The tasks will change every year, but you have been working on some typical questions in this section so far. Here are two more examples.

Short question [16 marks] 25 minutes	*Your local council has asked for suggestions for a new leisure facility for teenagers in your area. Write a letter suggesting an idea and why you think it would be good.*
Longer question [24 marks] 35 minutes	*Explain why you would or would not like your local town to be a car-free zone. Think about:* • *The advantages of getting rid of cars* • *The disadvantages of getting rid of cars* • *How you feel about cars in your local town* • *The overall effect of the change on your lifestyle*

Exploring Sample Responses

ACTIVITY

Read the extract on the following page from a student's response to the longer question above.
As you read it, decide how good it is.

Here are the key questions an examiner would look to answer:
- How clearly and effectively has the writer communicated his/her ideas?
- How well organised are the ideas and information ?
- How accurate are the sentences, spelling and punctuation?

Example 1

We should get rid of cars. I know we all think we need them but they are a pain too.

Our local town is just completely clogged up with traffic mainly at school times and Saturdays when people go shopping. You can hardly cross the road at school times. Still kids have to get to school and there aren't enough buses and some live a long way away. It means using a car most of the time.

On the other hand there are some buses and we could use them. Kids could get these buses and they could lay on extra ones. If it took cars off the road that would be good. Another thing is pollution. Basically cars give out lots of gases and pollute the atmosphere and if you live by the side of the main road it's really unhealthy. Having more buses might save the world.

Having said that if we tried to get rid of cars all together, that would cause problems for people who live outside the town. Like old people who can't walk to the bus-stop which is miles away. They might need the car. We have to think of them too.

Perhaps electric cars might be one solution. They are cars, yes, but they are very different. They are healthier for a start. It means people could get around without polluting, but they also go more slowly so there wouldn't be as many deaths on the roads. And pedestrains wouldn't be choking on fumes.

Getting rid of cars would not have a big effect on my lifestyle now because I can't drive. But my mum and dad do have to take me by car to lots of football games so it would effect them and me. If we couldn't take the car through town I might cycle more. Or I would walk to the bus-stop. The effect would be good on my fitness because I would walk or cycle more and I quite like being fit so overall it would be a good thing.

You know, I think we should do it. We should get rid of cars in the town.

Examiner feedback

The candidate has answered the task set and has given his/her opinion. However, the paragraphs do not build logically into a convincing argument: the response flits from idea to idea. Simple spellings are correct but there are some errors in more complex words ('completly', 'pedestrains'). Sentences are mostly accurate if a little dull and often short. In terms of style, the answer is reasonably formal but sometimes chatty ('kids', 'they are a pain'), and feels at times as if the writer might be talking to a friend rather than writing an exam response ('You know').

Suggested grade: D

Based on the examiner's comments, how would you improve the article to Grade C standard? Discuss these questions with a partner:

- How could the opening paragraph be improved?
- Can you find some sentences that might be joined together to make more complex sentences?
- Can you find all the spelling errors?
- Where could you introduce a rhetorical question or a quotation to interest the reader?
- How could the final paragraph be improved?

Now read this response to the same question by a different candidate.

Example 2

Introduces subject →

The idea of getting rid of cars from our local town is an interesting one and there are advantages and disadvantages.

On the one hand it would be great to get rid of cars. For a start it would ← First paragraph deals with pollution

mean air pollution is not so bad. Also there would be less noise because if you live by the side of a main road it is horrible hearing cars racing by.

Good link to last paragraph →

Another advantage would be to fitness. If we had to walk more or cycle more then it will improve health. This would mean the health service and hospitals would save money. We would need cycle lanes and more walking areas which would cost money but this would be worth it I think.

New paragraph to deal with disadvantages →

On the other hand there are some disadvantages. For example what if you are a pensioner or disabled? You might need your car and not be able to get to a bus-stop. Of course there could be special cases for people like that.

Another point is shops and businesses. If you were a shopkeeper you might be well annoyed if people didn't come to the town anymore. They could go to

A bit informal →

the enormous out-of-town supermarket which would mean driving even more! ← Use of exclamation mark to emphasise point

Also your business might be based on cars – like delivery or taxis. What would you do? In fact, this is quite a problem.

Covers the last bullet point in the task →

Finally there is the effect on my life. I know I can't drive yet but I want to learn. I don't want to rely on my mum and dad. They already get fed up taking me everywhere! Also we live miles from a bus-stop so I am not sure how practical it is. I could cycle I suppose but am I really going to do that when it's raining cats and dogs. I don't think so. Perhaps the solution is electric cars. ← Electric cars idea could go in separate paragraph

Then we wouldn't have to worry about making the town car-free. Electric cars are quiet and don't pollute.

Overall I think it would be a bad idea to get rid of cars altogether. Too many people would suffer like old and disabled people and you can't have buses going everywhere. I think cars are here to stay and whether we like it or not people need them for work, taking kids to school, and just general laziness. Besides I want to drive and have my own car which would be really cool. ← Last paragraph sums up but new point at end seems strange

Examiner feedback

This is a well-organised and clear response to the task with (most of) the paragraphs dealing with separate points for both sides of the topic. The points are quite well developed. Towards the end, the response does not have such a logical progression, which means the conclusion is not as effective as it could be. However, the vocabulary and sentences are varied and there is some thoughtful use of punctuation for effect. The writing is mostly accurate.

Suggested grade: C

EXTENDED PRACTICE TASK

Write an article for the local paper persuading local businesses (shops, cafés, banks) to sponsor events at the school's next 'Comic Relief' charity day. You will need to write about:

- What the sponsorship is for
- What events the charity day will include
- What the school can offer businesses in return

If you only do five things...

1   Read the task carefully and plan your answer around the form, audience and purpose required. Use the conventions of the writing forms you know.
2   Grab your reader's attention with the first paragraph; end by linking back to the main point or points you have made. Develop your ideas: points you make will usually have other points within them that can be drawn out.
3   Use a clear, logical sequence of paragraphs, each covering a separate point. Vary your paragraph lengths, for example long followed by short, for effect on the reader.
4   Use a variety of sentences – both in terms of length (short and long) and in terms of type (simple, compound and complex). Whatever else you do, make sure all your writing is accurately punctuated, clear and logical and uses a range of sentences and paragraphs.
5   Make your vocabulary specific rather than general, and avoid repeating words or phrases when there are better alternatives available. Use powerful imagery – especially similes and metaphors – to make your writing come alive. Try to use a range of other language techniques, for example rhetorical questions and patterns of three, for effect on the reader.

TARGETING C IN THE HIGHER TIER EXAM

The Two Writing Tasks

- You will have to respond to two writing tasks in the Higher Tier exam.
- The most obvious difference between these two tasks will be in how much you might write in response. The first, shorter task is likely to be more straightforward, perhaps a letter to a friend, or something in which the format is short and more easily controlled. Whatever you do, don't spend more time on this than the longer second task.
- The second, longer task may ask you to consider different viewpoints or develop your ideas a little more.
- The tasks will change every year, but you have been working on some typical questions in this section so far. Here are two more examples.

Short question [16 marks] 25 minutes	*A family friend from abroad is coming to visit your home town or area. Write to them and describe what there is of interest to see and do.*
Longer question [24 marks] 35 minutes	*Some people think it is wrong that members of the public are allowed to be humiliated in talent shows by celebrity judges. Write an article for a magazine in which you argue for or against this idea.*

Exploring sample responses

ACTIVITY

Read the extract on the following page from a student's response to the longer question. As you read it, think about whether it is closer to a D or a C grade, and why.

Here are the key questions an exam marker would look to answer:
- How clearly and effectively has the writer conveyed his/her ideas?
- How appropriate and well-chosen is the vocabulary?
- Does the structure and organisation guide the reader fluently through the ideas?
- Does the range of sentences, choice of language features, etc. have a strong impact on the meaning?
- Overall, does this text engage and interest the reader throughout?

Example 1

Talent shows are excellent

Talent shows have been around for quite some time and people love them. They stay in on Saturday night to watch them. I stay in myself to watch them. Whether it's X Factor or Britains got talent or even Celebrity Come Dancing they are all good. Let's face it, it's good to see people making an idiot of themselves. And some of them are actually quality – look at Leona Lewis for a start.

Some people have been saying we shouldnt be laughing at people who arent very good, but singers like Susan Boyle are a bit specal and if we didn't have the programmes we wouldnt ever hear from them. That is why I think the programmes should be kept on TV so it gives a chance to everybody. Even I would like to go on if I got the chance.

It's not fair at all that others criticise the judges. What have they ever done wrong? They have to say what is best and what is not so good about the performers and nobody is forced to go on so they have to take what the judges say and it shouldnt upset them. In fact, Simon Cowell is about the most popular man on television (I think he is) so that must mean that veiwers like him. We don't want to stop him doing what he does best. It's great when he gives that little look and you know he is hating what he is watching.

If people dont like talent shows they dont have to watch and if people dont want to be shown up they dont have to go on them. it's as simple as that. No one is being forced to do anything so the do-gooders who want to get things banned should be banned themselves. Then the rest of us can get on with watching what we like and laughing if we want.

Examiner feedback

This piece responds to the title and is satisfactorily, if mechanically, paragraphed. There is a range of ideas and a rhetorical question is used to add interest. However, there are some technical errors (punctuation and spelling) and the sentences and vocabulary lack variety. The student could, perhaps, have checked the writing more carefully and could have improved it to interest the reader more.

Suggested grade: D

With a partner:
- Identify and correct all the spelling and punctuation errors.
- Choose one paragraph and re-write it, improving the vocabulary and sentences and developing the ideas, adding detail where appropriate.

Now read this response to the same question by a different candidate.

Example 2

Headline grabs attention →

Celebrity rudeness

We all love talent shows such as 'X Factor' and 'Britain's Got Talent'. These shows show people making fools of themselves as well as showing off their talents, such as singing and dancing. 'Best thing on the box,' my dad says, but my view is that it has all gone a bit too far and OTT. It's fine to have some criticism if you need to improve and you are not singing as well as you could, but if you are a poor person with some trashy job with no real talent, it's not fair to make you feel like a dummy.

States one main line of argument

Use of quotation for effect

Expresses personal opinion

Gives reason why the show is, perhaps, not acceptable

Uses short sentence for effect →

Sometimes, what is even worse is that the person who is criticised doesn't even realise what is happening. **That is terrible.** It is like a private joke between the celebrities and the audience. I think it is like bullying in school behind someone's back when they don't notice. For example, calling children a horrible name but not to their face.

States opposite point of view →

The thing is, the shows would not work unless they had people making fools of themselves. If it was just people with talent it would be boring, and I admit that I am watching when these programmes come on. So I am as bad as the programme makers I suppose.

Uses connective to give sense of progression →

But you can't really stop people wanting to take part and no one really knows until someone opens their mouth whether they are going to be an idiot or a genius. I suppose you could choose not to show the really stupid ones, but probably some of them don't mind. **Perhaps they would rather be on telly even if it's making themselves look stupid?**

Uses rhetorical question for effect →

ctd.

> This leads me to my final point. You would need to be from a different planet not to know what goes on in these shows. Everyone knows what they are letting themselves in for – nobody is completely innocent are they? And perhaps they like being shouted at by Simon Cowell. In fact, it might be the highlight of their lives, which is pretty sad – but it's their choice. No one forced them to sing out of tune or dance clumsily!
>
> So, as long as there are people willing to humiliate themselves, I guess it's OK. I will continue watching and maybe one day I will be the daft one on stage making a fool of myself! Simon Cowell beware!

Exclamation at end of paragraph makes point strongly

Shows range of vocabulary

Effective conclusion and memorable finishing sentence

ACTIVITY

Before you read the examiner feedback, note down any improvements you think the student could make to his/her response. In particular, identify where and how some imagery might be used and a greater range of sentence lengths and types.

Examiner feedback

This is generally a clear, well-argued article with accurate sentences and linked and organised paragraphs. There is a good beginning and ending, and the candidate uses some variety of sentences, sometimes to good effect. There is a sense of how the text might affect the reader and the article is slightly informal only occasionally. The language is generally clear and there is some variety to keep the reader interested - the ending is unexpected and leaves a smile on the face of the reader.

Suggested grade: C

EXTENDED PRACTICE TASK

You are helping to organise a charity day at school to raise money for a hostel for homeless youngsters. Write a letter which will be sent to all parents, persuading them to come along to the charity day. [24 marks]

If you only do five things...

1 Read the task carefully and plan your answer around the form, audience and purpose required. Use the conventions of the writing forms you know.

2 Grab your reader's attention with the first paragraph; end by linking back to the main point or points you have made. Develop your ideas: points you make will usually have other points within them that can be drawn out.

3 Use a clear, logical sequence of paragraphs, each covering a separate point. Vary your paragraph lengths, for example long followed by short, for effect on the reader.

4 Use a variety of sentences – both in terms of length (short and long) and in terms of type (simple, compound and complex). Whatever else you do, make sure all your writing is accurately punctuated, clear and logical and uses a range of sentences and paragraphs.

5 Make your vocabulary specific rather than general, and avoid repeating words or phrases when there are better alternatives available. Use powerful imagery – especially similes and metaphors – to make your writing come alive. Try to use a range of other language techniques, for example rhetorical questions and patterns of three, for effect on the reader.

Unit 2 **Speaking and Listening**

What's it all about?

We can all speak and listen, but if we develop our skills, we can communicate much better throughout our lives. Speaking and listening involves many skills that can be used elsewhere in English work and offers an immensely enjoyable change from reading and writing.

How will I be assessed?

You will get 20% of your English Language marks for your Speaking and Listening ability.

You will have to complete three Speaking and Listening controlled assessments.

You will be marked on your

- presenting
- discussing and listening
- role playing.

What is being tested?

Your teacher will be judging your ability to

- speak clearly and purposefully
- organise your talk and sustain your ideas
- speak appropriately in different situations
- use standard English and a variety of techniques when speaking
- listen and respond to what others say and how they say it
- interact with others, shaping meanings through suggestions, comments and questions and drawing ideas together
- create and sustain different roles.

Presentations

Introduction

This section of Chapter 3 shows you how to

- give a presentation to an audience
- select a topic and structure your talk
- consider what content you might include
- use a range of techniques to boost your performance.

Why is it important to develop good presentational skills?

- We can all talk about topics, but to get good grades you need to demonstrate a range of skills.
- You will be more successful if you plan and structure your presentation and make it as lively as you can.
- You will use similar skills in other parts of your English course, such as when you are required to write in the examination.
- You may well use these presentational skills throughout your working life.

A **Grade E** candidate will

- give straightforward accounts and begin to adapt their talk for different audiences
- generally use Standard English appropriately
- show some variety in vocabulary and language structures.

E

A **Grade D** candidate will

- use different strategies to engage the listener's interest, with an increasing variety of vocabulary, appropriate for the task
- understand the need for Standard English.

D

A **Grade C** candidate will

- adapt their talk to the situation, using Standard English confidently
- engage the listener through their use of language so that information, ideas and feelings are communicated clearly
- the presentation will have a clear structure and interest the reader.

C

Prior Learning

Which of their techniques might you be able to use?

Before you begin this unit, think about

- times when you have heard someone talk in a formal situation

- which speakers have interested you most and why

- how you have been taught to structure your formal essays.

When you watched someone on a news programme or in assembly, or had an outside speaker in school, how did the speaker try to hold your attention? How did they begin and end their talk?

Which of the techniques could you use when preparing and delivering a presentation?

Understanding your audience

Learning objective

- *To consider what an audience expects and how to respond to its needs.*

What does understanding your audience mean?

Thinking about your **audience** is vital when making a presentation. You might be talking to a class, an individual, a group of people outside school or an assembly.

You need to **understand** what type of presentation is required. Is it

- factual
- argumentative or persuasive (supporting a point of view)
- entertaining?

Checklist for success

- You need to be clear about who you will be talking to and what is expected of you.
- You need to make sure your language, content and style are right for your audience.

ACTIVITY

You are going to make a presentation on how your school's rules should be changed.

How would you vary your style and content for these audiences?

1 the headteacher
2 your classmates
3 a meeting of interested parents.

In each case, ask yourself

- What will they already know?
- What do I need to tell them?
- How can I convince them to share my views?

Focus for development:
Choosing the right words and style

You will gain marks by using a wide **vocabulary**. However, it must be right for the people you are talking to.

ACTIVITY

This Grade C presentation uses words that are appropriate for the audience.

> We all know what's wrong with the school rules. It doesn't take a genius to see that things need to be changed. Take the shirt rule for a start... Who decided that we can't learn anything if our shirt is out? How stupid is that?

Discuss with a partner:

- Who do you think the speaker is talking to? Give reasons.
- Why is the style right for this audience?

Glossary
Style: the way you speak or write; how you deliver what you want to say.

ACTIVITY

Improve this extract from a Grade E presentation. The student is struggling to find interesting vocabulary.

> I know lots of you don't like 'Scrubs' but I do. I watch it with my mum and dad. My dad loves it. I love it too. We watch it on Sky. The programmes are crazy but they are good. That's why I laugh at them. It's about doctors and what they are thinking and amazing things happen all the time. Sometimes there are, like, amazing dream sequences and everything.

Examiner's tip ✶

Always vary your words. It will be much more interesting than using the same words again and again.

Rewrite the extract, trying to improve the

- **choice of words:** especially when they are repeated
- **sentences:** many are short
- **content:** is some of it unnecessary?
- **style:** can you make it sound more interesting?

ASSESSMENT FOCUS

Write a presentation explaining what is best about your school.

You are going to make the presentation to visitors at parents' evening. Make it appeal to this audience.

In your actual assessment you will not be allowed to read from notes!

Remember

- **Use different styles and approaches for different audiences.**
- **Focus on your choice of content, style and vocabulary.**

Choosing a topic

Learning objective

- To understand why a sensible choice of topic increases your chance of success.

★ **Examiner's tip**

Some speaking tasks are more difficult than others. For example, it is harder to persuade someone that your football team is the best than to describe what happened during a match. You gain more credit for tackling something harder.

Why is choice of topic important?

If the **topic** is something you feel comfortable with, because you know about it, your presentation will flow better and be more detailed.

Checklist for success

- You need to choose your topic and approach carefully, so it interests your audience, not just you.
- You need to know as much as possible about your topic.

ACTIVITY

If you were choosing a presentation, which of these topics could you talk about most successfully? Why?

1 Argue that knife crime is (or is not) a real threat for young people.
2 Advise the parents of primary school students to send their children to your school.
3 Explain why teenagers prefer technology to real life.

Focus for development: Successful topics

ACTIVITY

- If you were choosing your presentation topic, what would it be?
- How would you approach your topic? Would you be describing, persuading your audience or putting forward an argument, for example? Give reasons why.

Discuss with a partner and decide why this Grade C response is better than the Grade D. Think about

- how the ideas are organised
- which says more interesting things.

Some ideas are given to start you off. The Examiner's tip on the right will help you too.

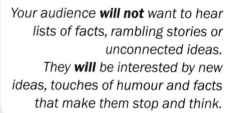
Grade D

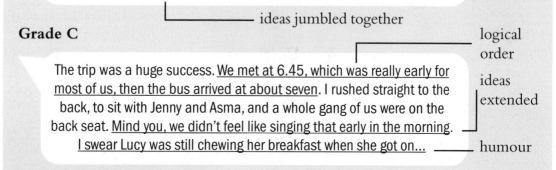

I like school trips! When we went to Alton Towers, it was great. We weren't home until after eight. <u>I went round with Chesney and Squilly and we didn't see a teacher once</u>. It was fantastic. <u>Some of the rides were awesome and we had burgers for lunch</u>. They cost a fortune though…

⌐ random
⌐ ideas

ideas jumbled together

Grade C

logical order

The trip was a huge success. <u>We met at 6.45, which was really early for most of us, then the bus arrived at about seven</u>. I rushed straight to the back, to sit with Jenny and Asma, and a whole gang of us were on the back seat. <u>Mind you, we didn't feel like singing that early in the morning</u>. <u>I swear Lucy was still chewing her breakfast when she got on</u>…

ideas extended

humour

ASSESSMENT FOCUS

You are making a presentation to your class about school trips.
Decide on

- the main points you will make
- details you could use to support your points.

You might want to

- describe what is good or bad about school trips
- compare them with school days
- persuade your audience they are fun and educational.

Remember

- **You must know about a topic to talk about it confidently.**
- **You will be rewarded for showing your knowledge.**

Researching and developing content

Why is it important to think carefully about content?

Unless your presentation has interesting **content**, you will not appeal to your audience.

Listening is different from reading. Points must be clear and easy to understand. If the audience misses a point, they can't go back to hear it again.

If the audience loses track of what you are saying, you will lose their attention.

Checklist for success

- You need to have enough information about your topic so that you can stay focused on the subject.
- You need to have details and examples to support your main points.

ACTIVITY

This extract is from a Grade C presentation: Muhammad Ali – why he was 'The Greatest'. The student has researched the topic well so she is clearly comfortable with it:

Muhammad Ali is considered by many to be the greatest boxer of all time. He was first called Cassius Clay and he won the gold medal at the Rome Olympics in 1960 with that name. He became world professional champion later. When he became a Muslim, he changed his name to Muhammad Ali and refused to fight in Vietnam, in the war. He had his title taken from him, but he came back, some years later and won the world crown on another two occasions.

Discuss with a partner:

- How many facts does she include?
- How well chosen are the facts to show that Ali was 'The Greatest'?

Focus for development:
Selecting effective content

Be careful about what you choose to say. Just because you find a detail interesting doesn't necessarily make it vital to your presentation.

For example, the talk on Muhammad Ali only includes relevant facts that

- give a clear picture of what he achieved
- indicate he was a great fighter.

It also stays focused on the man because it is a presentation about why he was called 'The Greatest' – so it doesn't talk about the rights and wrongs of boxing, for example.

ACTIVITY

You have been asked to review a film you have seen recently and present it to your class.

With a partner, decide which of the following points you would include, and why.

Character details	Your range of hobbies
When you saw it	Why you watched it
Your favourite forms of entertainment	Length
Storyline	Best/worst moments
Themes	The last production you saw before this one
Opinions of others about it	Alternative ways of spending your time
Comparison with other similar productions	

(Of course, in a review you don't only get marks for your main points, but also for how you comment on them.)

Compare these extracts from two student reviews. Discuss with a partner:

- What does each review tell us about the programme?
- Are all the details relevant to the topic?
- Why is the second review better?

Grade D

I like *Boys will be Boys* and, obviously, most of you like it too. It's on twice a week on Mondays and Wednesdays, but you know that. It has three main characters, who are Steve, Imran and Ben. I was watching it with Jenny last week on Wednesday and we couldn't stop laughing. Jenny even knocked over a glass of water and we just howled. Her mum wasn't pleased, though...

Grade C

I think *Boys will be Boys* is a programme that would appeal to anyone. I thought about my own brothers when I was watching it. I laugh at them, and I laughed at the boys on the screen. The show made fun of Steve, Imran and Ben, but I have to say the girls seemed ridiculous too: Maeve with her hair and Sammy with her turned-up nose. She tries to be *so* superior...

Effective research

Because you will prepare your presentations in advance, you can always do some **research**. As you read about the subject, you need to be selective, finding information which best suits your purpose.

If you were researching the talk about Muhammad Ali and how he became a hero, which of these websites do you think might be useful? Why? Discuss with a partner.

1 Biography Channel – Muhammad Ali
http://www.thebiographychannel.co.uk/biography_home/741:0/Muhammed_Ali.htm

2 Muhammad Ali Trivia
www.whosdatedwho.com/celebrity/ trivia/muhammad-ali.htm

3 Muhammad Ali Timeline
http://www.infoplease.com/spot/malitimeline1.html

Having found relevant material, you need to decide how to put it across effectively to your audience. For example, you might use

- diagrams or pictures
- PowerPoint slides
- anecdotes.

Ending well

ACTIVITY

Organise these facts into a conclusion for a presentation which argues that Ali deserves to be known as 'The Greatest'.

Write a conclusion that

- summarises your argument
- only includes relevant details
- leaves the audience with a positive impression of Ali (and of you as a presenter!).

> Voted top sportsman of the 20th century.
>
> World champion at the age of 22 in 1964.
>
> In 1996 lit the flame at the Olympics in Atlanta.
>
> Three times world champion. Finally retired in 1981.
>
> Won 56 fights and lost 5.
>
> Said he could 'Float like a butterfly, sting like a bee'.
>
> Parkinson's Disease diagnosed in 1984.

ASSESSMENT FOCUS

You are preparing to talk to your class about your favourite hobby. Complete a table like the one below, which is about running.

Summarise

- the points you would select
- why you would choose them
- how would you develop them.

Point	Why	Development
Running is healthy	Health issues important at any age	How much weight I lost / How my life changed as I became healthier
15 million British people run	Pleasure / Competition / Feeling of well-being	Age no barrier: Constantina Dita became world marathon champion at 38; Buster Martin ran in the London marathon aged 101

Remember

- **Content needs to be appropriate for your purpose and audience.**
- **Research if necessary but be selective in what you use.**
- **Using content well is the key to success.**

Structuring your presentation

Learning objectives

- *To understand the importance of organising your ideas for maximum effect.*
- *To learn about effective openings and endings.*

What does structuring your presentation mean?

In a **well-structured** presentation, the speaker knows what they are going to say, and in what order. Planning a strong opening and a memorable ending is part of the structuring.

Checklist for success

- You need to prepare your presentation in detail.
- You need to consider the different ways you can begin, develop and end your presentation.

ACTIVITY

You have been asked to give a short presentation about your favourite subject at school.

- List the points you might make.
- Put them into a logical order.
- How would you begin your presentation?
- How might it end?

A student writes…

Surely planning a presentation is just like planning an essay.

Answer…

In many ways, they are alike. However, when you are talking, you can interact with your audience, develop ideas on the spot and use different tones of voice.

Focus for development:
Planning, openings and endings

A bulleted plan can contain all the information you need – and you can use it as a prompt while speaking.

ACTIVITY

Complete a table like this, developing your ideas about your favourite subject.

Main idea	Points to be included
Teachers	Miss Spivey (obsessed with Crimean War) Mr Jenkin (anecdote about haunted mansion)
Lessons	Lots of videos Fun quizzes
Trips	Warwick Castle Tower of London Portsmouth

Openings

Your opening **sets the tone** for what follows. It is vital to attract your audience's attention from the start. Here are some opening ideas for a presentation about going to the dentist:

- **rhetorical questions**:'Have you ever had the wrong tooth extracted?'
- **relevant humour**:'Have you heard the one about the dentist, the missing tooth and the court action for damages?'
- **powerful facts**:'Last year in Britain, 57% of children under the age of 10 had at least one tooth extracted.'

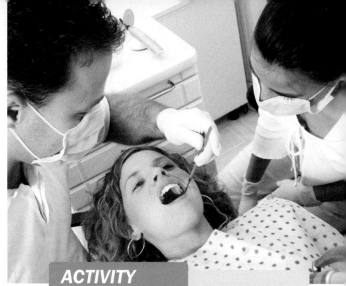

ACTIVITY

Use these techniques to write three different opening sentences for your presentation about your favourite subject.

Endings

A memorable ending can leave a powerful impression upon your audience. You could try

- a summary of your argument
- one final, convincing point
- a joke.

Which of these you choose will depend on your topic, purpose and audience.

Examiner's tip ★

Practise your delivery. Powerful words are wasted if they are not delivered well.
You can present to a friend, to a mirror, or you could record yourself then judge your own performance.

ACTIVITY

Look at this ending and decide with a partner

- what was the purpose of the talk
- how the speaker hoped to impress the audience at the end.

Decide how the ending could be improved.

Grade D

So there is much we can do to help the environment. It's easy to leave it to everyone else but that's not what we should be doing. If you join with us today, we can work together tomorrow. Come and help us. Thanks.

ASSESSMENT FOCUS

Go back to the plan for your presentation on your favourite subject and decide how much precise detail you need to add.

Make sure it will interest the audience throughout.

Remember

- **A detailed plan is essential for success.**
- **Openings and endings are vital parts of any presentation.**

Using standard English, imagery and repetition for effect

Learning objectives

- *To understand the importance of standard English in presentations.*

- *To understand how imagery and repetition can add to the quality of performances.*

Glossary

Standard English: the form of English which is grammatically correct – not the more casual, chatty form you might use with friends.

Imagery: the use of imaginative comparisons, such as similes and metaphors.

Similes: the use of words 'as' or 'like' to make the comparison: 'She was as brave as a lion.'

Metaphors: the direct comparison of one thing with another: 'Her hair was a flowing mane.'

What does using these techniques for effect mean?

Using **standard English** will add a more formal tone, which is expected as part of your assessment.

Including **imagery** and **repeating** words or phrases will help engage your listeners and stress your key points.

Checklist for success

- You need to understand the differences in grammar and vocabulary between talking informally to friends and speaking in more formal situations. Listen to news presenters on television, to remind you what standard English sounds like.

- You need to plan some imagery and repetition into your presentation to create more of an impact.

ACTIVITY

Look at this extract.

With a partner:

> See, it's clear, init? There's them that's got the cash, sitting on it like some big greedy thing, and them that 'asn't. You gotta find some guy with big wads – and I'm talking major league money now, and make 'im cough up his big wads. Then yer charity's got wads of stuff to work with...

- Identify the similes and metaphors.
- Find an example of repetition. Does it make the extract more or less interesting?
- Re-write the piece more formally in standard English, as if it was spoken by a BBC presenter.

Focus for development: standard English

Presenting in standard English means using correct grammar and avoiding very informal language, or **slang**.

- Try to speak in full sentences.
- Use 'school' vocabulary rather than street language.

Imagery and repetition

Imagery will make your presentation more interesting, while repetition can be used to touch your audience's emotions or hammer home a point.

Look at this extract from a Grade C presentation.

> I met a refugee from a country in Africa where the people have no freedom. She was like a scared rabbit. There was no sign of hope in her eyes. I felt really sorry for her. I felt sorry for her people too. That's why I'm doing this talk today. We have to help people like Mende. Without our help they will have no future, no tomorrow at all...

Use a table like this to list the imagery and repetition in the extract. Explain the effect of each example.

Imagery and use of repetition	Effect (how audience is expected to react)

A student writes...

We've always been told to avoid repetition because it makes it seem as if you've run out of ideas.

Answer...

When you're using repetition for effect to hammer home a point, it will be seen as a strength, not a weakness.

Prepare the opening of a presentation about the job you would like to have when you are older.

Use standard English, some imagery and at least one example of repetition for effect.

Remember

- You will be expected to use standard English in most presentations.
- By including imagery and repetition for effect, you will make your presentation more impressive.

Using rhetorical questions, humour and exaggeration for effect

Glossary

rhetorical question: a question asked to involve the audience, without expecting a reply – 'How could anyone ever think that?'

exaggeration: making things seem bigger to hammer home a point – 'I've told her a million times not to exaggerate.'

What does using these techniques for effect mean?

Using **rhetorical questions**, **humour** and **exaggeration** will help engage your listeners and bring variety to your presentation. You need to think about what each technique will make your audience feel or respond.

Checklist for success

- You need to use rhetorical questions, humour and exaggeration sparingly and only when suitable for your topic or audience.
- You need to plan in advance which of these techniques you will use.

ACTIVITY

Read this extract from a presentation to a group of headteachers.

With a partner, decide which questions, humour and exaggeration are inappropriate.

> So, how are you guys doing? I've got to say, you look pretty bored: I suppose you always do. Anyway, I've managed to cheer up thousands and thousands of conferences like this one, so it was worth your while turning up today. Actually, it's just as well you came today, because I don't suppose many of you will be around much longer. I bet your doctors are pretty busy, aren't they?

Focus for development:
Making presentations more interesting

Rhetorical questions

Rhetorical questions challenge the audience to think more actively about something. For example:

'Can this ever be acceptable?' – probable reaction: 'No!'

'Why, then have these changes been introduced?' – probable reaction: 'Tell me more.'

ACTIVITY

Add two rhetorical questions to this extract to add interest.

> The royal family is something we should admire. They stand above politics and make us proud. Without them, the world would think less of Britain. Not only that, increasingly they seem so human: the two princes are just like ordinary young men you might meet anywhere.

Not everyone finds it easy to be funny. However, if you can add witty touches it often keeps the audience listening.

You could try using a funny **anecdote** (or short story) to support your point, for example: 'I caught measles on holiday. Well, actually, measles caught me. What happened was…'

ACTIVITY

With a partner, try to add a funny follow-on to these sentences.

- Anyone can dress well if they know where to shop.
- I try to help my cousin. Well…

Exaggeration

Don't over-use exaggeration, but it can have considerable impact. For example:

Crack SAS commandos couldn't track down and bring back my father when he's out for a night on the town.

ACTIVITY

Which of these exaggerations is more effective? Why?

- 'You'd have to go to the ends of the earth to find a better movie than this.'
- 'Literally millions of different kinds of bugs crawled out when we moved the stones to set up our tent.'

ASSESSMENT FOCUS

Write the opening of a speech about a person you admire – someone you know well, or someone famous.

- Explain why you admire them.
- Use rhetorical questions, humour and exaggeration.
- When you've finished, identify each feature by underlining it.

Remember

- Using rhetorical questions, humour and exaggeration can make your presentation more interesting.
- These features should only be used occasionally and if appropriate for your audience or topic.

Delivering your presentation

Learning objective

- *To be best prepared to deliver a presentation.*

★ Examiner's tip

Make sure any props that you pass round during your talk don't distract your audience.
Use PowerPoint to show your main points or to illustrate ideas, with photographs, diagrams or a short video. It will help guide you through your talk as well – but don't use it as a script. You get no marks for reading from the screen!

★ Examiner's tip

Making regular eye contact with your listeners shows confidence. A smile helps too.

How do you deliver a presentation well?

If you have **structured your ideas** and planned to use some **language techniques**, you should be ready to deliver your presentation with style. If you are not prepared, you could underperform.

Checklist for success

- You need to organise your presentation so that you know what to say in what order.
- You need to know how to handle your audience: this is crucial for your success.

Speakers deal with audiences in different ways: a stand-up comedian is likely to move around and joke with the audience, while a presenter at an awards ceremony will be more serious.

Focus for development: Establishing and maintaining a good impression

First impressions

First impressions count. If you seem calm and prepared, you will impress your audience. People notice body language: try not to look nervous.

ACTIVITY

In groups of four, improvise two scenes where a young person has a job interview at a supermarket.

- One interviewee knows about the job and is enthusiastic.
- The other knows nothing about the job and shows no interest.

Talk about the different impressions created.

Sustaining your role

Having created a good impression, you need to keep your confidence going throughout. Remember:

- Listeners can get bored quickly.
- A strong opening is wasted if it's followed by a muddle of points.
- Move through your planned material and head towards a clear ending.

Dealing with questions

You will probably have to answer questions from your audience at the end of your presentation. Try to think ahead to what they might be.

Good answers can often lift a Grade D presentation up to Grade C level.

ACTIVITY

Why is the Grade C answer to this question better?

> **Question:** What more *can* we do to help old people?

Notice that the Grade C answer has

- humour
- an extended idea (how to make them feel wanted)
- no irrelevant thoughts, such as 'sometimes I just give up'.

Grade D answer

> We can do some things and try to help. Of course, they are usually grumpy so that's often it. I try sometimes, but sometimes I just give up. Whatever happens, we shouldn't though, because it's good to do their shopping and stuff like that...

Grade C answer

> We can carry them across the road! No, seriously, we need to care more about them, take time to talk to them... All that stuff. They are happier if they feel wanted...

ASSESSMENT FOCUS

Create an impressive opening to the presentation:

My life out of school

Deliver the opening, then take questions. Ask for feedback on how you performed.

Examiner's tip ★

If you anticipate some likely questions, you can have the information ready.

Remember

- **Prepare thoroughly.**
- **Impress your audience from the start.**
- **Sustain their interest to the end.**

Grade Booster

Extended Assessment Task

Produce a detailed plan for a presentation to your class, entitled:

> **What is the best sort of day out?**
> *Persuade your audience to accept your point of view.*

Or, you could choose one of these topics:

- **Argue that there is no such thing as a good day out.**
- **Argue that it would be better if people concentrated on making everyday life better rather than being obsessed with holidays.**
- **Offer advice on how to enjoy your time on holiday and avoid problems.**

Make a note in your plan of the language techniques you will use at various stages, to interest your audience.

Pay particular attention to your opening, how you develop your ideas and your ending.

Deliver the presentation and ask for feedback.

Evaluation – What have you learned?

With a partner, use the grade checklist below to evaluate your work on the Extended Assessment Task.

C
- I can organise and deliver a structured presentation for a given audience.
- I can use presentational techniques and appropriate and effective language.
- I can hold the attention of my audience from start to finish.
- I can answer questions using some detail.

D
- I can plan and deliver a presentation to a given audience and use different techniques to interest them.
- I can begin and end relevantly and talk for an appropriate length of time.
- I can answer questions using some detail.

E
- I can express straightforward ideas.
- I can use some variety of vocabulary appropriately.
- I can begin to adapt talk for particular audiences.

F
- I can express ideas and use detail to add interest.
- I can use straightforward vocabulary and grammar and some standard English.

You may need to go back and look at the relevant pages from this section again.

Discussing and Listening

Introduction

This section of Chapter 3 shows you how to

- prepare for a discussion with one or more people
- speak and listen effectively in group situations
- improve your discussion skills.

Why is it important to spend time improving discussion and listening skills?

- Although we all talk and listen each day in many different situations, many people do not understand how to discuss topics effectively and skilfully.
- Discussion is not about simply making your point of view known; it is also about listening, responding and possibly changing previously held views.
- Persuading someone to agree with you is a skill that can be developed.
- Listening sensitively and accepting other people's views is a sign of maturity.

A **Grade E** candidate will

- make relevant contributions to discussions and respond positively to what others say
- follow discussions and ask straightforward questions.

E

A **Grade D** candidate will

- stay involved right through a discussion
- make effective contributions
- show they understand by responding appropriately to what is said.

D

A **Grade C** candidate will

- communicate clearly, using language that is appropriate to the situation
- listen carefully, developing their own and others' ideas and making significant contributions to discussions
- they are likely to ask questions, stimulate the discussion and are able to summarise what is said
- they stay focused on the subject.

C

Prior learning

Before you begin this unit, think about

- discussions you have watched on television.
- discussions you have taken part in at school
- discussions with friends

Who has appeared to be in control? How do they direct the conversation? Which people seem left out, and why?

How successful have they been? Why have they sometimes ground to a halt or not produced a conclusion? What can go wrong?

Who do you most like to talk with, and why? When do you find conversations with friends annoying?

Preparing for discussion

Learning objectives

- To understand how preparation can improve some discussions.
- To practise preparing for a discussion.

⭐ **Examiner's tip**

Notes are fine but you should never read directly from them.

What is there to prepare?

The kind of preparation needed will depend on the topic. For example, if you are discussing teenage crime, you may gather facts, figures and opinions from the Internet. If you are asked how your local area could be improved, you would probably collect other people's ideas and opinions.

Checklist for success

- You need to know what you will be discussing and, if appropriate, what your role in the discussion will be.
- You need to prepare ideas and information and note them down.

ACTIVITY

What would you find out in advance, to help you in this discussion?

> *In a group of four or five, come to an agreement about the five greatest-ever recording artists.*

Focus for development: Roles and research

Some discussions just happen naturally in class; preparation can help with others.

Chairing the discussion

You might be asked to chair a discussion. As chair, you need to have questions ready to ask and information ready to keep the discussion going. You must also be prepared to adapt to what anyone else says.

ACTIVITY

You have been asked to chair a discussion about how £5 million should be spent to improve your school.

Draw up notes you might use. For example:

- How will you start? (You could offer a range of ideas to be discussed).
- Will each person speak in turn?
- Will there be summaries?
- How will you end (in general terms)?

Adopting a point of view

You may be asked to take a particular point of view. If so, you need to be clear about what this is and prepare how you are going to support that viewpoint.

ACTIVITY

Imagine you are to be involved in the discussion about spending the £5 million.

You are supporting the view that half the money should be spent on new sports facilities and half on new teachers. Prepare your notes.

A student writes…

We did the £5 million discussion. I found some facts, figures and quotes to use and it was the first time I've performed like a 'star' in English.

ASSESSMENT FOCUS

Your teacher has warned you that you will be involved in a group discussion about whether there is still time to save the world from global warming.

You can choose whether to agree or disagree.

Make notes that

- support your opinion
- are in a logical order
- include some relevant facts, opinions and examples.

Remember

- **Prepare for discussions as much as you can, so you have more to say.**
- **Never read from scripted notes.**
- **Adapt your notes as the discussion develops.**

Developing strategies for confident talk

Learning objective

- *To understand how to be, and appear, more confident in discussions.*

How can anyone become more confident?

Confidence is important in all speaking and listening activities, including group discussions. If you are well-prepared (see page 134–5) you will show confidence in the way you speak.

Checklist for success

- You need to be prepared to offer views, listen carefully and ask questions.
- You need to work with people you feel comfortable with wherever possible.

Focus for development:
Improving your confidence

Speaking with confidence does not just mean speaking clearly. You also need to sound as if you **believe** in what you are saying.

Some hesitation is natural, because we think as we speak, but hesitating all the time would be a problem in an assessment.

ACTIVITY

Look at this short extract from a discussion.

The students are analysing advertisements they have just been given.

Who is more confident, Abi or Jenny? Why?

Abi:	So, does this advertisement work or not?
Jenny:	Well… there's the picture…
Abi:	Yes. *(Raises her eyebrows to Jenny)*
Jenny:	And the colours are good. I like them… Some of them…
Abi:	Do they have any effect though? Do they make us think?
Jenny:	Yes. No… Some… I don't know really…

Asking questions

Asking **appropriate questions** – which link with what someone has just said – can make you seem more in control and shows you are listening.

For example, you might

- ask for extra information: 'So, if maths is so wonderful, can you tell me why we need to learn about equations?'
- encourage reluctant speakers to join in: 'James – can you add to that point?'
- challenge people: 'You honestly believe that Spiderman exists?'

ACTIVITY

What questions might you ask in each of these cases?

> **Steph:** I've read some Shakespeare and the stories are utterly unbelievable.
>
> *(Ask for extra information.)*
>
> **Anna:** I think she's right. Probably.
>
> *(Ask a question to encourage Anna to say more.)*
>
> **Steph:** We shouldn't have to read Shakespeare; it's just a waste of our time.
>
> *(Ask a question to challenge what Steph has said.)*

A student writes…

I never feel I'm saying enough in discussions. Other people say a lot more than me. But I think what I'm saying is important.

Answer…

Confidence is not just about talking at length. Careful listening, followed by a sensible comment or a good question, can show your confidence just as well.

ASSESSMENT FOCUS

To improve your confidence, discuss this topic in groups of three.

> ***Should we should bring back hanging?***

- One of you should be the chair and introduce the discussion confidently.
- The others should take opposing viewpoints.
- The chair will use questions at different stages to help the discusssion.
- The chair will sum things up clearly.

Remember

- **Show confidence in a discussion and you will gain more marks.**
- **Be well-prepared and you should be at ease in the discussion.**
- **Know when to speak and when to listen.**

Developing and supporting ideas

Learning objectives

- *To learn how to develop ideas in discussion.*
- *To understand how to argue effectively.*

What does supporting and developing an idea mean?

In conversation people often state an idea simply but fail to support what they say.

Being able to extend ideas or offer alternatives to ideas put forward by others moves the discussion on and gains you credit.

Checklist for success

- You need to know what you are talking about and to extend ideas in a discussion if you are going to be convincing.
- You need to listen carefully so that you can challenge or support what others say successfully.

ACTIVITY

If the points below were made in a discussion, how would you develop them (add information) and argue against them?

Copy out and complete the table.

Statement	Development	Opposite argument
'Football is a total waste of time.'		
'Nothing in life is more important than love.'		

Focus for development:
Extending and opposing ideas

Extending ideas

Discussions are usually better if you can make your ideas more detailed and encourage others to make their ideas clearer.

To improve your own points, add some supporting comments. For example:

- evidence (facts, statistics, details)
- anecdotes – short stories or examples to illustrate an idea
- others' opinions.

What evidence could you use to develop this point? Jot down some ideas.

> *Everyone should take more care to avoid sunburn.*

Add some **facts** and an **anecdote**. You can invent what you need.

To extend the ideas of others, you can use phrases like

- 'True! What else..?'
- 'And can you take that idea one stage further?'

To develop one of your own ideas, you can use phrases like

- 'Yes. And that reminds me of when…'
- 'Yes, I agree. Not only that, but…'

Opposing ideas

Discussions involving opposing views should not become disagreements. To argue your point in a controlled way, you can

- support a viewpoint
- try to change other speakers' minds sensitively.

Discuss with a partner:

Why is Mandy more successful in this argument that Dave?

Dave:	I think the advertisement is good.
Mandy:	Really? Why? Have you seen that picture?
Dave:	'Course I have. That's why I like it.
Mandy:	Typical. There's a pretty girl in it so you think it's good. I mean, yes, she's pretty but does the picture go with the product?
Dave:	Who cares?
Mandy:	Lots of us do, actually. Look at what it's saying…

ASSESSMENT FOCUS

Write down what you would say in response to these statements. Use the techniques you have learnt to develop ideas and challenge other views with tact.

> *There is only one good place to live: Australia. Australia has everything anyone could ever want. Only a fool would choose to live anywhere else.*

Remember

- Extend and develop your ideas to make them more convincing.
- If you challenge other people's ideas tactfully and in detail, it is more likely to make them change their mind.

Responding to talk

Learning objectives

- To understand how to respond to others' talk.
- To understand how you can show you are listening closely.

What does responding to talk mean?

You are assessed on your ability to **talk** *and* **listen**. Your physical reactions will suggest how well you are listening, and what you say will show how well you have understood the discussion.

Checklist for success

- You need to remember that both speaking and listening skills are vital in any discussion.
- You need to focus on listening carefully because what you hear affects how well you respond.

ACTIVITY

Think back to the last assembly you attended. Discuss with a partner:

- What were people in the audience doing which showed they were not listening? Think about students and staff.
- What was said in the assembly? What can you remember?
- How well did you and others **listen** on that occasion?

Focus for development: How you respond

Physical reactions

It is easy to identify who is not listening carefully, because of the way they behave. Try to avoid

- gazing out of the window
- muttering to someone else
- doodling.

Faces can be revealing too. Someone who is listening might

- raise eyebrows
- open or narrow their eyes slightly
- smile
- bite a lip.

What you say

What you say reveals how well you are listening because you respond appropriately. Poor listeners are easily spotted.

Read this extract from a group discussion about who we should respect.

Shabnam:	OK. So we're going to put these people into order of importance. Lucy, can you start?
Lucy:	Princess Diana.
Steve:	I think she was over-rated. No one talks about her now. When did she die…?
Lucy:	There's Martin Luther King too. He was good.
Steve:	They all were, weren't they?
Shabnam:	My dad never liked Margaret Thatcher. What was she like?
Steve:	First woman Prime Minister…
Lucy:	President Kennedy… I don't know anything about him…

Discuss with a partner:

- How are Lucy's listening skills limiting this discussion?
- Why are the others better?

ACTIVITY

If you **listen effectively**, you can take in others' ideas and develop new ones. Andi is a Grade C student. How do her listening skills show here?

Melody:	Let's face it, fashion isn't *that* important.
Andi:	Because? (*She looks quizzical and opens a palm, asking for clarification.*)
Melody:	There are lots more serious issues to think about.
Andi:	(*Andi shakes her head, smiling.*) But fashion brings people pleasure, doesn't it?
Melody:	Not much…

ASSESSMENT FOCUS

Discuss this in a group. Record the discussion, then play it back.

How often did you

- 'disappear' from the discussion? (Were you still listening?)
- argue effectively?
- develop an idea?

Is fashion really important?

Remember

- In discussions, listening is as important as speaking.
- Your listening ability will be clear in what you do and say.

141

Reacting to suggestions and summarising

Learning objectives

- To recognise what people are suggesting.
- To learn how to summarise.

What does reacting to suggestions and summarising mean?

Responding sensitively – not only to what people **say directly** but to what they **imply** – shows you are a good listener.

People often say things which **suggest** or imply something else: for example, 'I love your new dress. It's so… different.'

Summing up briefly what has been said in a discussion shows you have listened and understood well. It also helps to round off the discussion.

Checklist for success

- You need to listen carefully and show that you understand how to react to what is said.
- You need to be able to sum up what has been said.

Focus for development: Showing listening skills

Reacting to suggestions

Responding to what others are suggesting shows good listening skills – but your response must be appropriate.

ACTIVITY

In the discussion below, what is suggested by:

Jenny at A   Daniel at B   Daniel at C?

Daniel:	Geography's like RE – a total waste of time.
Jenny:	I agree. I've hated it since Year 7. I've had Mrs Bates every year and she's always had it in for me. (A)
Daniel:	Too right. And I've had Mrs Cowen. How can she teach? She's too old to even know what's going on. (B)
Maisie:	She said, 'An understanding of geography is vital if we are to understand the world around us.' You don't have to have a degree to know that's rubbish.
Daniel:	She said, 'You've got to work hard to achieve anything.' That's like something my grandma would say. (C)

Examiner's tip

Look out for what other speakers are suggesting, and challenge them if necessary.

Summarising

If you listen closely, you will be able to

- sum up what has been said in a discussion so far
- explain the main points of view at the end.

Making brief notes though the discussion will help, so nothing is missed. Notes are useful to

- group members, for weighing up different opinions
- the chair, for maintaining the balance between people with different views
- the summariser for commenting at the end.

ACTIVITY

Watch a current affairs programme in which there are guests representing opposing viewpoints.

- Note down the main points made.
- Summarise the viewpoints.

Examiner's tip ★

To summarise, use phrases like: 'On the one hand… whereas on the other hand…'. This shows you are balancing the views.

ASSESSMENT FOCUS

In a group, discuss this statement:

> *Out of school, most teenagers waste most of their time.*

- Whilst discussing, look out for suggestions and respond to them.
- Each member of the group can then summarise the discussion.

Remember

- **Good listeners will spot suggested ideas, and respond to them.**
- **If you can summarise accurately, you show you have been listening.**

Making significant contributions

What are significant contributions?

You are making a significant contribution if you

- support others in the group
- show understanding of others' ideas
- comment sensibly, helping to move discussions forward.

You need to be prepared to help direct discussions and sort out disagreements.

ACTIVITY

Working on your own, match these examples with the speaking and listening skills.

Examples	Skills
1 Right, to kick things off: why don't we like this story?	**A** Summarising
2 Are you sure, Satish? Let's just look at …	**B** Getting the discussion back on track
3 That's agreed, then. We think …	**C** Opening the discussion
4 Well, that's a totally different point. For now, can we get back to …?	**D** Challenging an opinion and focusing the discussion again

Focus for development:
Directing the discussion

A good performer will support others and, despite their own viewpoint, will ensure that all views are heard and all participants feel comfortable.

ACTIVITY

The extract on the next page shows the difference between two students working at Grade E, Cyndi and Jamie, and a Grade C student, Kylie.

Kylie:	So, is single-sex education a good thing or not? Jamie?
Jamie:	It's unnatural. We should all be together, right?
Kylie:	OK.
Cyndi:	Boys are a pain in school.
Jamie:	That's stupid. We're not any worse than the girls. They mess about with hair and stuff…
Kylie:	OK. So, you don't really agree. But wouldn't you both be happier if it was single sex? Jamie, if the girls are always messing about – you'd be away from them. Yes?
Jamie:	Not really. I like girls…
Cyndi:	I get sick of boys…
Kylie:	Could you both go to different schools then? A mixed one for Jamie, a girls' school for Cyndi?

Discuss with a partner:

- How does Kylie help the discussion? Look at each of her contributions.
- How might the others react to her suggestion at the end? Explain.

A student writes…

I like working in groups but I'm hopeless at leading the others. I always get swamped by their ideas.

Answer…

If you can't lead the whole discussion, try to guide the group through parts of it. Brief notes might help you stay in touch.

ASSESSMENT FOCUS

- In a group of three, have a discussion in which two take directly opposed viewpoints and the third guides the others to a friendly outcome. Choose from these topics:

    Football is more important than anything

    or

    … is the best band the world has ever known

- Then repeat with a different topic and different roles.

Remember

- **When guiding a group discussion, the priority is to try to avoid conflict and get agreement.**
- **Sensitive listening and the ability to encourage involvement and understanding make significant contributions to discussion.**

Grade Booster

Extended Assessment Task

Working as a group, prepare a discussion on the topic to the right. Then hold the discussion.

> *From the age of 14, young people should have much more freedom in every area of their lives.*

Each member of the group should
- decide on their initial viewpoint
- produce some bulleted notes and/or other materials for discussion
- come to the discussion with an otherwise open mind.

It is likely to help if
- one member chairs the discussion
- at least one person takes each side of the argument
- one member summarises the discussion for the rest of the class.

Evaluation – What have you learned?

With a partner, use the grade checklist below to evaluate your work on the Extended Assessment Task.

C
- I can listen closely and sympathetically.
- I can ask relevant questions and make significant contributions.
- I can also engage with others' ideas, recognising bias and using precise detail.
- I can stay focused throughout the discussion, offer detailed and relevant ideas and have the ability to summarise what has been said.

D
- I can sustain involvement and make effective contributions.
- I can show evidence of understanding and respond appropriately to what is said.
- I use some detail to clarify my ideas and listen throughout. Most contributons are relevant.

E
- I can respond positively to what is said.
- I can ask for clarification and make relevant contributions.
- I can also follow ideas and ask straightforward questions.

F
- I can make contributions and respond appropriately to the contributions of others.

You may need to go back and look at the relevant pages from this section again.

Adopting a Role

This section of Chapter 3 shows you how to

- approach the task when adopting a role
- develop a role successfully
- improve performances.

Why is it important to be able to adopt a role?

- It is one of the three tasks you must complete for the Speaking and Listening section of the exam.
- If you can adopt a role successfully, it shows understanding of the character you are portraying – and understanding others is a skill for life.

A **Grade E** candidate will

- show some understanding of aspects of characters and situations
- meet the basic requirements of different roles by using simple patterns of speech, gesture and movement.

E

A **Grade D** candidate will

- be able to prepare a performance and perform a role in a believable manner
- be able to interest the audience through intonation, movement and gesture.

D

A **Grade C** candidate will

- develop and sustain roles through appropriate language and effective gesture and movement
- engage watchers' interest by showing understanding of characters, ideas and situations
- give performances of appropriate length in which the character will be sustained throughout.

C

Prior learning

Before you begin this unit, think about

- soap operas and/or television series or films you watch

- how the characters were portrayed in any live theatre you have seen

- what the acting was like in any amateur drama you may have seen.

What is memorable about your favourite characters? How are facial expressions and gestures used? How are the most memorable lines delivered, and why?

How were they made convincing?

How might the characters have been made more realistic and interesting?

Getting into role

Learning objectives

- To learn how to explore a role and what is required when improvising it.

- To think about what can be done to improve performances and be more successful.

What does getting into role mean?

In your Speaking and Listening assessment, you will be asked to **improvise a role** using drama techniques. You might have to play a character from literature or someone from real life such as a doctor or cleaner, or you might have to represent a viewpoint in a discussion – supporting a new leisure complex, for example.

You need to prepare in advance to create and develop a **convincing character**.

Checklist for success

In order to portray a character convincingly, you need to explore

- their **history**: what has happened to them
- their **behaviour**: how they speak to others and act
- their **relationships**: with people around them
- their **motivations**: why they behave as they do.

★ Examiner's tip

Some improvisations are disappointing because they have no 'depth'. To succeed, you need to know as much as possible about your character, so that you can think and behave as they would.

ACTIVITY

Choose a character from a novel, play or poem you have studied.

- Make notes about this character for each of the areas listed above.
- In a group of three, imagine that your characters meet in heaven. Introduce yourselves, describing your life.

Focus for development: Planned improvisations

Look at the improvisation below, based on this situation:

A headteacher is meeting an angry parent whose child has been excluded for fighting.

What advice would you give these two **Grade D** performers, to improve their marks?

Think about what they say and their movements.

Paula:	(*sitting at her desk*) Hello, Mrs Garvey, please sit down.
Dawn:	Thanks. I wanted to see you. (*She sits down.*)
Paula:	What can I do for you?
Dawn:	I'm unhappy about Alice.
Paula:	I expected that. Could I get you a cup of tea?
Dawn:	No, thanks. I want to talk about Alice, she's very important to me.
Paula:	Fair enough. So, what can we do? (*She sips a cup of tea.*)
Dawn:	I thought you would know. I want our Alice back in school. She hasn't done anything wrong. (*thumping the desk*) You're the Head. Do something. You think she causes all the trouble. That's not true. You should look after her.
Paula:	Well, we'll see what we can do, Mrs Garvey…

ASSESSMENT FOCUS

With a partner, act out your own headteacher/parent interview.
Choose your own topic.

- First, make notes to help you play your role.
- Then decide together roughly how the conversation will start – develop – finish?

After performing, decide which were the most successful parts of your performance and why.

Improve any details and try again. Ask yourselves:

- Do we need to know more background about the characters or the situation?
- Could we change the mood to increase the interest for the audience?
  For example by building gradually to a big finish?

Remember

- **Careful planning for your characterisation is essential.**
- **Try to make your character convincing.**
- **Preparing well with your group will help make your performance better.**

Speaking in role

Learning objective

- To learn how to develop a role through what you say.

A student writes…

How precise should we be about preparing our performance?

Answer…

You need to know enough before starting so that no one in the group will be surprised by events and everyone is aware of roughly what will be said. Beyond that, you improvise!

What does speaking in role mean?

Your performance will be more believable if you think carefully about a character's background.

However, to be really convincing you also need to pay attention to **how** your character speaks and **what** you say. Try to reveal what you **think and feel** through your words, not just say things which move the story along.

Checklist for success

Before you practise your performance, ask yourself:

- Have I prepared properly?
- Have I thought through what will happen and what I need to do at every stage?

After a practice run-through, ask yourself:

- Have I worked effectively as part of the group?
- What can I do to improve my performance?

Before the final performance, ask yourself:

- Do I know roughly what I will be saying at each stage?
- Am I secure in my character? Do I know how I will react?

ACTIVITY

In these extracts a father, who is a single parent, is talking to his ex-wife …

Both students tell the audience similar information.

Discuss with a partner why the second one is better.

How does it

- express emotion?
- create a 'speaking voice' that sounds real?

Grade D answer

I need some more money to help me feed the kids. Because you're their mum, it's reasonable that you should help to support them. They need shoes and new clothes. I can't do everything.

Grade C answer

They're not just my kids. They're yours too. I need you to help support them because you know I simply don't have enough money. My wages can't stretch far enough and it's hard to even feed them properly, never mind buy new clothes…

Focus for development:
Speaking in character

Obviously you need to speak clearly, but you also need to speak in the way your character would. This means you won't always use Standard English.

ACTIVITY

Look at this **Grade C** improvisation in role as the Nurse in *Romeo and Juliet*. Discuss with a partner what features of her speech make it successful.

> Phew! I've had a hard day, I can tell you. I've been rushing around from morning 'til night. No rest! Not a chance. Everybody in this house wants something doing. And they ask muggins here to do it. Nobody cares about me. Couldn't give two hoots about old Nursie. None of 'em.

ASSESSMENT FOCUS

Work with a partner, each choosing two different characters from literature, the media or real life.

Demonstrating clearly how they speak, make a 30-second speech by each character.

Then your partner will criticise your performance, picking out

- what was convincing
- what was unconvincing, in terms of the character's personality and the words used.

Remember

- Focus clearly on **what** you say and **how** you say it throughout your improvisation.

Developing a role through expression and movement

Learning objective

- To understand how words can be supported by actions.

How can I develop a role through expression and movement?

As well as thinking carefully about the words your character would use (see page 150), you can develop a character by adding physical actions. This might be a limp, a mannerism such as furrowing your brows or showing anger with the jab of a finger.

However, to develop a role successfully though **gesture** and **movement**, you first need to understand the character's feelings.

Checklist for success

You need to observe people closely – their expressions, their movements and their peculiarities. Notice how they

- show feelings on their faces
- stand
- move
- show feelings in their mannerisms (for example, scratch their head, play with their fingers).

Focus for development:
Expression and movement

ACTIVITY

Choose someone both you and a friend should recognise from television. Make notes about them for each of the areas listed.

Then mime them doing something and ask your friend to recognise who they are.

ACTIVITY

Look at these **expressions**. Explain how you think each person is feeling.

Read these two statements:

- I'm happy here. There's nothing more I want from life than this.
- Things have got to change if we are going to get through this.

Create very different characters by speaking each of these statements as

- an old person
- a confident business person.

Concentrate on giving your characters physical characteristics, such as a bad leg or a habit of smoothing their hair. Make your facial expressions convincing.

Gestures and movements add to the feelings you want to show. For example:

- Hugging someone shows affection.
- Hands to the mouth could show shock.
- Arms wide apart could show welcome.
- A waved fist demonstrates anger (or triumph).
- Sitting down suddenly could register dismay.
- Walking away could show a struggle to accept what has been said.

ASSESSMENT FOCUS

With a friend, act out the extract below, using expression and movements.

- The first time, A is drunk and B is confused.
- The second time, A is frustrated and B is happy.

A: When the guy walks in…

B: Yeah… What?

A: Make sure it's safe…

B: It's safe?

A: Yes, safe.

B: Then what?

A: Get him.

B: Get him?

A: Yes. Are you stupid? Get him!

ACTIVITY

Imagine someone says each of these lines to you. Mime your reaction.

- We have no money left. We will have to move away, I'm afraid.
- She simply stepped into the road without looking. It wasn't the driver's fault. He couldn't stop.

What gestures and movements will you use?

Remember

- **Create an impression by how you react and move – but don't overdo it.**
- **Show your feelings even if you are not speaking.**
- **Support your words with expressions and movements.**

Maximising the impact

What does maximising the impact mean?

To maximise the **impact** of your performance, show aspects of your character, sustain your role and finish strongly, leaving a clear impression of your character.

Checklist for success

- Plan exactly what you will do, what you will be talking about and how you will move and behave.
- Think seriously about how you will begin, maintain your role, and finish in a memorable way.

ACTIVITY

You are auditioning for a part in *Hollyoaks*. The part is a teenager who has just moved into the area and comes from a rich family but does not get on with their parents.

You have to walk into the café for the first time. How will you make an impact?

- What aspects of your character will you want to show?
- How will you behave towards the owner and other customers?

Focus for development: Making an impact

The opening

Performances can **start in different ways** but the opening is likely to establish your character.

ACTIVITY

You are 24 and have just arrived on holiday with a friend. You know no one else in the hotel. Your friend has gone out to look around and you go down to the pool.

In a small group, you are going to act out your first entrance. Imagine the people by the pool all go silent as you arrive. What will you do? What will be the first thing you say and to whom?

You might want to

- tell them about yourself
- tell them about your journey
- ask about the resort.

⭐ Examiner's tip

Talk to the people around you, but remember the audience too. Sometimes, actors on stage talk directly to the audience when they have something important to say.

The middle

Stay focused on your role:

- React in a convincing way, using speech, expression and movement.
- Keep focused and don't become distracted by the audience.
- Don't allow yourself to be excluded from the main action.

The ending

Your final appearance or your final speech will be your last chance to create an impact. It will help you if you can

- make a significant final contribution
- show you are the same person but, perhaps, also show how you have been affected by what has happened.

Glossary
monologue: an uninterrupted speech delivered by one person.

155

Interviews

When might I have to take part in an interview?

This might be in your **presentation** task – dealing with questions.

Or it might be a **role** you are asked to adopt.

Checklist for success

You need to be successful as an interviewer and interviewee.

- A successful interviewer asks probing questions.
- An effective interviewee gives detailed answers.

ACTIVITY

Watch two different interviews on television, one involving a TV personality and one a politician.

Which interview is better and why?

What impression do we get of each interviewer and each interviewee from

- the language they use
- their facial expressions
- their body language?

Focus for development:
Good questions and good answers

Interviewing

ACTIVITY

In this extract, what does Sarah, the interviewer, do badly? Then what does she do well?

Sarah: Tell us about your early life. —— standard opening

Beata: I was brought up in Warsaw, then we moved to England.

Sarah: What did you first think of—— sudden switch
university?

Beata: I had a terrible time…

Sarah: Yes. I think we all know that story. You have apologised, of course: but will the public ever forgive you for what happened…?

Being the interviewee

Prepare fully for the interview so that you know your subject well.
You need to be able to give detailed answers that will interest listeners.

ACTIVITY

What details and opinions does this **Grade C** student use to add interest to their answer?

Interviewee:
I had a great time as a kid. I was brought up in California. It was all sunshine and beaches. I loved it. When my parents said they were coming back to England, I was gutted. I didn't know anyone here and didn't know anything about the country either. I'd always been an American before.

— gives opinion in role

— good detail

ASSESSMENT FOCUS

Imagine you are a famous person of your choice.
Prepare to answer these questions in role.
Make up any necessary details.

- What are your earliest memories?
- Tell us about your time at school.
- How has fame affected your life?

Remember

- **You are assessed on your speaking and listening skills, so show both.**
- **Interviewers must be fully involved and interviewees must interest the audience.**

Grade Booster

Extended Assessment Task

In a group of three or four, plan an improvisation set in a workplace. A valuable item has gone missing and one person is accused.

Work though these stages:
- Plan what will happen.
- Divide the improvisation into scenes and decide what will happen in each one (or decide what will happen in one scene, if that is all there is).
- Make detailed notes on your character.
- Decide how you will play your role.
- Practise as a group.
- Discuss improvements.
- Have another run-through.
- Perform for the rest of the teaching group.

Take feedback on the performance, discuss it with your group, then improve your performance in the light of what you have learned.

Evaluation – What have you learned?

With a partner, use the grade checklist below to evaluate your work on the Extended Assessment Task.

C
- I can sustain and develop a role.
- I can use effective language, gestures and movement and show I understand how the character thinks and feels.
- I am convincing throughout and offer more than just simple characteristics.

D
- I can prepare a performance, perform in role and use appropriate language, gestures and movement.
- My role is believable and clearly different from the person I actually am.

E
- I can attempt to perform in role and can use simple patterns of speech, gesture and movement.

F
- I can create simple characters and react to situations in appropriate ways.

You may need to go back and look at the relevant pages from this section again.

Controlled Assessment Preparation
Speaking and Listening

Introduction

In this section you will

- consider examples from students' Speaking and Listening assessments
- look closely at how other students have responded to the tasks
- identify the strengths and weaknesses in their responses.

Why is preparation of this kind important?

- The example responses in this section allow you to take time to think about how well others speak and listen.
- It is important to learn from the examples of others.
- Taking the opportunity to consider and discuss how activities can be approached and how others have performed will help you to improve the quality of your own performances.

Key Information

Unit 2 is the Speaking and Listening assessment.

- It has three parts: **Presenting**, **Discussing and Listening**, and **Role Playing**.
- The three activities are worth **20% of your overall English Language GCSE mark**.

What will the assessments involve?

You will have to

- make an individual presentation
- discuss and listen as part of a group
- play a role.

You are likely to complete more than one assessment in each of the three areas, with your best mark in each case being used.

It is crucial that you avoid reading from notes in any of the activities. You are allowed to use notes if they are appropriate (for example, in the presentation), but you are expected to refer to them as you talk, not simply read them.

The Assessment

The assessment objectives for Speaking and Listening (AO1) state that you must be able to do the following:

- Speak to communicate clearly and purposefully; structure and sustain talk, adapting it to different situations and audiences; use standard English and a variety of techniques as appropriate.
- Listen and respond to speakers' ideas and perspectives, and how they construct and express meanings.
- Interact with others, shaping meanings through suggestions, comments and questions and drawing ideas together.
- Create and sustain different roles.

Targeting Grade C

Some of the key features of Grade D and Grade C answers are as follows:

Grade D candidates	See example on page 161 and 163–4
<ul><li>interest the listener in different ways</li><li>use an increasing variety of appropriate vocabulary</li><li>understand the need for standard English</li><li>make effective contributions throughout discussions</li><li>respond appropriately to what is said</li><li>perform in role in a believable manner and interest the audience through intonation, movement and gesture.</li></ul>	

Grade C candidates	See example on pages 162–3 and 165
<ul><li>adapt their talk to the situation</li><li>use Standard English confidently</li><li>interest the listener through their use of language</li><li>communicate clearly</li><li>listen carefully and develop their own and others' ideas</li><li>make significant contributions to discussions</li><li>develop and sustain roles through appropriate language and effective gesture and movement, and interest watchers by showing understanding of characters, ideas and situations.</li></ul>	

Exploring Sample Responses

Individual presentation

This is an extract from a presentation about 'Why Work Experience is a good experience'.

Example 1

I had a great time on my work experience and I would recommend everyone to do it. I was working in a hospital in the kitchen and although I spent a lot of every day washing up, it was still fun. For a change, they let me clean the floors sometimes and although that sounds awful it could be great fun because I got the chance to use one of the scrubbing machines and they are really cool. You kind of lean to one side to make them go that way. The cleaners use them in school and they don't look like anything special but it can be a good laugh.

I also met some pretty good people and they helped me and showed me what to do. The other kitchen porter with me was called Raymond and he didn't have any teeth at all. He must have had pretty hard gums, because he seemed to eat most things. How can you get through life without teeth? There was also Annie who was about a million years old and she showed me how to rip the stem out of a lettuce and then turn it upside down and run water through it and all the leaves get cleaned at once. Pretty magic, that...

Examiner feedback

The response was delivered using only bulleted notes. It is focused on the title and suggests throughout that it was a good experience, though the examples given seem a little trivial – there might have been more important benefits to the student. There are some interesting touches about the people, though they are not developed as character studies. The opening and the language could have been improved.

Suggested grade: D

ACTIVITY

How might the response have been improved to Grade C level?
Think about

- how the opening could have been improved
- which vocabulary might have been made better
- what other kinds of details and ideas you might expect the speaker to include later
- how the speaker could really interest the listeners.

Now read this response to the same presentation title by a different candidate:

Example 2

rhetorical question → *Is work experience a good thing? I would say it is, and I have no doubts about that. I had a wonderful time working for Boots and I'd go back there every week if I could. They looked after me well: I had my supervisor, who told me what to do and kept checking that I was OK and knew what I was doing; and the other workers all treated me as if I was part of the team. I found out about what it is like to work in a big store and now know what it will be like when I leave school and enter the world of work.* ← situation established

why it was worthwhile →

I want to start by talking about the interesting people you meet. You find out that adults can be fun to be with (and even that they can be childish at work when no one is around!) and going to work is great when you feel as if you have friends there. ← sense of order in the talk

an interesting aside →

One of the girls – Annette – who worked on cosmetics was amazing. Looking at the layers of make-up she always wears, you would think that she was not real at all, but she had a fabulous sense of humour and made me laugh every day – ← individual as example

presents picture →

complex sentence well controlled → *much more than I ever do in school. One day an area manager was coming in, and you wouldn't believe what she did …* ← start of anecdote

Examiner feedback

This begins well, giving some ideas about why the experience was positive, and then begins to work logically though them, starting with the people. Examples are used effectively. There is some variety of expression here (everything is not just 'good' or 'great') and the speaker gives a real sense of having enjoyed what happened – for example, the aside in brackets. At the end of the extract, she is moving on to deliver an anecdote. The style seems formal enough, sentences are varied and this is a good opening.

Suggested Grade: C

Discussing and Listening

This is an extract from a group discussion about transport and what could be done to improve it.

summarises Janey's opinion

Kane: So, you're saying we need more roads and it's as simple as that. Is it really just about building more roads and getting rid of more fields?

questions to get more information

Janey: Yeah… I think so… It would solve the problems… Simple.

Kane: But we have to think about the environment too.

a new angle

Janey: You're going to say we've all got to start riding bikes. Then we'll all get killed by the cars.

disagrees without offending Janey

Kane: Not if we're all on bikes. There won't be any cars, will there?

Janey: So how do we get to London? Grow wings?

Kane: No, grow more trains. Public transport's what we're supposed to be using, isn't it? Buses, trains, trams… that's the future.

touch of humour

Janey: I think that is just stupid.

helping Janey clarify

Kane: Why?

Janey: Because it is. I want to learn to drive and travel around and so does everyone else and I want to fly to holidays abroad. I don't see why I should miss out on everything.

own opinion challenges her

Kane: I think you'll have to. There's all this global warming stuff and transport's part of the problem. You know that. We have to change the ways we travel.

Janey: I hate all the grannies on the bus.

doesn't want to offend

Kane: Yeah. I know. Maybe we could have special buses for teenagers. You know, music on board and a disco upstairs and a make-up room for you.

lightens the conversation again

Janey: Hey…

Kane: OK. For you and your friends… with mascara on tap…
and lipstick racks on the walls…

Janey: Actually, that would be great!

Kane: And if it helped save the world, it would be worth every penny…

links back to what he feels is important

Examiner feedback

Janey is making useful contributions to the discussion and is following what is said. When she comments on us all riding bikes but getting killed by the cars, she is not perfectly logical. She develops a couple of points slightly and co-operates well with Kane.

Kane sustains the conversation and tries to impose some logic and development. He summarises and uses questioning effectively. His humour towards the end appeals to Janey, and he still manages to link it back to the main focus of the discussion.

Suggested grades: Janey D, Kane C

ACTIVITY

For each of these points made by Janey, decide how she could have developed them:

- We should solve the problem by building more roads.
- The idea of using public transport is stupid.
- Buses are full of old ladies.

How might she have countered these points made by Kane?

- There won't be any cars if we're riding bikes.
- Transport's part of the problem of global warming.

Adopting a role

Example 1

This student is speaking in role as Lennie, from *Of Mice and Men*.

JOHN STEINBECK'S
CLASSIC NOVEL COMES TO THE SCREEN

Everyone has a dream, few dare to follow it.

Lenny did!

OF MICE AND MEN

(Sitting on a chair, facing the audience)

Me and George travel around together and we've been together for years. I used to live with my Aunt Clara but then me and George started travelling and we've been to lots of places. We were in Weed for a while and I made friends with a little girl there but then we had to leave and George made me hide in ditches and places and he said I'd done a bad thing but it's only 'cos I like to pet soft things. Sometimes I keep mice and then George makes me throw them away. He told Aunt Clara he'd look after me. When we got to the ranch, I made friends with Slim. He's a good guy. I don't like Curley though, but I like his wife 'cos she's purty. Candy had an old dog when we got there but that was shot. And we made friends with Crooks, but he lives in a room off the stable. He's on his own all the time, not like me and George.

Examiner feedback

The student has an understanding of Lennie's life and can talk as the character (in terms of the sort of details he might include, but also using 'purty'). Although some of the ideas are not well linked, that might be how someone who is not very clever might speak. However, it would have been better if the points were not quite so random and there was more development of ideas. There is no evidence here of Lennie using movement or gesture – he might have been better demonstrating his character by using more than just words to show what sort of person he is.

Suggested grade: D

In this second example, a student speaks as George, from *Of Mice and Men*.

Example 2

throughout, moves indicate feelings

effective opening captures how the character speaks

not proper sentences, but a speaking voice

questions show his torment

beginning to develop the character's thoughts

(Wandering round the bunk house)

Gee, it's hard. I loved that guy. I told his Aunt Clara I'd look after him, and now look what's happened. I loved that guy and now he's dead and it's my fault. *(Head in hands)* How am I gonna live now? That ranch? No, not now. Who cares about keeping rabbits if there's no Lennie around any more? Candy said we can still get the ranch, but that won't happen. *(Stands, close to tears)* I shot the guy and now there's nothing for me. I might just hand myself in and let them hang me. There's nothing left. But that woman lured him in. I knew she was bad. *(Stares out of the window)* I told him to stay away from her 'cos I knew she was poison. And she poisoned everything – I was right...

emotional from start

repetition for effect

links to detail in novel

simple sentences demonstrate the simple reality for George

sense that it is now not just his fault: development again

Examiner feedback

The student enters well into George's character – we get a clear impression of what the character is thinking through what he says and through his movements. We recognise his sorrow and possibly anger towards the end and the ideas seem to flow logically. The character is sustained and developed.

Suggested grade: C

Read through Example 1 on page 164 again, then act it out. There is no need to change the actual words. Just go through it putting in movement and gesture and notice how it is improved. If you can attempt an American accent, that would make it even better.

EXTENDED PRACTICE TASK

The local council has come up with an idea: there is to be a street festival in your area. Planning committees have been formed.

In a group of four, plan the grand procession. You need to have colourful floats which

- represent the community and the area
- will draw in people from outside the district.

You need entertainers who

- can move along with the procession
- offer a variety of skills and performances.

You will also have to consider, for security

- a police presence
- road closures.

Finally, you need to consider

- food and drink requirements for those taking part *and* those watching
- the route itself.

In your group, take on the roles of

- the chair who leads the discussion
- the festival organiser who also summarises the decisions at the end
- a local police officer
- a local business person.

Before you hold the discussion do some initial planning and make brief notes.

During the discussion, use the techniques and approaches you have learnt in this chapter.

If you only do five things...

1 When you are undertaking assessment tasks, avoid the temptation to use only simple words and short sentences – remember that you are rewarded for variety.

2 Attempt to speak appropriately in any given situation: formally, perhaps, for a presentation; speaking more 'normally', perhaps, if you are playing a character from a literary text.

3 If you are given the opportunity to plan, grasp it with both hands, because it will prove to be time well spent when you have to perform.

4 In discussions, pay attention to what others say: don't forget that listening is rewarded as well as talking. In role-play, try to really get into the character. Your performance will be more believable if you are thinking like the person and moving as they would move.

5 Take speaking and listening seriously. The 20% of marks awarded to it can be the difference between success and failure.

④ Unit 3A **Extended Reading**

What's it all about?

Exploring longer texts in detail means you can read, discuss and write thoughtfully about really interesting ideas and characters.

How will I be assessed?

- You will get **15% of your English Language marks** for your ability to respond to one extended text. This might be a play, novel, poem or work of non-fiction.
- You will have to complete a Controlled Assessment task on **one** extended text (such as a novel) over the course of 3–4 hours.
- You will be marked on your writing of **one** written response taken from a choice of two task areas (**Characterisation and voice** or **Themes and ideas**).
- The recommended word limit is **1200 words**.

What is being tested?

You are being examined on your ability to

- read and understand texts, selecting material appropriately to support what you want to say
- develop and sustain interpretations of writers' ideas and perspectives
- explain and evaluate how writers create particular grammatical or linguistic effects (for example, imagery) to influence or engage the reader
- explain and evaluate how writers use structural or presentational features (such as rhyme patterns in poetry) to influence or engage the reader.

Characterisation and Voice

Introduction

This section of Chapter 4 shows you how to

- understand what a 'Characterisation and voice' Controlled Assessment task requires you to do
- develop responses to different forms of texts.

Why is it important to learn about characterisation and voice?

- Texts can be looked at in a range of ways, and focusing on characterisation and voice sometimes requires a different approach from a focus on themes and ideas.
- Characters are at the centre of most of the texts we read. Your understanding and enjoyment of a text can be increased by exploring how a writer creates characters or presents ideas through a specific voice.
- Looking at how writers create character and voice will provide a model for your own creative writing.

A **Grade D** candidate will

- show some understanding of how a character has been presented
- use appropriate quotations to support their points
- interpret what the writer has to say
- offer explanations that show understanding
- understand some features of language and structure.

A **Grade C** candidate will

- show clear evidence of understanding the main ways in which a character has been presented
- support points with relevant and appropriate quotations
- become involved in the content of the texts and interpret them
- offer clear explanations of the writer's presentation of character
- display understanding of various features of language and structure.

Prior learning

Before you begin this unit, think about

- what you already know about analysing character and voice
- any recent text you have read in which a particular character made an impression on you.

What do you think these terms mean?

What do you remember about the character? Did you empathise or engage with the character's feelings, actions or viewpoint on life?

What was it about the *way* the character was presented that made him or her memorable and kept you interested?

Characterisation

Learning objectives

- To understand the ways in which writers create character.
- To consider the features of a good response on character.

What does characterisation mean?

Characterisation is the way in which a writer creates and develops a character.

Checklist for success

- You need to comment on **how** a character is created by the writer.
- You need to consider the development of characters (if and how they change over the course of a text).

Judging character

As readers and watchers, we make judgments about characters by looking at these pointers:

- what they say
- what they do
- how others speak about them (the writer or other characters)
- how others behave towards them
- in particular, their first and last appearances in a text.

For example, in Shakespeare's *Macbeth*:

Character pointers	What these might tell us about the character
What Macbeth says Macbeth says: 'False face must hide what false heart doth know.'	This tells us Macbeth is prepared to hide his murderous thoughts from the outside world; *he is two-faced!*
What he does Macbeth murders the King who has rewarded him for his loyalty.	He is *disloyal* – and *treacherous*.
How others speak about him Someone calls him 'this fiend of Scotland'.	He is *devilish*.
How others behave towards him His soldiers desert him during the final battle.	He is *unloved*, and because of his terrible acts no one will support him.

ACTIVITY

- Note down which of the four character pointers the response on the page opposite refers to when discussing Curley's wife. (She is a character from John Steinbeck's novel *Of Mice and Men*.)
- What is the effect of these descriptions, according to the student?

Candy, the old man in the story, says that he thinks Curley's wife is 'a tart'. George also criticises her saying she's a 'tramp'. These descriptions create a picture of Curley's wife as someone disliked by many in the story. However, Lennie does say, 'She's real purty' (pretty).

Focus for development: Choosing quotations

Here, the narrator of the novel *Martyn Pig* by Kevin Brooks, is describing his father.

> Did I hate him? He was a drunken slob and he treated me like dirt. What do *you* think? Of course I hated him. You would have hated him, too, if you'd ever met him. God knows why Mum ever married him.

ACTIVITY

Write one sentence about how Kevin Brooks characterises Martyn. You will need to

- **make a point** about Martyn – for example, how he feels about his father
- **support the point** with a quotation – choose the best one from the extract
- **develop the point** – could you say something about the strength of Martyn's feelings by referring to another phrase or word in the extract?

You could start:

The writer shows us that Martyn ...
Try to embed the quotation in the sentence. Look back at how the student writing about Curley's wife does this well.

Examiner's tip ★

If you can point to a specific technique a writer has used to create a character, it will improve your response. For example, look at how Martyn uses direct questions to the reader to make him sound almost like a friend. The writer has chosen to do this to create this effect.

ASSESSMENT FOCUS

Choose a character who interests you from a novel you have read. Write a paragraph explaining how he or she is characterised through their actions, their speech, their own and others' opinions.

Remember

- **Writers create characters in a range of ways.**
- **Focus on the character pointers to help you find your 'evidence'.**
- **Try to go beyond a basic explanation and develop your points.**

Developing character

Learning objective

- To understand how writers use language techniques to reveal character.

What does developing character mean?

You have seen how the author of *Martyn Pig* uses questions to make it sound as if Martyn is chatting, or confiding in us, almost like a friend. What other techniques might a writer use?

ACTIVITY

Here is another extract from *Martyn Pig*. Here, Martyn is talking about a girl he knows called Alex.

> It wasn't that I was jealous. Well, I suppose I was a bit jealous. But not in a namby kind of way, you know, not in a snotty, pouty kind of way. No, that wasn't it. Not really. That wasn't the reason I was glum. All right, it was *partly* the reason. But the main thing was – it was just *wrong*. All of it. Alex and Dean. It stank. It was wrong for her to spend time with him. It was a waste. He was nothing. It was wrong. Wrong. Wrong. *Wrong*. She was too good for him.

Make notes with a partner of what you notice about

- the **style of language** – what makes it informal and chatty?
- the **length of the sentences** – do they vary and why (or why not)?
- other features to do with the way Martyn 'speaks' – for example, the use of **repetition**.

What is the **effect** of these language choices? Discuss these three possibilities.

- Martyn comes across as lively and funny because of the way…
- Martyn's strength of feelings for Alex is shown by …
- Martyn still seems chatty and friendly as a result of …

Now choose one of the possibilities and complete the sentence, using a quotation and further explanation.

The novel *Of Mice and Men*, mentioned on page 170, concerns two men, George and Lennie, who find work at a ranch in the 1930s in California. It was a time of high unemployment. Curley is the ranch boss's son.

Read this longer extract about Curley's wife.

A girl was standing there looking in. She had full, rouged lips and wide-spaced eyes, heavily made up. Her finger nails were red. Her hair hung in little rolled clusters, like sausages. She wore a cotton house dress and red mules, on the insteps of which were little bouquets of red ostrich feathers. 'I'm looking for Curley,' she said. Her voice had a nasal, brittle quality.

George looked away from her and then back. 'He was in here a minute ago, but he went.'

'Oh!' She put her hands behind her back and leaned against the door-frame so that her body was thrown forward. 'You're the new fellas that just come, ain't ya?'

'Yeah.'

Lennie's eyes moved down over her body, and although she did not seem to be looking at Lennie, she bridled a little. She looked down at her finger-nails. 'Sometimes Curley's in here,' she explained.

George said brusquely, 'Well, he ain't now.'

Glossary
rouged: red-coloured

mules: flat, backless shoes

bridled: drew back

brusquely: abruptly, almost rudely

Using the character pointers on page 170, write two paragraphs in response to this task:

How does John Steinbeck use language to present Curley's wife?

Comment on:
- specific physical details – the adjectives and nouns chosen to describe how she looks
- significant repeated ideas which might represent something
- particular similes or other uses of imagery.

In each case, explain the effect these create.

Remember

- Refer to the language the writer uses.
- Make sure you say what effect it creates in terms of how we see a character.

Writing about voice

Learning objective

- *To explore how writers create a particular voice for characters.*

What is voice?

In some texts, especially ones which are told in the first person ('I') or have a particularly strong main character, writers try to create a very distinctive voice. This allows us to empathise with a character (understand how they think).

Voice can come across strongly in **poems**, which are often told from a particular point of view.

ACTIVITY

Read the beginning of this poem by Stevie Smith, which a student has begun to annotate. With a partner, jot down answers to these questions.

- Who is speaking in this poem?
- What is unusual about him/her/it?

> **The River God**
> I may be smelly and I may be old,
> Rough in my pebbles, reedy in my pools,
> But where my fish float by I bless their swimming
> And I like the people to bathe in me, especially women.
> But I can drown the fools
> Who bathe too close to the <u>weir</u>, contrary to rules.
> And they take a long time drowning
> As I throw them up now and then in the spirit of clowning.
> <u>Hi yih, yippity-yap</u>, merrily I flow,
> O I may be an old foul river but I have <u>plenty of go.</u>

River point where water is often deeper, faster moving

Sounds Native American – like a chant of a tribal chief?

Sounds child-like – very simple

This response to a task about the voice in this poem mentions character but has not said enough about the voice created.

> *The writer characterises the river god as cruel and kind at the same time as it will sometimes 'bless' swimmers and then 'drown the fools'.*

- Add a further sentence or two about the voice of the river. Focus on what it sounds like, whether it is simple or complicated.

Focus for development: Language structures and techniques

In 'The River God' the poet gives a voice to an imaginary being or god. Other poets have done a similar thing. Read the opening of the poem, 'Medusa' by Carol Ann Duffy. A student has begun to make notes around the verses about the language structures Duffy has used.

Medusa

A suspicion, a doubt, a jealousy ← *Pattern of three builds up idea of Medusa's feelings*

grew in my mind,

which turned the hairs on my head to
   filthy snakes

as though my thoughts

hissed and spat on my scalp.

My bride's breath soured, stank

in the grey bags of my lungs.

I'm foul mouthed now, foul tongued,
   yellow fanged.

There are bullet tears in my eyes.

Are you terrified?

Be terrified.

It's you I love,

perfect man, Greek God, my own;

but I know you'll go, betray me, stray
   from home.

So better by far for me if you were
   stone.

Medusa talks directly to her lover

Metaphor is a violent one

ACTIVITY

Based on the verses you have read, make notes on the following points.

- What are Medusa's **feelings** about her 'Greek God'? For example, does she trust him, love him or hate him?
- What **picture** is conveyed of Medusa's appearance through the description? Is it a pleasant one? Why / Why not?

The language used is key to understanding Medusa's voice. Just look at some of the verbs.

> 'My bride's breath *soured, stank*'
> 'as though my thoughts
> *hissed* and *spat* on my scalp.'

or the adjectives she uses to describe herself:

> *'foul mouthed', 'foul tongued', 'yellow fanged', 'filthy'*

It's not a pretty picture!

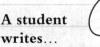

⭐ **Examiner's tip**

Look out for language techniques from other forms of writing, too. For example, note how Duffy uses patterns of three (from persuasive writing) to stress or develop an idea: 'perfect man, Greek god, my own'.

ACTIVITY

Use the following structure to write three paragraphs based on the notes you have made.

Paragraph 1 could introduce the background to the poem like this, saying who Medusa was and perhaps something about how Duffy has updated it:

> *The poet presents the reader with an updated version of the mythological creature Medusa who …*

Paragraph 2 could focus on an aspect of Medusa's voice – and the picture of her it gives us – like this:

> *In the first verse, Medusa is shown as …*

Make sure you refer to a language choice the writer makes, and the effect it creates.

Paragraph 3 could link from this idea to more comment on Medusa's voice, like this:

> *This links to verse … in which Medusa says that …*

Focus for development: Adopting a voice

Duffy has **taken on the voice** of 'Medusa', rather than describing her in more traditional ways. She could have written:

> A suspicion, a doubt, a jealousy,
> grew in *her* mind
> which turned the hairs on *her* head to filthy snakes.

176

But by using the **first person**, she enables the reader to relate more closely to what is being said.

Other poets use the same technique to create a voice for an object. For example, in the poem 'Mirror', by Sylvia Plath, the mirror describes itself and its effect on those who look in it.

> ### Glossary
> **Personify**: to give human characteristics to an object or idea.

Mirror

I am silver and exact. I have no preconceptions.
What ever I see I swallow immediately
Just as it is, unmisted by love or dislike.
I am not cruel, only truthful—

ACTIVITY

- How does Sylvia Plath **personify** the mirror?
- What words does she use to bring out its feelings and voice?

ASSESSMENT FOCUS

One good way of understanding how poets create a voice for an object or other being is to write a similar poem yourself. Choose one of the following and write a short verse from its point of view.

- The wolf from 'Little Red Riding Hood'
- A Christmas tree
- A football.

Write two verses of four lines each.

- In the first verse, describe the object or creature starting 'I am …'
- In the second verse, describe your effect on those you meet or who come into contact with you.
- Use personification in the same way that Sylvia Plath does in 'Mirror'.

Remember

- Writers use a range of techniques to get inside the skin of a character and create their voice.
- These techniques can have the effect of bringing the reader closer to their thoughts and feelings.

Writing about character development

Learning objective

- To learn how to trace the ways a character develops over a whole text.

Why is tracing character development important?

When you are reading longer texts, especially novels, there is a good chance that key characters will develop over the course of the story. To appreciate this development you need to look at

- what the character is like at the start
- what he or she is like at the end
- key events that change or affect them.

Often, stories which focus on a young person growing up or 'coming of age' show clear character development. In these stories, young people's view of things is changed by an event or experience.

Read this summary of the story 'The Darkness Out There' by Penelope Lively, from your AQA Anthology, *Moon on the Tides*.

> *A teenage girl called Sandra agrees to help out an old woman, Mrs Rutter, who lives near the local woods where Sandra played when she was younger. Sandra thinks in rather simple terms of old people who need helping and is happy to lend a hand. Sandra arrives at Mrs Rutter's cottage with a teenage boy called Kerry whom Sandra doesn't like much and thinks is a bit rough and silly. While they are there, Mrs Rutter tells them about her husband who died in the war and about the night a German war-plane crashed in the woods. She tells the two teenagers that one of the crew, a young German man, survived – but with terrible injuries. She and another local woman left him to die, slowly, over the course of two nights, even when he asked for help. On the way home, Kerry expresses his hatred of the old woman and seems shocked. Sandra, too, is affected by what she has heard and shares his disgust.*

ACTIVITY

Based on this summary, discuss these questions with a partner.

- What key incident or new information from the story is likely to have had a big effect on Sandra?
- How might it have changed her view of people?

Read these two extracts from the story. As you do so, pick out any examples of **imagery** used by the writer to show how the characters feel. In particular, look at the way the woods are described.

On the way to Mrs Rutter's house

When they were small, six and seven and eight, they'd been scared stiff of Packer's End. Then, they hadn't known about the German plane. It was different things then; witches and wolves and tigers. Sometimes they'd go there for a dare, several of them, skittering over the field and into the edge of the trees, giggling and shrieking, not too far in, just far enough for it to be scary, for the branch shapes to look like faces and clawed hands, for the wolves to rustle and creep in the greyness you couldn't quite see into, the clotted shifting depths of the place.

But after, lying on your stomach at home on the hearth rug watching telly with the curtains drawn and the dark shut out, it was cosy to think of Packer's End, where you weren't.

After they were twelve or so the witches and wolves went away.

Leaving the cottage, after Mrs Rutter's story

The boy said, 'I'm not going near that old bitch again.' He leaned against the gate, clenching his fists on an iron rung; he shook slightly. 'I won't ever forget him, that poor sod.'

She nodded.

'Two bloody nights. Christ!'

And she would hear, she thought, always, for a long time anyway, that voice trickling on, that soft old woman's voice: would see a tin painted with cornflowers, pretty china ornaments.

'It makes you want to throw up,' he said. 'Someone like that.'

She couldn't think of anything to say. He had grown; he had got older and larger. His anger eclipsed his acne, the patches of grease on his jeans, his lardy midriff. You could get people all wrong, she realized with alarm. You could get people wrong and there was a

darkness that was not the darkness of tree shadows and murky undergrowth and you could not draw the curtains and keep it out because it was in your head, once known, in your head for ever like lines from a song. One moment you were walking in long grass with the sun on your hair and birds singing and the next you glimpsed darkness, an inescapable darkness. The darkness was out there and it was a part of you and you would never be without it, ever.

She walked behind him, through a world grown unreliable, in which flowers sparkle and birds sing but everything is not as it appears, oh no.

ACTIVITY

Now look at how one student has commented on the first extract, summing up what we learn about Sandra from it.

> As a child Sandra played games in the woods, pretending that there were witches and wolves in them. But then she grew up and they went away. The writer says, 'After they were twelve or so the witches and wolves went away.' This means her fears went away.

This explains something about how Sandra feels, but it

- misses a chance to write about the powerful imagery: for example, 'the clotted shifting depths of the place'
- does not embed the quotation fluently
- explains the quotation, but hasn't grasped the underlying idea – that the wolves and witches weren't real but part of the innocence of childhood
- does not link this to the change in Sandra.

How is this second response better? Find at least two ways.

> By the end of the story, Sandra has a different view of the woods, which now have an 'inescapable darkness'. This is a metaphor for growing up as she cannot hide away from the bad things in the world.

Add a further sentence or two to the paragraph above, saying something more about how Sandra cannot stop thinking about what Mrs Rutter did. Comment on the writer's use of

- the image of a river, suggesting Mrs Rutter's voice going on and on
- a simile to say how the memory of what Mrs Rutter did stuck in Sandra's head
- personification to describe the 'world' now.

Read the whole story in *Moon on the Tides* AQA Anthology. Then write a full response to this task.

> **How does the writer present the way Sandra changes as a person over the course of the story?**

You could use this structure to help you plan your key points and draft your ideas.

Structure for response	Add possible quotation to use
Opening: Write about who Sandra is and her situation at the start of the story. Include details about how she describes herself.	
Development: Explain how Sandra used to feel about the woods at Packer's End as a younger child and how she has changed (even before meeting with Mrs Rutter).	
Development: Explain how Sandra feels and behaves when she • first sees Kerry • arrives at Mrs Rutter's.	
Development: Focus on the significant moment in the story when Mrs Rutter tells them about the dying German airman. Comment on how Sandra's thoughts and feelings are conveyed.	
Conclusion: Write about how Sandra is described at the end as she walks back with Kerry. Try to link back to how she was at the start of the story and how she has changed.	

Remember

- Identify key events that have a big effect on the main character.
- Choose appropriate quotations to support your points.
- Offer detailed comment on the changes in the character.
- Focus on specific language techniques the writer uses to put ideas across.

Grade Booster

Extended Assessment Task

Write a response of around 1200 words to this task.

> *Explore how the first person narrative voice is used to present the main character in any text you have studied.*

Draw on what you have learned about detailed analysis and response.

- How can you make general comments about the character, linked to detailed specific examples, evidence and exploration?
- Consider alternative or personal interpretations of the character.
- Write a developed response that goes beyond basic points.

Evaluation – What have you learned?

With a partner, use the grade checklist below to evaluate your work on the Extended Assessment Task.

C
- I can clearly understand the way character is portrayed and presented.
- I can explain these main ideas in clear and logical ways.
- I can understand how language features and structure work, and can support comment on character with relevant quotations.

D
- I can show some understanding of how character is presented by the writer.
- I can support my ideas with quotations and evidence but these are not always well chosen or appropriate.
- I can make my own points but they are not developed in as much detail as they should be.

E
- I can show some awareness of the ways a character has been presented.
- I can use quotations to support ideas, but often they are not as relevant as they could be.
- I can make simple and basic points but I do not say enough about how the writer uses language techniques.

You may need to go back and look at the relevant pages from this section again.

Themes and Ideas

Introduction

This section of Chapter 4 shows you how to

- understand what a 'Themes and ideas' Controlled Assessment task requires you to do
- develop responses to different forms of texts.

Why is learning about themes and ideas important?

- Understanding and considering a text's hemes and ideas will add to your enjoyment of reading it.
- Texts can be looked at in a range of ways, and focusing themes and ideas will sometimes need a different approach from a focus on characterisation and voice.
- The ways in which writers put forward their ideas or explore particular themes that interest them will provide a model for your own creative writing.
- Themes are usually at the core of the text: they deliver the 'message' that the writer wants to get across.

A **Grade D** candidate will

- understand the texts and use appropriate quotations most of the time
- try to interpret what the writer has to say about themes and ideas
- offer explanations that show understanding of what the writer is trying to do
- support points with some relevant quotations.

D

A **Grade C** candidate will

- show clear evidence of understanding the main ways in which themes or ideas have been presented
- be able to explain writers' presentation of ideas clearly
- display understanding of various features of language and structure used by writers to convey ideas and themes
- support points with relevant and appropriate quotations.

C

Prior learning

Before you begin this unit, think about

- what you already know about analysing a writer's ideas and themes
- any text you have read recently in which a particular idea or thematic focus made an impression on you.

Decide what you think these terms mean.

What do you remember about the theme of the text? Did you agree with the writer's viewpoint or enjoy the way ideas were presented? What made it interesting?

Exploring themes and ideas

Learning objective

- *To learn how to respond to writers' themes and ideas.*

Checklist for success

- You need to show how an idea or theme **develops** throughout a text.
- You need to understand how a writer's **language choices** and decisions about **structure** help develop a theme or idea.

ACTIVITY

On your own, decide which of the questions below is a 'character' question and which is a 'theme/idea' question.

Question 1: Explore the way childhood is presented in the story, 'The Darkness Out There'.

Question 2: Explore how the character of Mrs Rutter is presented in the story through what she says and does.

The key thing is that when you are writing you must keep to the idea and theme and not start

- retelling the story too much
- talking about a character without making it relevant to the theme or idea.

Here is part of a **Grade D** response to Question 1.

> *Sandra remembers being a young girl and playing in the woods in the story and this shows she has changed and is beginning to grow up, but she doesn't really change until she meets Mrs Rutter.*

This focuses too much on Sandra and doesn't mention the theme word 'childhood' at all. A better response would begin:

> *The idea of childhood is important to 'The Darkness Out There' because we see how ...*

Examiner's tip

The key thing is to refer to the theme or idea regularly as you are writing.

ACTIVITY

- Complete the second paragraph above by adding something about Sandra and how she changes.
- Bear in mind that, if you were actually answering this task, you might also comment on
  - Kerry and how the theme is presented through him
  - other references to children or childhood in the story.

Focus for development:
How writers present themes

Writers can encourage the reader to think about particular ideas in a number of ways, for example through

- the events of a story
- carefully-chosen language that perhaps implies or suggests things
- the particular characters and locations selected (for example, a story with a child and a forest in which a plane has crashed could well focus on the idea of childhood fears).

We can see this in 'The Darkness Out There', as Sandra is walking towards Mrs Rutter's house. She has already been thinking about the rumours of ghosts in the woods at Packer's End and is trying to focus on collecting flowers and doing 'nice things' as she approaches the cottage.

She would pick a blue flower and examine its complexity of pattern and petal and wonder what it was called and drop it. She would plunge her face into the powdery plate of an elderflower and smell cat, tom-cat, and sneeze and scrub her nose with the back of her hand. She would hurry through the gate and over the stream because that was a bit too close to Packer's End for comfort and she would…

He rose from the plough beyond the hedge.

She screamed.

'Christ!' she said, 'Kerry Stevens you stupid so-and-so, what d'you want to go and do that for, you give me the fright of my life.'

He grinned. 'I seen you coming. Thought I might as well wait.'

ASSESSMENT FOCUS

Write a short paragraph in which you explain

- how the writer presents childhood fears in the extract on the left
- how she uses language to surprise and create tension in order to keep us reading.

You could use this structure for your paragraph.

> The author focuses on the idea of childhood fear in the way she describes Sandra's thoughts as she …
> This is emphasised when …
> The short sentences create the effect of …

Include relevant quotations to support these points.

Remember

- Longer texts like 'The Darkness Out There' can have several themes.
- Writers use almost 'film-like' techniques to engage our attention.

Tracing the development of themes and ideas

Learning objective

- *To explore themes and ideas in a different text.*

Checklist for success

- You need to show you can trace the development of an idea or theme through a text.
- You need to make well-supported judgements about the themes or ideas presented (answering questions such as 'Why has the writer drawn them to our attention?').

The novel *Of Mice and Men* contains several themes, but what are they and how can you find out about them?

Start with some background to the novel:

- The novel is set in 1930s California during a time of job shortages and economic depression.
- Lennie and George are two homeless men moving from ranch to ranch looking for work.
- Lennie is rather backward and slow. George tries to keep him out of trouble. He feels both responsible for him and irritated by Lennie's child-like behaviour.
- The title comes from this line from a Robert Burns poem: 'The best laid schemes o' mice an' men/Gang aft agley' ('often go wrong').

ACTIVITY

Based on this background information, would any of the following themes seem likely? Why / Why not?

Growing-up   Dreams   Friendship   Family conflict

Now read the following three extracts from the novel. As you read, think about what similarities they share, if any, and consider these questions:

- What do we find out about the characters, their feelings and so on?
- Would a key theme here be pride or love? Or a theme from the list above?

Extract 1

Lennie and George spend the night outside before they go to a new ranch. Lennie asks George if they can talk about their plans for when they make some money.

> …. 'Tell about how it's gonna be.'
>
> 'Ok. Some day – we're gonna get the jack together and we're gonna have a little house and a couple of acres an' a cow and some pigs and ——'
>
> *'An' live off the fatta the lan',*' Lennie shouted. 'An' have *rabbits*. Go on, George! Tell about what we're gonna have in the garden and about the rabbits in the cages and about the rain in the winter and the stove, and how thick the cream is on the milk like you can hardly cut it. Tell about that, George.'

Extract 2

At the ranch, Lennie is talking to the stable-hand, Crooks, and has let slip his and George's plan to get their own ranch some day.

> 'You're nuts.' Crooks was scornful. 'I seen hundreds of men come by on the road an' on the ranches with their bindles on their back an' that same damn thing in their heads. Hundreds of them. They come, 'an they quit an' go on; an' every damn one of 'em's got a little piece of land in his head. An' never a god-damn one of 'em ever gets it. Just like heaven.'

Extract 3

Later, Lennie is in the barn. Curley's wife comes in and starts telling him how she feels about living on the ranch.

> 'I tell you I ain't used to livin' like this. I coulda made somethin' of myself.' She said darkly, 'Maybe I will yet.' And then her words tumbled out in a passion of communication, as though she hurried before her listener could be taken away. 'I live right in Salinas,' she said. 'Come there when when I was a kid. Well, a show come through, an' I met one of the actors. He says I could go with that show. But my ol' lady wouldn' let me. She says because I was on'y fifteen. But the guy says I coulda. If I'd went, I wouldn't be livin' like this, you bet.'
>
> Lennie stroked the pup back and forth. 'We gonna have a little place – an' rabbits,' he explained.

ACTIVITY

Write a short paragraph, explaining what you think a key theme of the novel could be, based on these extracts.

Comment in detail, using evidence from the extracts.

Focus for development: Developing ideas about a key theme

ACTIVITY

Try writing a first paragraph about the theme of 'dreams' in *Of Mice and Men,* based on the three extracts on page 187. This will be an introductory paragraph, so begin with a broad statement, and then add a more detailed example of the theme. For example:

> Dreams are a key element of …
> A key idea is how people are desperate to …

Think carefully about these dreams. What is it exactly that George, Lennie and Curley's wife want?

Now, consider how you could deal with each extract in turn. Plan out your ideas.

Paragraph 2: Explain what Lennie and George's dream is. *For Lennie and George, their dream is pretty simple. It is to* … (choose quotation)
Paragraph 3: Comment on what Crooks has to say about it. *However, not everyone shares their hope. Crooks says that* … (choose quotation, preferably referring to the image of 'heaven')
Paragraph 4: Comment on Curley's wife's dreams. *Others have dreams, too. Curley's wife describes how, when she was young, she* … (choose quotation)
End, perhaps, with a personal interpretation – how these dreams make us feel about the characters or their situation.

A student writes…

I can find evidence of key ideas and themes in the text but writing about them is difficult. How do I make sure I say more than 'the story is about childhood' or whatever?

Answer…

You need to develop your comments on themes. For example, you could say in a first paragraph about the story, 'The Darkness Out There':

Broad theme →
Specific idea →

> One of the key ideas the writer of 'The Darkness Out There' is interested in is <u>childhood</u>, in particular <u>how our view of people develops and changes as we get older</u>, in response to important events or experiences.

Embedding quotations

When writing on themes and ideas it is vital to use quotations in a fluent way. Take this useful quotation about dreams from an earlier chapter in the novel. Curley's wife is explaining why she keeps on coming into the workers' rooms 'looking for her husband'.

> 'Well, I ain't giving you no trouble. Think I don't like to talk to somebody ever' once in a while? Think I like to stick in that house alla time?'

You could make the point and add a suitable quotation as follows:

Curley's wife dreams of escaping the boredom of the ranch. 'Think I like to stick in that house alla time?' she says.

This is fine, but better still would be to embed part of the quotation within the point you are making, like this:

Curley's wife dreams of escaping the boredom of the ranch and is fed up that she has 'to stick in that house alla time'.

ACTIVITY

Take one of the paragraphs you planned above and try to write it so that the quotation you chose is embedded, where possible, in the point you want to make.

ASSESSMENT FOCUS

Write up the response you planned about the theme of dreams in *Of Mice and Men*. Make sure you

- open with a broad statement about theme
- follow your plan, introducing your detailed examples of how the theme is presented
- use evidence from the novel, embedding the quotations you selected into each of your main points.

Remember

- Themes can usually be traced across several scenes or chapters in a text.
- Say something specific about the theme rather than just making a general comment.
- Choose appropriate quotations and embed these, where you can, in the point you are making.

Presenting themes through settings and symbols

What does presenting themes through settings and symbols mean?

Sometimes simple descriptions of a place, of weather or objects, can convey a particular feeling or idea within a story.

For example, *Touching the Void* is an account by a mountaineer of surviving against the odds after he falls, breakS his leg, and is left for dead. The two climbers are trying to scale an unconquered peak in the Andes. The main themes emerge as friendship, suffering and survival.

Read this simple sentence from halfway through the text.

> *A slight breeze ran through the crevasse and I felt it on my cheek, a chill, deathly brush from somewhere deep below me.*

ACTIVITY

In the description above, how does the writer give a clue that the book will feature survival in the face of death?

Focus for development: Exploring description of place

The description of setting or creation of atmosphere in a text can often reflect its main themes and ideas.

In the extract opposite from the novel, *Lord of the Flies*, a group of schoolboys have been stranded on a desert island. As the novel unfolds, the boys form tribes and several of them are killed or hunted down. It is a novel about fear and violence, childhood innocence coming to an end, and about how living in an island paradise becomes a nightmare.

How is the idea of a paradise turning into a nightmare presented in this description? With a partner, make some basic notes in a grid like the one below.

Use the annotations around the extract to help you.

> Soon the darkness <u>was full of claws</u>, full of the unknown and menace. An interminable dawn faded the stars out, and at last light, <u>sad</u> and grey, filtered into the shelter. They began to stir though still the world outside the shelter was impossibly dangerous. The maze of the darkness sorted into near and far, and at the high point of the sky the cloudlets were warmed with colour. A single sea bird flapped upwards with a hoarse cry that was echoed presently, and <u>something</u> squawked in the forest. Now streaks of cloud near the horizon began to glow rosily, and the feathery tops of the palms were green.

Must mean in their heads?

Makes the light seem human

Fear of the unknown?

Idea	Quotation
Paradise	'the horizon began to glow rosily' 'cloudlets warmed with colour'
Nightmare	

ASSESSMENT FOCUS

Now, working on your own, try to turn this into a paragraph about the idea of nightmare and violence on the island. You need to

- use words such as 'suggest', 'convey' and 'imply' to express your ideas
- refer to language features such as adjectives, personification, images.

Remember

- **Look out for descriptions of setting and weather that reflect the key themes or ideas in a story or an account.**
- **Pay attention to language features, such as powerful adjectives and verbs. They often reveal a great deal about a theme.**

Investigating clues and connections

Learning objective

- *To understand how texts can provide clues and anticipate events or ideas.*

Checklist for success

- You need to read texts very closely, looking for hints and clues about themes, and exploring what they might imply.
- Sometimes themes are clear, for example fear in 'The Darkness Out There', and *Lord of the Flies*. At other points, writers use more subtle skills. If you can refer to these, you should get a higher mark.

ACTIVITY

- Read this extended extract from 'The Darkness Out There'. Bear in mind that we have not yet found out that the old lady, Mrs Rutter, left a young German airman to die from his injuries in the woods.
- With a partner, decide what clues in the extract suggest that this will not be a sweet, innocent story.

She seemed composed of circles, a cottage-loaf of a woman, with a face below which chins collapsed one into another, a creamy smiling pool of a face in which her eyes snapped and darted.

'Tea, my duck?' she said. 'Tea for the both of you? I'll put us a kettle on.'

The room was stuffy. It had a gaudy lino floor with the pattern rubbed away in front of the sink and round the table; the walls were cluttered with old calendars and pictures torn from magazines; there was a smell of cabbage. The alcove by the fireplace was filled with china ornaments: big-eyed flop-eared rabbits and beribboned kittens and flowery milkmaids and a pair of naked chubby children wearing daisy chains.

The woman hauled herself from a sagging armchair. She glittered at them from the stove, manoeuvring cups, propping herself against the draining-board. 'What's your names, then? Sandra and Kerry. Well, you're a pretty girl, Sandra, aren't you. Pretty as they come. There was – let me see, who was it? – Susie, last week. That's right, Susie.' Her eyes investigated, quick as mice. 'Put your jacket on the back of the door, dear, you won't want to get that messy. Still at school, are you?'

Focus for development: Simile and metaphor

Mrs Rutter and her room are described in a range of ways in the extract above. Look at these **metaphors**, for example:

'a cottage-loaf of a woman'

'a creamy smiling pool of a face in which her eyes snapped and darted'

ACTIVITY

- Can you find a further description of Mrs Rutter in the form of a **simile**?
- How is the room described? What is the general impression you get of it?

None of these things, on their own, state openly that 'Mrs Rutter has another side'. Everything is hinted at. If you were writing a themes and ideas response about this, you would need to refer to these language techniques.

How does this response miss the clues in the extract?

> *There is no hint of the darkness or shocking revelation to come in this scene. Mrs Rutter is very sweet and kind, offering the children tea in her comfy, if rather old-fashioned room.*

ACTIVITY

Try rewriting the response, referring to the description of Mrs Rutter and her room, and the hints at darker things. This student has begun by referring to the 'cottage-loaf' description.

> *The idea of the 'darkness out there' – the reality that the world can be a harsh place – is hinted at by the clues that Mrs Rutter is not quite as sweet as Sandra thinks. The metaphor of Mrs Rutter as a 'cottage-loaf' reminds us of Hansel and Gretel and the house made of sweets which hides murder inside …*
>
> *The next image, of her 'creamy smiling pool of a face', implies that …*

ASSESSMENT FOCUS

Write a longer response to the extract that would be part of the answer to the question:

> ***How are things not as they seem in 'The Darkness Out There'?***

Remember

- **Look for subtle clues in the language – are themes or ideas anticipated?**
- **Try to link specific descriptions to themes or ideas.**

Grade Booster

Extended Assessment Task

For any novel or play you have studied, consider one of the key themes or ideas. It could be 'how friendships develop' or 'dreams and disappointments', or whatever you choose. Jot down notes in these areas:

- how the idea or theme is presented at the start of the text (including subtle hints and suggestions)
- how the theme or idea is developed or changed through the text by important incidents, moments or situations
- how the theme is presented through choice of language, setting, key detail and imagery.

Write a response on this theme or idea of about 1200 words, using direct evidence from your chosen text.

Evaluation – What have you learned?

With a partner, use the grade checklist below to evaluate your work on the Extended Assessment Task.

C
- I can show I clearly understand main ideas and themes.
- I can explain these main ideas and themes in clear and logical ways.
- I can understand how language features and structure work.
- I can support my main ideas with relevant quotations and explanations.

D
- I can show some understanding of main themes and ideas.
- I can support these ideas with quotations and evidence but quotations are not always well chosen or appropriate.
- I can make my own points but these are not developed in as much detail as they could be.

E
- I can show some awareness of main themes and ideas.
- I can sometimes support these ideas with quotations and evidence but they are not always well chosen or appropriate.
- I can make a few of my own points but these are often not developed in any detail.

You may need to go back and look at the relevant pages from this section again.

Controlled Assessment Preparation: Extended Reading

Introduction

In this section you will

- find out what is required of you in the Extended Reading Controlled Assessment task
- read, analyse and respond to two sample answers by different candidates
- plan and write your own answer to a sample question
- evaluate and assess your answer and the progress you have made.

Why is preparation of this kind important?

- If you know exactly what you need to do, you will feel more confident when you produce your own assessed response.
- Looking at sample answers by other students will help you see what you need to do to improve your own work.
- Planning and writing a full written response after you have completed the whole chapter will give you a clear sense of what you have learned so far.

Key information

Unit 3 Section A is 'Understanding Written Texts: Extended Reading'.

- The controlled part of the task will last **3–4 hours**, and is worth **30 marks**.
- It is worth **15%** of your overall English Language GCSE mark.

What will the task involve?

- The task will be based on **one extended text** you have studied (fiction or non-fiction).
- This text can be the same as one you have studied for English Literature but **the task must be different.**
- If you wish, you can use the **AQA Anthology** of poetry and short stories, *Moon on the Tides*.

What does the task consist of?

- You will be asked to respond to **one task**. You will have to write about either **Themes and ideas** or **Characterisation and voice**.
- The task will be done under 'controlled conditions' – in silence, in an exam room or in your own classroom.
- The recommended word limit is 1200 and you will be allowed up to **four hours** to complete the task.

Here are some example questions based on the general task areas set by the exam board.

Characterisation and voice	How is a central character presented in a text you have studied? *Consider how Shakespeare presents the development of Macbeth once he has killed the king.* *How do poets you have studied create a range of different voices in their poems?*
Themes and ideas	Relationships: *Explore how friendship is an important theme in a story or novel you have read, and how the writer uses particular language techniques to develop it.*

The Assessment

The assessment objective for this unit (AO3) states that you must

- read and understand texts, selecting material appropriate to purpose
- develop and sustain interpretations of writers' ideas and perspectives
- explain and evaluate how writers use linguistic, grammatical, structural and presentational features to achieve effects and engage and influence the reader.

Targeting Grade C

Some of the key features of Grade D and Grade C responses are as follows:

Grade D candidates will	See example on pages 197–8
<ul><li>show some evidence of understanding key meanings in the text with an attempt to interpret some ideas</li><li>show some familiarity with writers' ideas, supported by some relevant textual detail</li><li>display some understanding of language features used and support points with some relevant textual detail.</li></ul>	(D)

Grade C candidates will	See example on pages 199–200
<ul><li>show clear evidence of understanding key meanings in the text, with some ability to look for more significant or deeper interpretations</li><li>write clearly about writers' ideas, supported by relevant and appropriate evidence/quotation</li><li>display understanding of language features used and support points with relevant quotations.</li></ul>	(C)

Exploring Sample Responses

ACTIVITY

How is a central character presented in a text you have studied? Consider how Shakespeare presents the development of Macbeth once he has killed the king.

As you read it, think about whether it is closer to a Grade D or a Grade C, and why.

Consider the key elements a marker would look for:

- How clearly and effectively has the student put forward his/her ideas?
- Are the author's and the student's ideas shown?
- How well has the student commented on the language used?
- How well does the student support the point he/she makes?

Example 1: Characterisation

I think Shakespeare shows how Macbeth changes once he has killed the King.

When we first actually meet Macbeth we are told it is with the witches on the heath. This is when they tell him he will be Thane of Cawdor and King after that. He talks to the witches and wants to know what they think. He also says that:

'My thought, whose murder yet is but fantastical ...' [Act I Scene 3]

Once he has actually done the killing, everything changes. At first, it all seems the same. Shakespeare presents Macbeth as a character who has lots of doubts and feels guilty even after he has killed the king. He tells his wife Lady Macbeth that he won't go back to the king's room because of all the blood 'cos he is too afraid to think what he has done. He tells her this when Lady Macbeth tells him to take the daggers covered with blood back into the bed chamber so that it will seem like the king's servants killed him. Shakespeare wants us to see that Macbeth and blood kind of don't go together at the start, but that he gets used to it later.

But not long after he is able to pretend he's innocent when Macduff asks him if the king has woken up, and is even able to chat with Lennox about the bad weather in the night. He is even able to think quickly and murders the servants so they cannot say they were innocent. This is the beginning of Macbeth murdering others to hide what he's done.

But Shakespeare makes a key change come in his actions in Act 3 Scene 2. There is a major change in the way Macbeth and his wife share responsibility for the killing. When the king was killed, Lady Macbeth did lots of the planning for Macbeth. Now when they talk about having to kill Banquo and Fleance Macbeth doesn't tell her what he has planned for Banquo. Here is a quote about what he says.

'Be innocent of the knowledge, dearest chuck/Till thou applaud the deed'

This means you don't need to know until I have actually killed the people. He has organised everything himself this time. You could say at this point that he is the same, in that he still needs his wife's support, but he is now acting much more on his own.

Shakespeare uses language to show Macbeth's character in the early scenes. He says lots about Macbeth's mind, like when he talked earlier about fantasy thoughts. But now Macbeth says to his wife, 'O full of scorpions is my mind'. This is a great sentence because it shows a nasty side to Macbeth...

Examiner feedback

This response answers the question and makes some valid points, such as the way Macbeth's doubts give way to a more confident approach as the play progresses. These points, however, are made in rather a clumsy way, with separate quotations, and are not always fully explored (for example, the 'scorpions' quote shows more than just a 'nasty side' to Macbeth but also the torment in his mind). Each paragraph contains worthwhile points but sometimes slips into too much retelling of the story rather than focused analysis. Finally, the expression is sometimes too informal (for example, 'cos' and 'kind of') and could be more fluent and formal.

Suggested grade: D

ACTIVITY

List
- The valid points in the response
- Things that could be improved.

Read the following extract from a response to this task.

> *How do poets you have studied create a range of different voices in their poems?*

Select three sections or sentences and improve them by adding more detail or explanation.

Example 2: Characterisation and Voice

Refers to poet's skills →

Reasonable summing up of poem's main story →

Good; refers to how Medusa is created →

Reasonable quote, clumsily included

Could say more about repetition of words starting with 'f'

Picks out structural change in poem →

Develops and links to previous ideas →

Carol Ann Duffy **uses a wide range of ways** *to create an unusual voice in her poem 'Medusa', which presents us with the* **thoughts and feelings of a woman abandoned by her husband.** *The poem is based on the Greek myth of Medusa, which is basically about a beautiful but monstrous creature who turns men to stone by looking at them after she was attacked by a god, Poseidon. However, this is a modern update and is not the same story.*

The characterisation of Medusa *comes from lots of things. For example, it is written in the first person, so it's like we are inside her head experiencing what she feels, like ...*

' **a suspicion, a jealousy, grew in my mind'.** *Also it's not like a monster, more like a real woman who is jealous of what her husband might be doing.*

The poet shows us the strength of how Medusa feels when she describes how her thoughts, 'hissed and spat on my scalp.' The characterisation is developed by more physical descriptions which Medusa herself tells us about, like how she is **'foul mouthed, foul tongued, yellow fanged'.** *These three descriptions paint a pretty horrible picture!*

Then Duffy makes a big change by Medusa now speaking to us directly with the line 'Are you terrified?' *like we are her husband who has been cheating on her or whatever. This really draws us into the poem.*

Then, by having more patterns of three descriptions, like 'perfect man, Greek God, my own' Duffy emphasises how he has let her down.

Another key *to understanding how Duffy creates the character is in the repeated lines in verses 4, 5 and 6 when she 'glanced', then 'looked' and then 'stared'. After each of these her* looks turned things to stone and Duffy creates very vivid images like, how a **ginger cat becomes a 'housebrick' and a bee a 'dull grey pebble'**.

Make more of the images?

The structure of the whole poem helps too to help us see what happens to Medusa. At the beginning Duffy shows her as jealous but she is crying with the **metaphor of 'bullet tears'**, then it shows how she feels about her Greek god. Later as each verse goes on she is turning things to stone till she finally looks in a mirror and she is now turned to stone. This might mean like in real life we say that we have no feelings – or just very cold – but then it says she also sees a 'dragon' so that might be a bit like when a woman is described as an 'old dragon' meaning dead nasty and nagging.

Could explain why is this an especially apt quotation

Bit unclear and rambling

However, the last verse really completes what Duffy wants to say about Medusa because now she is asking her lover 'wasn't I beautiful?' and she wants revenge because she says 'look at me now' which if he does means he will die! Which is what she wants.

Overall, Duffy presents a very vivid character with strong feelings and powerful description who is like the original Medusa but modernised to be like a wronged woman who speaks about revenge on the man who will 'betray me, stray far from home.'

Good conclusion and nice quote to end

Examiner feedback

Plenty of interesting points are made, mostly supported by relevant quotations, but on occasions a bit rambling and unfocused. Some lines are included without really saying what their effect is, or how they add to characterisation. References to language techniques are fairly widespread although perhaps there could have been more on the rhyme scheme, sound and structure. A good beginning and a useful conclusion to this part of the response, although perhaps a little more on the betraying husband and the metaphors of the 'sword for a tongue' and 'shield for a heart' would have been good. The student would go on next to discuss the voices used in more poems they have studied.   **Suggested grade: C**

ACTIVITY

Read the extract on the page opposite from a response to this task.

> ***Relationships: explore how friendship is an important theme in a story or novel you have read, and how the writer uses particular language techniques to develop it.***

This response is an improvement on both the previous examples and is pushing towards a Grade B answer. Identify what makes it work well.

Example 3: Themes and ideas

'We kinda look after each other,'

So says George when he and Lennie first meet Slim in the bunk-house of the ranch. Is this a good description of their friendship though? After all, it seems to be mostly George who looks after Lennie, a bit like a father with a silly child.

Anyway, the point is that the whole book is really centred around the idea of friendship. This is not just Lennie and George but the friendships of the men at the ranch, or perhaps their loneliness would be a better word.

What do we learn about friendship from the writer? Firstly we see that friendship is not very easy. When George is angry with Lennie in Chapter One he tells him how he could 'get a job an' work, 'an no trouble'. Steinbeck is presenting the idea that friendship isn't easy and is a burden sometimes. Of course this is seen at the end of the story.

The friendship that the two men have is probably based on guilt, too. For example, George explains how he used to almost bully Lennie and once how he nearly drowned because of him. He obviously feels bad as Steinbeck says how his 'voice took on the tone of confession'. This comparison to telling a priest that you have sinned makes it sound like George is trying to make up for his bad treatment of Lennie.

The essay task refers to how friendship as a theme develops. I think this means that at the start of the book George and Lennie are sort of on their own, but the writer then brings in new characters. Some could be friends of George and Lennie, some are not suitable. Carlson is pretty nasty, but Slim seems decent. He is the one who comforts George at the end after he has killed Lennie and says, 'You hadda, George, I swear you hadda'. It's like Slim is to George what George was to Lennie. Perhaps they will be friends though it won't be the same really.

ctd.

Friendship in the story is seen in some key moments. The first of these is when Lennie breaks Curley's hand. It is clear from this that Lennie is really dependent on George, like an animal to its master.

'Suddenly Lennie let go his hold. He crouched cowering against the wall. 'You tol me to, George' he said, miserably.'

This shows that Lennie even with all his strength is just a child inside. The second important moment is when George has to shoot Lennie at the end. We can tell from the way George is described by Steinbeck of the strength of feeling he has for Lennie really, for example in the way his 'hand shook violently' as he prepares to pull the trigger. The adverb 'violently' conveys how strongly George feels. Also, before that the tragedy of the friendship ending can be seen in the description of the surroundings. It says how the 'shadow in the valley was bluer, and the evening came fast'. Perhaps this is a reference to death coming, like how the night is linked to death and darkness?

Friendship (or lack of it) is also explored through the other characters. For example through the description of the bunk-house Steinbeck suggests...

Examiner feedback

This is a generally very confident and effective response. It would be easy to just describe George and Lennie's characters but the student comments with some good examples on their relationship and what it says about their friendship and what this depends on. It is a good beginning with a quotation, although there may be an argument for a more general introduction. Quotations elsewhere are usually used effectively and the points developed sufficiently, although the idea of friendship as a 'burden' could have been explored more fully. The extract ends with the student signposting clearly the next aspect of friendship that he is going to explore.

Suggested grade: C borderline B

EXTENDED PRACTICE TASK

Explore the way conflict is presented in a text you have studied.

You could write about how a writer explores conflict as a theme in a novel you have studied, in short stories or in several poems from the AQA Anthology *Moon on the Tides*.

If you only do five things...

1 Make sure you are fully aware of what the terms 'characterisation', 'voice' and 'themes' mean.

2 Read your chosen texts closely so that you know them well in terms of story. It can save you a lot of time during your Controlled Assessment task.

3 Read your texts in the particular light of 'character' and 'themes', making clear, well-organised notes on these aspects in particular.

4 Plan to use some professional language in your response, trying out phrases such as 'the writer conveys…', 'this idea reflects…' and 'the central action is…' to impress the examiner.

5 Don't forget that your personal response matters: have you thought about the text on your own, or just simply noted down what you are told?

5 Unit 3B **Creative writing**

What's it all about?

Writing creatively really enables you to 'show off' your most imaginative ideas, original thinking and the very best writing techniques.

How will I be assessed?

- You will get **15% of your English Language marks** for your ability to write creative texts.
- You will have to complete two written pieces in a Controlled Assessment task over the course of **3–4 hours**.
- You will be marked on your writing of **two** written responses taken **from a choice of three**.

- These two creative texts will **total up to 1200 words**.

What is being tested?

You are being examined on your ability to

- write for specific creative purposes
- communicate clearly, effectively and imaginatively
- organise information in a structured and inventive way, using a range of paragraphs
- use a variety of sentence structures and styles
- use a range of linguistic features for impact and effect
- write with accuracy in punctuation, spelling and grammar.

Re-creations

Introduction

This section of Chapter 5 helps you to

- explore the creative writing area of 'Re-creations', in which you take one text and transform it into another form or type of text
- understand what a Controlled Assessment task in this area is asking you to do
- develop creative writing responses to a range of texts
- practise and develop extended responses.

Why is it important to learn about re-creating texts?

- The best writers know how to adapt, transform and re-work ideas and texts to create impact and effect.
- Being 'creative' in writing does not just mean writing fictional stories or poetry; creative approaches to non-fiction can have real impact on readers too.
- Approaching written tasks in a creative way is enjoyable, and it feeds back into your understanding of reading.

A **Grade D** candidate will

- make an attempt to use and adapt conventions, though not always successfully
- use some variety in sentences, paragraphs and vocabulary but not always for a deliberate effect on the reader
- come up with ideas but will not develop them sufficiently
- include accurate spelling and punctuation.

D

A **Grade C** candidate will

- understand how the basic conventions of texts can be adapted
- engage the reader's interest with a variety of sentences and vocabulary
- write in a structured and coherent way, using paragraphs, so that ideas are clear to the reader
- spell and punctuate accurately.

C

Prior learning

Before you begin this unit, think about

- any texts you know in which features of texts are mixed or adapted
- what makes a piece of writing 'creative'
- different types of text that have been inspired by a recent event, for example 9/11 or the war in Afghanistan
- how you would turn the first verse or two of a poem into another form of text.

Can you think of a fairy tale used in advertising?

Can you come up with five ideas?

Take a poem you know and try turning the first verse into a story, report or diary entry.

Re-creations – from poem to letter

Learning objective

- To explore ways of taking a text and re-writing it in a new form or style.

What does re-creating a text involve?

When you re-create a text, you take its main elements (its story, its setting, or its central idea) and you turn it into something new. This usually involves changing the **form** of the writing. For example, you could turn a poem about a battle into a newspaper report.

Checklist for success

- You need to decide what to keep from the original text and what to change.
- You need to use the typical features of the new form you choose (for example, a newspaper article should include a headline).
- You need to have a clear purpose and match what you say to your intended audience (for example, describing the realities of war clearly in a newspaper article).

ACTIVITY

A student was given a war poem to turn into a different form. Here are some of the ideas he came up with.

> A **letter** from a soldier's mother to a newspaper

> A **news report/article** from a war reporter in a newspaper

> **WAR POEM ABOUT BOMBING IN AFGHANISTAN**

> An **advert** for a charity that helps injured soldiers

> A **short play** for teenagers about the horrors of war

Write down:

- the four **types of text** the student has come up with as possibilities
- any **features** you know you would have to use if you wrote these texts (for example, paragraphs and the first person 'I' in a letter)
- which of these forms you would feel most confident writing – and why.

Focus for development:
Re-creating a poem

Here is the opening of Carol Ann Duffy's poem 'The Twelve Days of Christmas', which was the basis of the student's re-creation spider-diagram:

*On the first day of Christmas,
a buzzard on a branch.*

*In Afghanistan,
no partridge, pear tree;
but my true love sent to me
a card from home.
I sat alone,
crouched in yellow dust,
and traced the grins of my kids
with my thumb.
Somewhere down the line,
for another father, husband,
brother, son, a bullet
with his name on.*

ACTIVITY

With a partner, re-read these first few lines and decide

- what we find out about the person 'speaking' in the poem
- how what he receives is rather different from what others might receive at Christmas
- what references he makes to the famous Christmas song. How do these ideas contrast with the reality of life in Afghanistan?

ASSESSMENT FOCUS

Who might a British soldier write a letter to, while at war? Come up with three possibilities, and then decide on the person you will write to.

Think about:

- how a personal letter is written
- what details you will include
- what the purpose of the letter is.

> How will it start? What 'voice' will it be written in?

> Would you tell your reader everything you have done/seen? Go back to the poem – could you use any of these details?

> Is your purpose to reassure everyone that you are safe; to let them know how you are feeling; to complain about something?

Now write a first draft of your chosen letter.

Remember

- **Keep to the features of your chosen form.**
- **Use details from the poem as a starting point.**
- **Have a clear purpose for the letter.**

Re-creations – from poem to newspaper report

Learning objective

- To take elements of a poem and re-use them for a newspaper report.

Checklist for success

- You need to select carefully those elements from the poem you can re-use and develop.
- You need to be clear about what suits a newspaper report, and what doesn't.

Sometimes, poems you are given to work with will have lots of rich ideas that you can use and adapt. But be careful – older poems may have unfamiliar words that we do not use much these days, or use features such as rhyme that would not suit a story, a news report or a letter, for example.

Read this poem.

Spellbound

The night is darkening round me,
The wild winds coldly blow;
But a tyrant spell has bound me
And I cannot, cannot go.
The giant trees are bending
Their bare boughs weighed
with snow.
And the storm is fast descending,
And yet I cannot go.
Clouds beyond clouds above me,
Wastes beyond wastes below;
But nothing drear can move me;
I will not, cannot go.

Emily Brontë, 1818–1848

Glossary

tyrant: a cruel, powerful leader

waste: wilderness

drear: bleak and depressing

Discuss with a partner:

- What are the weather conditions like in the poem?
- Are they getting worse or better? How do you know?
- Does the poet want to stay or leave?
- What features of the text make it clear this is a poem?

Focus for development: Adapting the text

Now imagine a student has been told to turn the poem 'Spellbound' into a news report about a rescue from the storm. With a partner:

- Quickly read the student's opening to the news report below.
- Discuss how similar and different the report will be in form and content to the poem.
- What features are clearly common to the openings of newspaper reports?

> SNOWBOUND!
>
> Thirty-year-old Emma Brown was tonight rescued in blizzard conditions from a small cottage near Haworth in Yorkshire.

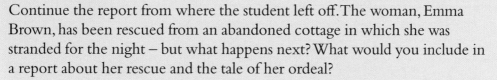

Continue the report from where the student left off. The woman, Emma Brown, has been rescued from an abandoned cottage in which she was stranded for the night – but what happens next? What would you include in a report about her rescue and the tale of her ordeal?

One key difference to bear in mind: in the original poem, the poet explains her attraction to the wild weather. What viewpoint, if any, do you think the newspaper report might take?

Use this planning grid to note down some ideas.

Structure	Advice	Your ideas
Headline for article	Make it catchy!	
Paragraph 1: opening	Cover the main facts: what happened, to whom, where and when.	
Paragraph 2	Explain what actually happened: how the rescue team found Emma.	
Paragraph 3	Give details about the conditions in the mountains/moors, and how bad the storm was (use ideas from the poem).	
Paragraph 4	Give details about Emma and where she was staying. Add a quotation from Emma about why she didn't leave when the weather became worse.	
Paragraph 5	Include a quotation from an eye-witness or member of mountain rescue team.	
Paragraph 6: conclusion	Include what Emma says about future holidays and expeditions.	

You will also need to think about getting the **style** right for a newspaper report.

A student writes…

What does 'getting the style right' actually mean?

Answer…

In this case, for a **Grade C** you will need to use

- **logical paragraphs**: this means making sure each one makes a separate point or puts across new information

- **a mix of sentence lengths**: perhaps using some shorter sentences to stress important points

- **vocabulary to create an effect**: this means choosing your words carefully to help your readers see the scene in their minds and imagine how Emma felt

- **the right tone**: this means using the right 'voice', for example a newspaper report doesn't usually use the first person 'I' to explain what happened.

Remember, above all, to **match the style and form** to your **purpose and audience** and you won't go far wrong.

One student has started her response but hasn't got the style or content quite right.

- Read the response and the teacher's comments with it.
- What else could be improved? Look back at the planning grid on the previous page to help you decide.

Headline okay, but could be catchier

SNOWBOUND!

Thirty-year-old Emma Brown was tonight rescued in blizzard conditions from a small cottage near Haworth in Yorkshire.

She said she was walking when she got tired. So she went into a nearby old cottage. But it had no heating and no one there. She got very cold but when the storm started she decided to stay. 'It all looked lovely,' she said. I think she was mad and that is why I am writing this report.

Good quotation but is it in the right place?

ASSESSMENT FOCUS

- Re-write the first two paragraphs to the newspaper report.
- Then work with a partner to check progress against the Grade C criteria on the previous page, and the style points for a newspaper report above. Re-draft your paragraphs if you need to.
- Write the remaining paragraphs of the report to complete the re-creation.

Remember

- If you write a newspaper report, be sure it has a balance of key information and further detail.
- Keep it impersonal – don't use the first person 'I'.
- Make sure each paragraph makes a separate point.

Re-creations – from short story to play or website

Learning objective

- To learn how to take elements of a short story and use them in a range of formats.

A novelist writing a story about a particular city will need to know details about that place to make the story convincing. Someone writing a guidebook to the same city will also need to show their reader they know the place well.

Read this extract from the short story 'Something Old, Something New', by Leila Aboulela. It describes a British man's first impressions of Sudan, as he and his Sudanese bride-to-be drive from the airport.

> It was like a ride in a fun-fair. The windows wide open; voices, noises, car-horns, people crossing the road at random, pausing in the middle, touching the cars with their fingers as if the cars were benign cattle. Anyone of these passers-by could easily punch him through the window, yank off his watch, his sun-glasses, snatch his wallet from the pocket of his shirt. He tried to roll up the window but couldn't. She turned and said, 'It's broken, I'm sorry.' Her calmness made him feel that he needn't be so nervous. A group of school-boys walked on the pavement, one of them stared at him, grinned and waved. He became
>
>
>
> aware that everyone looked like her, shared her colour, the women were dressed like her and they walked with the same slowness which had seemed to him exotic when he had seen her walking in Edinburgh. 'Everything is new for you.' She turned and looked at him gently. The brother said something in Arabic.
>
> The car moved away from the crowded market to a wide shady road.
>
> 'Look,' she said, 'take off your sun-glasses and look. There's the Nile.' And there was the Nile, a blue he had never seen before, a child's blue, a dream's blue.

ACTIVITY

Discuss with a partner:

- What different views of Sudan do we get from the man and his fiancée?
- What descriptions does the writer use to make the setting come alive?
- How much idea do we get of the man's inner feelings from this text?

Focus for development: Transforming the story

If you were re-creating this text, there would be a range of possible forms you could consider. Look at these two examples.

Play form

> **Scene 1** Inside the car *(two sets of chairs on stage)*
>
> *The 'crowd' circle the car, walk in front of it, behind it, chatting. Man tries to wind window up.*
>
> **WOMAN**: It's broken, I'm sorry.
>
> *Man stares out of window.*
>
> **WOMAN**: *(gently)* Everything is new for you …

Website form

> Khartoum (Sudan's capital city) is a vibrant, lively and busy city with markets, shops and fascinating sights. It may take you a while to get used to the different way of life but when you do, you will be amazed by the people and the places. For a start, don't forget that this country contains the wonderful Nile – the most famous river in the world!

Both texts **describe** aspects of the country but the **purpose** of each text is different.

* The purpose of the play is to show actions and events, which reveal people's feelings and inner thoughts, as in the original story.
* The purpose of the tourist website is to *sell* the country, and inform the reader as to its key features, facts and attractions.

ASSESSMENT FOCUS

Taking one of these examples, plan how you would develop it further. You could

* read the remainder of Leila's story in your AQA Anthology, *Moon on the Tides,* or simply use the beginning to imagine how the scene might develop as a play
* research the Sudan further and try to create a tourist information site for UK travellers.

First, complete these spider diagrams about the conventions of plays and websites to get you started.

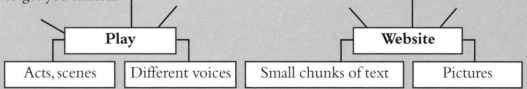

Then, draft the first two or three scenes of the play, or the rest of the home page for the website.

Remember

* **Use what you know about the features of a website or a play to assist you.**

Grade Booster

Extended Assessment Task

Write a response of around 600 words to this Re-creations task.

> *Take the poem 'Spellbound' and re-write it as a diary extract, written when the woman was trapped by the storm inside the cottage.*

Make sure you

- decide what content and ideas to include from the original poem
- plan the various parts to the diary entry (noting down what you will write about in each paragraph)
- take the opportunity to write creatively by using a wide, but appropriate, range of sentences, vocabulary and paragraphs.
- show clear understanding of the content and conventions of diary writing (for example, the style, use of first person, reference to personal feelings).

Evaluation – What have you learned?

With a partner, use the grade checklist below to evaluate your work on the Extended Assessment Task.

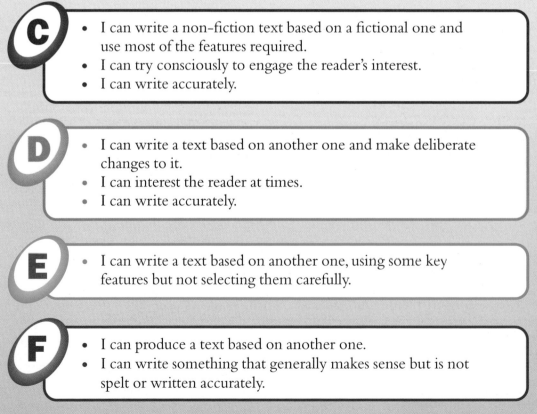

C
- I can write a non-fiction text based on a fictional one and use most of the features required.
- I can try consciously to engage the reader's interest.
- I can write accurately.

D
- I can write a text based on another one and make deliberate changes to it.
- I can interest the reader at times.
- I can write accurately.

E
- I can write a text based on another one, using some key features but not selecting them carefully.

F
- I can produce a text based on another one.
- I can write something that generally makes sense but is not spelt or written accurately.

You may need to go back and look at the relevant pages from this section again.

Moving Images

Introduction

This section of Chapter 5 helps you to

- explore the creative writing area of 'Moving images' in which you respond to films, television and other moving image sequences
- understand what a Controlled Assessment task in this area is asking you to do
- develop creative writing responses to a range of texts
- practise and develop extended responses.

Why is working on moving images important?

- Moving image 'texts', such as films, documentaries and TV adverts, have their own conventions and features, as does any writing about them.
- Commentary about moving images is widespread, in the form of film reviews or blogs.
- Writing about visual texts requires many of the same techniques that are used for commenting on printed texts.

A **Grade D** candidate will

- explain some ways in which a moving image text is put together, but might not use very specific or sufficiently professional language or terms
- use some of the conventions of reviews and other forms of writing about images, but not always clearly or relevantly.

D

A **Grade C** candidate will

- comment clearly on how a moving image text is constructed
- back points up with evidence
- use appropriate but not wide-ranging professional language
- know the main conventions of reviews and other forms of writing about images, and use them quite effectively.

C

Prior learning

Before you begin this unit:

- Watch a range of short news items and a selection of advertisements.
- Look over any previous reviewing or media studies work you have done.

> Jot down some basic notes on what you see on screen, who they are aimed at and whether, in your opinion, they are successful.

> Highlight what you did well, and what you needed to improve.

Writing about film

Learning objective

- To recognise and use the key features of film reviews.

Checklist for success

- You need to be able to write analytically, using the technical language of moving image texts.
- You need to hold the reader's interest by writing engagingly.

ACTIVITY

People write about films for different purposes. For example, read these two extracts about the same film.

With a partner, identify the text which is from

- the film review from a magazine or newspaper
- a promotional advert or trailer for the same film.

How do you know? What features tell you which is which?

Text 1

> *Fangman*, Cert 12
>
> This latest blockbuster from director Stephen Lucas stars Bruce Cage as Fangman, as he escapes from an LA zoo and chases a frankly bored-looking Kellie Ryan around the streets trying to persuade her he is not the brutal bearded beast he appears. Unfortunately, there is no chemistry between the two stars and although the gothic locations look good, the film just doesn't have enough bite.

Text 2

> Think you know what it means to be frightened? Think you know what the creatures behind the bars of the zoo are really thinking? Think again. From the makers of *Space Hostage* and *Forests of the Night* comes a new film that will blow you away. Starring Bruce Cage and Kellie Ryan, and directed by Academy Award winning Stephen Lucas. *Fangman*. In cinemas from Monday. Get ready. Be prepared. The fright of your life is coming.

- What is the writer's purpose – or purposes – in each case?
- How does each text attempt to appeal to the reader?

These different kinds of writing about film deal with similar content but use slightly different techniques. For example, Text 2 is more persuasive and uses **imperative verbs** (which tell you what to do, like 'Think' or 'Get').

Most reviews contain these features

- a summary of the basic storyline or key events
- reference to the main actors/characters (and possibly their performance)
- information on the feel or style of the film – its genre (thriller, for example)
- the opinion of the reviewer (this may not be present at all points in the review).

Focus for development: The language of reviews

The key to a good review is to use appropriate language. Reviews tend to be

- in the **present tense** ('the film *stars* Ashton Kutcher')
- **packed with detail** – sentences contain lots of information ('chases a *frankly bored-looking* Kellie Ryan')
- **vivid and powerful** – sometimes using **imagery** and vivid descriptions ('*dark, grimy streets* of gangland LA')
- always **full of opinion** and sometimes humorous.

ASSESSMENT FOCUS

Write the first two paragraphs of a review of a film you know well.

To focus clearly on the look and feel of the film, these phrases and vocabulary might help.

story	title, action, plot, tale, events, climax, shock, challenge, quest, coincidence, chance-meeting, flashback, future, past, storyline
genre	thriller, sci-fi, fantasy, historical, comic, rom-com, romantic, gothic, teen, farce, slapstick
style	fast-paced, reflective, moving, emotional, tragic, heart-rending, gentle, violent, sexy, disturbing, light-hearted, hilarious, thrill-a-minute, tense
people	character, lead role, pair, lovers, rivals, enemies, villain, hero, director

Make sure you don't just comment on what you think of the film, but also on how it works (or doesn't!). You could use this structure:

Paragraph 1: introduce the film by its title, explain who stars in it and something about its style or genre.

Paragraph 2: write about a specific aspect such as the storyline (without giving the end away) and hinting at what you think of it. Do this by adding simple adjectives (some of the 'style' words above) to the 'story' words (for example, 'a ridiculous chance-meeting' or a 'moving climax').

Finally, you could go on to finish the review, but make sure you plan the rest of it first.

Remember

- Keep your purpose in mind when writing about film (for example, independent reviews give an independent, personal viewpoint).

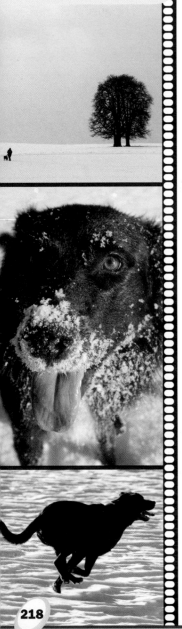

Analysing moving image texts

What does analysing moving image texts involve?

Film reviews are mostly written for a general audience and, although they contain specific 'film language', they do not usually use very technical terms. They focus more on the storyline, acting and so on.

However, if your job involved looking at how effective an advert was, you would need to focus closely on the way it was put together. For example, read this task:

> *You work for a dog-food company. Your boss has asked you to write a report on an advert for a new product. Explain what happens in the advert and how well it works.*

Here are two extracts from the report written by different students.

Extract 1

> There's a field, then they go to another pic and there's this dog who looks healthy. Then the dog sort of runs off, then it is back to the beginning and there's this man throwing a stick.

Extract 2

> First we see a long shot of a field. This shows a man walking his dog in the background, which tells us what the location is. It is obvious straight away that this is a healthy outdoor lifestyle.
>
> In the next shot, we see a close-up of the dog. He is panting, his teeth look white and his tongue looks pink – this also shows how healthy he is. The next shot has the dog in the centre of the screen as he runs away. It makes us feel like we are his owner.
>
> The final shot is of the dog food can, with the brand name. The point is clear – if you buy this brand, your dog will be happy and healthy.

ACTIVITY

Discuss with a partner what makes Extract 2 better than Extract 1. Identify where the writer

- makes his/her points clear in each paragraph
- uses more professional and technical language
- explains the effect of different camera shots.

Focus for development:
Analysing in more detail

Extract 2, which is Grade C standard, sets the tone for a good response by

- using a sequence word which makes clear what we are looking at and when: '**First** we see …'
- using a technical term which tells us exactly what is shown: 'a **long shot** of a field'
- developing the explanation to say what the overall effect is: 'This shows a man walking his dog in the background which **tells us what the location** is. It is obvious straight away that this is a **healthy outdoor lifestyle**.'

ACTIVITY

- Look at any advertisement from television you know well.
- Analyse it in three parts, using a grid like the one below.
- Make notes in each column. Try to say what the effect is on each occasion. Use the explanations in the glossary to help you.

	Content (what's in frame) including on–screen text	**Shots** or how one shot moves to another	**Music** or **voice- over**	**Effect**
How the advert opens				
How the advert develops				
How the advert ends				

ASSESSMENT FOCUS

Write the first paragraph of your analysis, using the notes in your grid.

- Explain how the advert opens.
- Comment on which camera shots are used, and with what effects.
- Begin with a sequence word or phrase (for example, 'Firstly', 'At the start').

Remember

- Use professional language when writing about moving image texts.
- Write about the effect of each image.

Adding voiceover to moving image texts

Learning objective

- To understand how the way you combine text with moving images can change the meaning of a moving image text.

What does 'voiceover' mean?

The spoken **voiceover** is the text chosen to go with images for a television programme (or an advert). The way the voiceover is written can really affect the meaning of moving image text.

To see this in action, look at these three images from a programme about global warming.

ACTIVITY

Cover the three images and read aloud this voiceover, revealing each image in turn.

> **Still 1**: 'Here is an image of the sky showing sun shining against the blue.'
>
> **Still 2**: 'Here's a polar bear; isn't it a lovely creature? Fluffy and white and so lovely to look at …'
>
> **Still 3**: 'Unfortunately, as you can see from the breaking ice, global warming is going to threaten polar bears.'

With a partner, discuss what is wrong with this voiceover and how it could be improved.

The secret is to let images speak for themselves – voiceovers are meant to **add meaning or information that isn't obvious from the image**. For example, for **Still 1**:

> *'The world is warming up.'*

This lets the viewer make the connection between the image and the voiceover.

Try writing a simple voiceover to match **Stills 2** and **3**, using these starters:

> *'All over the Earth, wildlife is …'*
>
> *'The effect could be …'*

Focus for development:
Changing the meaning

Consider the images on the previous page again. Could the voiceover be on a different subject or would it have to be about global warming?

ACTIVITY

Read this new voiceover with the same images.

Still 1: 'Is there a God?'

Still 2: 'In today's programme we will look at creation.'

Still 3: 'And how Darwin's work shattered what the Victorians believed.'

Can you see any links to the images?

ACTIVITY

Write three voiceover lines of your own to go with the three images. If you need help coming up with a different type of text, you could use one of these ideas:

- An opening to a news report about a missing ship.
- An advertisement for a new washing powder.
- A documentary about the Arctic.

ASSESSMENT FOCUS

- Watch a very short section from a wildlife documentary or news report (showing an event).
- Listen carefully to (or use a transcript of) a small section of the narration or voiceover.
- Write a commentary in which you explain how the images and voiceover work together. Focus on:
    - the purpose and audience for the programme
    - how much (or little) is said
    - how the images work with the voiceover or narration
    - the tone of voice of the speaker.

Remember

- **The images in moving image text need the voiceover, up to a point. But the words alone would make little sense without the images.**

Grade Booster

Extended Assessment Task

Produce a response of around 600 words in answer to this Moving Images task.

> *Write an analysis of an advertisement you know well, commenting on how the images and any text (spoken or written) combine to create effect and meaning.*

Complete the grid from page 219 [Analysing moving image texts spread], then write your commentary, using the structure of how it begins, develops and ends to help focus your analysis. You could use this writing frame for your first draft.

Firstly, the advertisement opens with
Next, we see
Then
Finally

Evaluation – What have you learned?

With a partner, use the grade checklist below to evaluate your work on the Extended Assessment Task.

C
- I can describe an advertisement, explaining clearly how it is constructed and some of the effects created.
- I can use appropriate language and try to develop my ideas or interpret the effect of particular choices.

D
- I can describe an advertisement's key features quite clearly, commenting on images, text and sound, with some reference to the effect.
- I can use some appropriate language but my ideas are not often developed as far as they could be.

E
- I can describe what I see in an advertisement and make some comments on images, text and sound.
- I can explain ideas in a basic way but don't develop them.

F
- I can describe what I see in an advertisement and attempt to make comments on it.
- I can only give very limited explanations.

You may need to go back and look at the relevant pages from this section again.

Commissions

Introduction

This section of Chapter 5 helps you to

- explore the creative writing area of 'commissions', in which you write to a given brief or set of guidelines
- develop creative writing responses to a range of texts
- practise and develop extended responses.

Why is learning about writing to a creative brief important?

- Being able to write to a set brief, with clear limits and a defined purpose and audience, is a key skill for learning and working life.
- Effective writers can turn their hand to most writing tasks they are set by others, such as employers or teachers.
- Learning how to adapt your writing so that it fits a clearly-defined purpose will help with your other written work.

A **Grade D** candidate will

- understand the task set and respond to the requirements, and begin to engage the reader's interest
- produce writing with a structure and using paragraphs, but which tends to be rather basic and without much variety
- create sentences that are mostly spelled and punctuated accurately.

A **Grade C** candidate will

- understand clearly the task set and write an appropriate response
- engage the reader's interest with a variety of sentences and vocabulary
- write in a structured and coherent way, using paragraphs, so that ideas are clear to the reader
- spell and punctuate accurately.

Prior learning

Before you begin this unit

- read a range of texts that have been professionally commissioned – for example, brochures for products, poems or speeches written for special occasions
- check out magazine websites to see if they have commissioning guidelines and what you have to do to submit an article.

Exploring a non-fiction commission

What does writing to commission involve?

A commission is when a writer is given a clear brief for a piece of writing. It will have clear features, usually a specific audience and content and sometimes a particular length, so it is vital to pay attention to the detail of the brief.

ACTIVITY

Below is an example commission given by the editor of a newspaper to one of the journalists. Imagine you are that journalist and your job depends on paying proper attention to what is being asked for.

Note down:

- what you have to write
- where it will appear
- what its subject will be
- what tone or style it should have
- any restrictions or limits on what you should produce.

From the editor

To: PG

Date: 7ᵗʰ April

As you know, our newspaper runs a section called 'Leisure Today' with a sub-section for teenagers.

I want you to write an article of between 500 and 800 words in which you recommend some positive ways of spending the summer holidays in your area. It should have a personal tone, with your own voice and ideas coming through.

Focus for development: Writing to the brief

This is the first paragraph from one student's article for the 'Leisure Today' section of the newspaper.

> *You might think that there is nothing to do in our local town, and that the best thing would be to fly off on a plane to somewhere hot and sandy. In fact, there is no need. There is a lot to do right on your doorstep if you look hard enough.*

This is a good **Grade C** response because

- it is clear and fits the subject set by the editor
- it has the personal tone as requested by the brief – 'You might think' … 'our town'
- it uses a range of sentence lengths to make sure the reader is interested.

ACTIVITY

Write a second paragraph for the article. It can be based on your home area or made up. It should focus on a specific attraction teenagers might enjoy.

- Use one **short sentence** for effect.
- Add imagery or vivid vocabulary, perhaps using **alliteration**, – for example, 'You could visit the *funky, fantastic new skate-park* …'
- Or try a **rhetorical question** – for example, 'Nothing worth seeing? You must be joking!'
- Or **patterns of three** – for example, 'Fancy a snack? There's Mac's tasty take-away, the cool i-Chat Café, and – cooler still – Dino's Ice-Cream Bar'.

Your could start your paragraph like this.

> *For a start, there is …*

ASSESSMENT FOCUS

Think of three or four other ideas for teenager-friendly attractions which you could write a paragraph about for your article. Try to complete a plan like the one below.

Paragraph 1: intro about my area

Paragraph 2: first thing worth doing

Paragraph 3: second attraction/thing to do

Paragraph 4: third attraction/thing to do

Paragraph 5: fourth attraction/thing to do

Paragraph 6: summary or conclusion

Use your plan to complete your article on attractions for teenagers for the 'Leisure Today' section of the newspaper.

Examiner's tip ★

As with any other piece of writing, adding detail to your plan will help you produce a more fluent response.

Remember

- Stick to what the brief asks you to do.
- Match what you say to the audience and purpose given in the brief.
- Use the features of the form you are asked to write in.

Developing a fiction commission

Checklist for success

- You need to match your response closely to the task set.
- You need to choose the most engaging content and ideas.
- You need to draw your reader in through a wide range of language devices, and sustain your tone, style and structure throughout.

ACTIVITY

Read this story brief. Quickly note down these key elements of the task:

- the form of the text
- where the text will appear
- what specific instructions there are about the word limit or format
- what restrictions there are
- what information about the content is given.

A website called 'All–people–together.com' has asked for contributions from young people about friendships between people of different cultures or about their positive experiences of different cultures.

> *We would like a short story in which two people from different cultures meet. It cannot be longer than 1000 words. It can be based on a real experience or be entirely fictional. Make it interesting to read.*

The content – where the story takes place and who the characters are – is entirely up to you.

One student came up with this basic idea for a short story.

A teenage boy in London discovers a young refugee mother and her baby hiding in a barge on the Thames.

Of course, it is just an idea and from here needs a **structure**. For example:

Paragraphs	Stage
Opening **2–3 paragraphs**	**Key setting**: the barge (**characters** = boy, woman/baby) **Opening**: Boy bunks off school, finds barge where he decides to hang out. Meets mother and baby.
Development **2–3 paragraphs**	**Key setting**: back home – the kitchen (**characters** = mum, boy) **Development**: They ask for his help and he decides to do what he can. Then is caught stealing food for them from home; is forced to tell mum what is going on.
Climax **2 paragraphs**	**Key setting**: river bank (**characters** = mum, boy, woman, baby) **Move to climax**: Goes to barge with mum; mother panics and threatens to jump into river. Mum persuades her not to.
End/Resolution **2–3 paragraphs**	**Key setting**: tube station (**characters** = mum, boy, woman, baby) **End/Resolution** (include a twist?): Mum agrees to help mother/baby but on the way to the police station, they run off and are not seen again.

Focus for development: Developing your own structure

ACTIVITY

Here are two other basic ideas for the short story. Using one of these, or one of your own, come up with a four-stage structure, like the one above.

Story idea 1: A boy/girl on a school trip abroad gets lost in a foreign city and is helped by a kind local person.

Story idea 2: A soldier in another country is searching for weapons in a village and finds some being hidden by a young girl/boy.

Remember:
- Keep it simple – not too many characters; a clear start and end.
- Create key settings/scenes to build your story round.
- Show development – something has to happen!
- Consider a twist or the unexpected.

Now plan out your basic story, adding the number of paragraphs you might write for each stage.

Examiner's tip

Stick to one or two main characters for a short story. You can mention other characters but don't develop them or give them too much speech or description. Stick to your main character's story – what he/she wants, what happens to him/her.

Focus for development: Improving your language

Look at these two openings based on the barge story idea.

Opening 1

Joey had decided to bunk off school. He was being bullied and was well fed up. He was small and shy, and didn't have many friends, so lots of times went for walks by the Thames. He liked watching the boats go by.

Then Joey saw the barge and it seemed like the ideal place to spend the rest of the day until it was time to go home and face his mum. He walked over to it and looked in but he couldn't see into it cos the windows were all broken up. He wondered what was inside it.

Opening 2

The barge lay half on its side in the brown mud, looking a bit like a dead whale. The window frames were rotten, and there was no glass remaining. Joey walked gingerly across the gang-plank that led to the barge's side. Perhaps he would sit inside the barge for a while, and kill the hours until it was time to go home. He would have to lie to his mum about where he had been. Another day off school, another made-up story.

He gazed sadly at the windows. Nothing moved. The barge was silent. Or was it? Could he hear something?

Examiner's tip

*It is better to **show** rather than **tell** the reader information. You will notice that the first extract tells the reader a lot, but shows us very little, so it is difficult to picture the scene.*

ACTIVITY

Discuss with a partner:

- Which of these two openings **shows us** the scene **most vividly?**
- Which provides the **most detail** about the barge?
- Which **holds back information** about Joey rather than telling us directly?
- Which uses a **powerful simile** to describe the barge?
- Which uses **short sentences** and paragraphs for effect?
- Which engages us through **suspense**?

Focus for development: Including speech and starting the story

Before you draft some paragraphs, consider again two areas that will improve your story.

Including speech

- Keep it simple and make absolutely sure it is accurately punctuated.
- Don't overdo 'he said' or 'she said'. Use alternatives.
- Make sure the dialogue adds something to the story and moves it on.

For example:

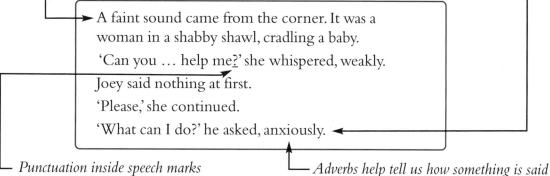

Sets scene for speech

New line/paragraph for each speaker

A faint sound came from the corner. It was a woman in a shabby shawl, cradling a baby.

'Can you ... help me?' she whispered, weakly.

Joey said nothing at first.

'Please,' she continued.

'What can I do?' he asked, anxiously.

Punctuation inside speech marks

Adverbs help tell us how something is said and add to our understanding of character

Starting – making an impact

There are a number of ways to start your story. Here are just three possibilities.

- The **place** – for example, 'The *bullet-riddled building looked empty*, but Johnson wasn't taking any chances.'
- The **person** – for example, '*Johnson, his AK-47 cradled in his arms, alert and tense,* edged towards the building.'
- **Dialogue** – for example, '*Anyone there? If there is, come out with your hands up!' Johnson's voice shook* as he stood by the bullet-riddled building.'

ASSESSMENT FOCUS

Now write the first two paragraphs of your story, or continue the barge story from one of the opening paragraphs on the previous page.

Remember

- **Provide twists or unexpected plot turns and suspense.**
- **Vary the length of sentences and paragraphs.**
- **Use imagery and a wide vocabulary.**
- **Give any speech you include a purpose and check it is accurately punctuated.**

Grade Booster

Extended Assessment Task

Write a full response to this Commissions task.

> A website called 'All-people-together.com' has asked for contributions from young people about friendships or experiences of people or places of a different culture.
>
> *We would like a short story in which two people from different cultures meet. It cannot be longer than 1000 words. It can be based on a real experience or be entirely fictional. Make it interesting to read.*
>
> The content – where the story takes place and who the characters are – is entirely up to you.

You may wish to complete your story from page 226 or begin an entirely new one.

Evaluation – What have you learned?

With a partner, use the grade checklist below to evaluate your work on the Extended Assessment Task.

C
- I can meet the main requirements of the task and write in a clear way.
- I can develop a coherent story idea with carefully thought-out stages.
- I can use language devices and techniques for effect, and engage the reader's interest.

D
- I can meet the main requirements of the task.
- I can come up with a clear idea for my story with several stages but these stages are not always as well-linked as they could be.
- I can try to use some language devices and sometimes make a conscious effort to engage the reader.

E
- I can write a story but it is not always focused on the task set.
- I can give my story a structure but it is not always clear or fluent and my beginning and ending aren't as strong as they could be.

F
- I can write a story which is based on the task set, but the structure of the story and my meaning are not always clear.

You may need to go back and look at the relevant pages from this section again.

Controlled Assessment Preparation
Creative Writing

Introduction

In this section you will

- find out the exact facts, demands and requirements of the Creative Writing Controlled Assessment task
- read, analyse and respond to three sample answers by different candidates
- plan and write your own response to a sample task
- evaluate and assess your response and the progress you have made.

Why is preparation of this kind important?

- If you know exactly what you need to do, you will feel more confident when you produce your own response for assessment.
- Looking at sample answers by other students will help you see what you need to do to improve your own work.
- Planning and writing a full sample written response after you have completed the whole chapter will give you a clear sense of what you have learned so far.

Key Information

Unit 3 Section B is 'Producing Creative Writing'.

- The controlled part of the task will last up to **four hours**, and is worth **30 marks**.
- It is worth **15%** of your overall English Language GCSE mark.

The Controlled Assessment tasks

- You have to complete **two** written tasks.
- The total number of words recommended for the two pieces is **1200**. The pieces do not have to be of equal length.

You will choose, or be provided with, two tasks from these three areas:

- Re-creations (transforming a text into a different form)
- Moving images (writing based on moving images)
- Commissions (responding to a set brief)

So, for example, you might re-create a poem as a letter in 500 words and then write an extended commentary on a piece of documentary film in 700 words.

These tasks will be done in 'controlled conditions', in the exam room or in your own classroom over a period of up to four hours.

The tasks in detail

Here are some example questions based on the three task areas set by the exam board.

Re-creations	Look at the poem 'Spellbound'. A woman, like the one in the poem, has been walking in some wild British countryside in winter, and while sheltering in a tiny cottage has been snowed in. Eventually, a rescue team find her and get her out. Write a newspaper report about the rescue.
Moving images	Write a review of a documentary you have seen, explaining how it got its message across, and how effective it was.
Commissions	The web host of a site for teenagers approaches you to submit some writing for it. This month's theme is 'Health = happiness'. You have complete freedom about how you approach the topic but it must be lively and engaging, and be no more than 500 words.

The Assessment

The assessment objective for this unit (AO4) states that you must be able to do the following:

- Write to communicate clearly, effectively and imaginatively, using and adapting forms and selecting vocabulary appropriate to task and purpose in ways that engage the reader.
- Organise information and ideas into structured and sequenced sentences, paragraphs and whole texts, using a variety of linguistic and structural features to support cohesion and overall coherence.
- Use a range of sentence structures for clarity, purpose and effect, with accurate punctuation and spelling.

Targeting Grade C

Some of the key features of Grade D and Grade C responses are as follows:

Grade D candidates	See example on page 235
<ul><li>adapt certain features of a new form when re-creating a text, but not always successfully</li><li>attempt a range of sentences and use a wider vocabulary but not always appropriately selected</li><li>use paragraphs with some sense of overall structure and with mostly accurate basic punctuation</li><li>show some basic understanding of form and genre</li><li>make an attempt to develop ideas, but these are not always sustained or followed through</li><li>use a range of language features, such as imagery, but not always with a sense of the effect on reader.</li></ul>	

Grade C candidates	See example on page 236-7
<ul><li>adapt one text and turn it into another, when re-creating, so that the new form is clear for its new purpose</li><li>use a range of sentences and a varied vocabulary to maintain the reader's interest</li><li>write in clear paragraphs that are well linked and with generally accurate punctuation and spelling</li><li>show clear understanding of form and genre</li><li>develop the subject matter in more detail than at lower grades</li><li>use a range of language features, such as imagery, with an attempt for conscious effect on the reader.</li></ul>	

Exploring Sample Responses

ACTIVITY

Read the extract below from a response to this Re-creations task.

> *Look at the poem 'Spellbound'. A woman, like the one in the poem, has been walking in some wild British countryside in winter, and while sheltering in a tiny cottage has been snowed in. Eventually, a rescue team find her and get her out. Write a newspaper report about the rescue.*

As you read it, think about whether it is closer to a Grade D or a Grade C, and why. Consider the key elements an examiner would look for:

- how clearly and effectively the writer has adapted the original text, the poem 'Spellbound', into a new version
- how clearly the student's ideas are conveyed
- whether the conventions of a new type of text (a feature article) have been followed
- how interesting the article is, in terms of the variety of vocabulary and sentences used.

Turn to page 208 to read the poem 'Spellbound'.

Example 1: Re-creations

SNOW IN MOUNTAINS

A woman got trapped in the mountains yesterday. She was walking when she saw an old cottage and decided to go in to get out of the bad weather.

The cottage was on the edge of some steep hillside near a village called Shepton but quite a remote place. No one had lived there for ages.

When she was in the cottage in fact the weather got much worse. The wind was really powerful and the snow started to fall. She felt that it all looked very beautiful and decided to stay where she was. She said, 'It looked so nice that I thought I was safe'.

But in fact it wasn't safe because the temperature dropped really low and the snow built up like huge rocks around the cottage. The cottage was an old, abandoned one so there was no heating. Her mobile phone was out of range too.

Then some of her friends in the village realised she was missing so they called the mountain rescue and they started to search for her. It was a long and hard search but eventually they found her.

The head of the rescue team said, 'She was dead lucky as the weather was getting worse. If we didn't find her she might have died. People should take more care.'

The woman whose name is Emma Brown was sorry for the trouble she caused. She said 'If I realised how bad the storm was then I could have been more careful.' The rescue team leader said 'people just don't think sometimes'. Emma is 32.

Anyway, it was a happy ending in the end and no one was harmed but it just shows how dangerous it can be in the mountains so you should really take care.

Examiner feedback

We can see the 'bones' of the original poem here and the paragraphs are reasonably clear and easy to follow, but they aren't linked well and are all the same length.

There is little variety in the sentences but speech is included. There is a headline but it doesn't really convey the main idea. Also, for a news article we would expect to see more of the key facts in the first paragraph – the woman's name, age, etc. The details only appear later in this response.

There is one attempt at a simile, 'like huge rocks' but it isn't very striking.

Suggested grade: D

Read the response below to this Moving images task:

> *Write a review of a documentary you have seen, analysing how it got its message across and how effective it was.*

Looking carefully at the annotations, decide how this is an improvement on Example 1.

Example 2: Moving images

Viewpoint established straight away

NO SHARKS FOR DOMINIC

'SHARK WATCHER' [9pm, Discovery channel]

There are just too many animal documentaries on television. It seems that if you want to get lots of viewers the television companies think **all you have to do is take a camera to some exotic location and put a celebrity in front of it**.

Good use of humour for effect

'Shark watcher' is a new documentary presented by Dominic Doran. He is that comedy actor who we see in some really stupid sit-coms. The first time we see him in this new documentary he is sitting on a lovely boat in lovely sunny weather, smiling **as if he has won the lottery**. Next moment he is telling us how dangerous it is watching sharks! Yes, Dominic, very **life-threatening!** You are in a safe boat with the camera crew!

Good simile

Vocabulary reasonably varied

The programme then shows Dominic as he fails to actually see any sharks at all. Instead we just get **long shots** of Dominic looking thoughtful as the sun goes down. This is very effective in promoting Dominic, but it drives me mad!

Appropriate reference to moving images

The programme is also irritating because **it uses the same old ideas**; Dominic interviews tribal people and pretends to be interested. Then Dominic phones home and tells his girlfriend he misses her. But there are no images of Dominic with sharks.

Shows knowledge of the conventions of such programmes

The only moment in the programme worth watching is when the camera crew actually do get some

Use of → *footage of sharks. There are **lots of them and they look really**
short   **healthy. Unfortunately they are not Great Whites**. This gives
sentence   *Dominic another excuse to say that they are under threat. What is*   ← Vocabulary a
and linking   *most worrying about this programme is that it is only the first*   bit limited
word   *episode in a six-part series. This means we will have to face*   here
                 another two and a half hours of Dominic.

                         Well, I won't because this is the one and only programme I will
                 watch. Bring back David Attenborough!   ← Good short
                                                                                            paragraph
                                                                                            to stress
                                                                                            final point

Examiner feedback

This is generally a successful account of the programme.

- We get a good sense of the reviewer's opinion, supported by some funny and well-argued points about the documentary.
- The writer usually uses appropriate language such as 'long shots', although a little more developed detail on how the images were constructed and how the programme appeared would have helped.
- Paragraphing is clear and generally linked, with some variety. Sentences are reasonably varied, too.
- Occasionally the language is a little dull, with repeated or rather weak descriptions, for example 'there are lots of them', when perhaps a richer vocabulary would have added impact.

All-in-all, a well-structured text with some attempt to engage the reader.

Suggested Grade: C

ACTIVITY

Read the response on the next page to this Commissions task:

> *The web host of a site for teenagers approaches you to submit some writing for it. This month's theme is 'Health = happiness'. You have complete freedom about how you approach the topic but it must be lively and engaging.*

Looking carefully at the annotations, decide how it is an improvement from Example 2.

Example 3: Commissions

HEALTH EQUALS HAPPINESS!

[pic of writer holding apple in one hand
and doughnut in the other]

Suits article's theme

Little descriptive details enliven text

There's a saying, 'You are what you eat'. In that case I ought to look like a doughnut. I wish I could say a **curvy sweet potato** but it is only just recently that I have changed my eating habits, thank god!

Nice use of humorous imagery

I can't quite believe how much better I feel since I rescued my **pink bike from dad's garage** and almost killed myself cycling to college. The first few times I felt like I'd done the Tour de France, but once I'd had a week or two of it I began to FEEL HEALTHY..

New paragraph develops the 'story' of why she changed

The thing that made me change my lifestyle came after my parents forced me to take the dog for a walk. I had to take Freddie for a walk round the block. **I can hear you saying, 'Around the block? That's not very hard'. Well, I can tell you that walking up Fisher Avenue is VERY demanding if you are as unfit as I was.** By the time I got to the top I was really out of breath and promised myself to exercise properly, cut out iced doughnuts except for Fridays, and eat the odd salad. After a rest on the kerb I walked back down the mountain **(ok, hill!)** except that when I got to the bottom I realised I'd left the dog behind. Mum saw how **knackered** I was and gave me a lift to the top to pick poor Freddie up. His tail was very low and he looked most upset with me!

Good sense of the audience and sharing thoughts with them

Use of humour in bracketed aside

This is a bit informal

Good link words

Since then I am a changed girl. I do still crave doughnuts and still have the odd one – like after I got my mock Science results (I didn't know 'U' meant 'ungraded'. I thought it meant 'utterly brilliant.') but I am now a keen cyclist, lover of **fresh air, food and fitness**. I can't wait to get out of the house.

Ends with comic anecdote which cleverly brings together school life and health

Pattern of three stresses point here

What is really funny is that I feel more confident too. There's this boy in Year 11 who keeps on looking at me strangely. I think he fancies the new me, but actually my best mate Cara says it's because I hadn't realised I still had my cycle–helmet on when I was chatting to him!

Examiner feedback

This is a good piece of writing which gets the tone and style right for the audience. It meets the commission well.

- There are some good references to the writer's own life which have been exaggerated and played with for entertainment value and to show creativity.
- The language succeeds in places in creating effects, for example the comic asides (in brackets) when talking to the reader as a friend.
- The variety in the sentence structures gives us a real sense of the writer's own personality.

In places, the vocabulary could be a little more varied but for the purpose and audience this is not too much of an issue.

Suggested grade: C borderline B

EXTENDED PRACTICE TASK

Commissions

A television company is looking to commission a new reality show featuring teenagers. It wants the show to have a serious message, issue or idea to explore. It will be on for one hour every night for 14 days, ending on a Sunday evening.

You have been approached by the producer to suggest what the show might be about, what its format might be and who might be involved.

Write a proposal of **no more than 600 words:**

- explaining your ideas clearly
- giving a clear vision of the look and feel of the programme
- saying why it would appeal to teenage viewers.

This proposal will be like a persuasive essay in which you set out what you would like to include and aim to get the television company to accept your ideas.

If you only do five things…

1 Make sure you use the main conventions or features that fit the style or form in which you are writing.
2 Take the opportunity to 'show off' your creativity through your ideas and detail.
3 Think carefully about the structure and order of your ideas – you don't have to tell the reader everything straight away.
4 Begin brilliantly, engaging the reader straight away. End brilliantly, by satisfying or surprising the reader.
5 Include a variety of vocabulary, paragraphs and sentences, using imagery and detail where appropriate.

Unit 3C **Studying Spoken Language**

What's it all about?

Spoken language tells us a lot about who we are, our relationships and our lives. We use talk to communicate feelings, influence others, tell stories, and give information, amongst other things. But what do we really know about our own talk?

How will I be assessed?

- You will get **10% of your English Language marks** for your ability to write about spoken language.
- You will have to complete **one** Controlled Assessment **task** of **800–1000 words** over the course of **2–3 hours**.
- You will be marked on your written response to **one** of these three topics:
  – **Social attitudes to spoken language**: how we and others respond to, and are affected by, the way people speak
  – **Spoken genres**: the patterns and features of talk in different situations (for example, in television interviews or in speeches)

  – **Multi-modal talk**: the way talk is changed or affected by a range of media (for example, mobile phones or the internet).

What is being tested?

You are being examined on your ability to

- show your understanding of changes in spoken and written language due to new technology or the way society changes
- explain how these changes in language reflect our own identity and culture
- write about how language is used in 'real life' (for example, attitudes about accent or how language is used in the workplace, or between particular groups or individuals)
- reflect thoughtfully on your own and others' uses of language, for example how you adapt what you say in different situations.

However, your response will probably only have to focus on one or two of these areas, depending on the topic you choose.

Talk – What's it all about?

Introduction

This section of Chapter 6 helps you to

- explore different types of research about spoken language that will be useful for your own work
- learn about transcribing talk
- investigate your own and others' spoken language.

Why is learning about talk important?

- Understanding how talk works can help you improve your own communication in everyday situations.
- Writing about talk may need different approaches from those you use for written texts.

A **Grade D** candidate will

- explore how they and other people use and adapt spoken language in different situations
- explore some features from spoken language data
- explore issues that arise from how we react to forms of spoken language but the explorations are likely to be under-developed.

D

A **Grade C** candidate will

- show some confidence in writing about spoken language
- begin to analyse how they and other people use language for particular situations
- begin to analyse some features of spoken language data
- begin to analyse how we react to forms of spoken language
- the response will be sustained and focused on the task.

C

Prior learning

Before you begin this unit, think about

- what you already know about your own spoken language

> How does it change when you are talking to parents, friends or teachers? Do you have an accent?

- what you know about other people's spoken language.

> Do any family members have a different accent? Do they expect you to talk in a certain way and why?

What is special about my talk?

Learning objective

- To explore your own talk, and understand some of your own attitudes to it.

What does exploring my talk involve?

Looking at the variations in the way you speak with different people – for example, your friends, parents or teachers – can provide really useful information for your spoken language study. You might even decide to take a closer look at your local accent or dialect.

ACTIVITY

Discuss your own 'talk' for up to 10 minutes in a group. Consider the following questions:

- **How do you speak with your friends?** Do you have special 'in-words' or phrases that you all share? What are they? Where did they come from? Would you use them in writing? Why/Why not?
- **Does your talk with others vary at all?** Do you speak differently to adults, and people you don't know so well? How do you feel when speaking in public or to unfamiliar audiences?
- **How would you describe your talk?** Do you have a particular accent? Is this related to where you live – or lived?

All these things that make up your own talk – including your pronunciation, dialect and use of vocabulary – are called your **idiolect**, a very important term in the spoken language work you will do. For example, you might say: 'My idiolect is recognisable by my Yorkshire accent and my habit of saying, 'like' lots of times. I also use a range of local dialect words.'

Key terms in spoken language study

Term	Meaning	Example usage
accent	Pronunciation of words according to place or society you are from (how words sound)	I have a southern accent which is noticeable when it comes to certain words like 'grass' which I pronounce with a 'long' A.
non-standard dialect	Vocabulary and grammar distinct to a place, group of people or, sometimes, country	My dad (from Somerset) still says 'Where's that to?' instead of 'Where is it?' and uses 'gurt' meaning 'very' or 'really' as in 'that's a gurt big burger you've got'.
standard English	The most widely-used form of language for educated speakers which is not specific to a particular location or region	In standard English I'd use 'We were going' not 'we was', and in vocabulary I'd use 'argument', not 'barney' or 'tiff'.
formal and informal	Usually, the types of language you would use when changing between professional or business situations, and talking with a friend or people you know well	I use more formal language when I'm doing my Saturday job. If customers come in, I have to say, 'Can I help you, sir?' Of course if a friend came in I might suddenly be more informal, and say 'All right, mate? What d'you want then?'
transcript	Written-out version of a conversation or talk as it actually occurred (includes pauses, hesitations and repetitions)	Well. I met our lass in, I mean, I fell, I mean, why, it sounds, it might sound old-fashioned, but I fell in love with her.

Focus for development:
Researching idiolect

Your discussion so far has been based on what you think about your talk. But are you right? What is your spoken language really like? One way to find out is recording some everyday language from your life.

Read this short piece of conversation. It was recorded by 'A' and then transcribed. (**A** is the student; **B** is his grandad.)

> **A:** So, grandad, how would you describe your accent?
>
> **B:** At one time me tink it was pure Jamaica! Me come from Jamaica in the sixties, wit your grandmother. We lived in Jamaica *long* time 'fore comin' here.
>
> **A:** Your accent is different to mine, then?
>
> **B:** Well, yu got traces too. Jus not so strong.
>
> **A:** Do you think your accent's important?
>
> **B:** It's important to know where yu from. Know your roots.
>
> **A:** Yeh – I don't wanna lose them.

ASSESSMENT FOCUS

Write one paragraph about the grandad's idiolect based on this short sample transcript between A and B. Try to refer to specific words or lines.

Remember

- **You will need to refer to at least three pages of transcription as part of your study.**
- **It doesn't have to be your own, but your own talk is a good place to begin.**

How others speak

Learning objective

- *To practise using different types of source material to research the spoken language of others.*

standard English: the most widely-used form of English, which is not specific to a particular location or region. For example, in Standard English you would say 'I'm not' rather than 'I ain't' and you would talk about a 'child' not a 'kid', a 'bairn' or a 'nipper'.

What does exploring how others speak involve?

A good starting point for your spoken language study would be to look at the different types of English that are spoken in your region and beyond, and collecting evidence of it.

ACTIVITY

Articles can be a good source of data on spoken language. Read the web text below and make brief notes about the regional dialect being explained.

- Where exactly is Geordie spoken?
- Where does the term 'Geordie' probably come from?
- What other dialects exist in the North East of England?

What is Geordie?

The word Geordie refers both to a native of Newcastle-upon-Tyne and to the speech of the inhabitants of that city. There are several theories about the exact origins of the term Geordie, but all agree it derives from the local pet name for George. It is sometimes mistakenly used to refer to the speech of the whole of the North East of England. Strictly speaking, however, Geordie should only refer to the speech of the city of Newcastle-upon-Tyne and the surrounding urban area of Tyneside. Locals insist there are significant differences between Geordie and several other local dialects, such as **Pitmatic** and **Makkem**. Pitmatic is the dialect of the former mining areas in County Durham and around Ashington to the north of Newcastle-upon-Tyne, while Makkem is used locally to refer to the dialect of the city of Sunderland and the surrounding urban area of Wearside. Although only 10 miles apart, the difference between Sunderland and Newcastle-upon-Tyne is, of course, extremely important locally, not least because of the rivalry between supporters of the two football clubs. For many people these different identities are expressed in the way they speak.

Discuss with a partner:

- When you speak to someone from your area, how do you tell exactly where they come from?
- Can you tell if they are from your own town or a nearby town? Make a note of any clues in their accent or vocabulary.
- What words or phrases can you think of from your own dialect? What do they mean in standard English? Make a list of them.

Focus for development:
Research from transcripts

Data could also come from actual speakers. Read this extract from the same site as the article on page 244.

> **Mark:** Well. I met our lass in, I mean, I fell, I mean, why, it sounds, it might sound old-fashioned, but I fell in love with her. You know. I still, I still, I'll always love our lass. I mean I love her stronger each day. I mean, you, the, them days you didn't, you didn't live with lasses. If, if a bloke was ganning with a lass and they weren't married, she, she had a bad name. You know. And everybody looked, looked down on people like that. And if a lass had a bairn, even if a lass had a bairn out of wedlock, she was, look, frowned upon, you know. I mean, I'm not saying that's right. But at the time they seemed right. I mean, people's att, your attitudes change now. I divn't think they're right now anyway. You know, when they live together. And they're having kids and, and they divn't want to get married and, I think you're, you're better being married. I mean it worked for me. But saying that, mind, uh, I got the right one. I was lucky; I got the right one. And it didn't work for my brother; he got the wrang one. So you cannot speak for other people really, can you? You know what I mean? I cannot. But I mean, I'm lucky. I've been lucky; dead lucky.

ACTIVITY

With your partner, note down from this transcript:

- any examples that show it is a record of a 'spoken conversation' (for example, repetitions, hesitations and pauses)
- examples of where local vocabulary has been used.

These two sources – the web article and the transcript – provide a great deal of information about local dialect. Other sources you could use include

- video or audio clips of people speaking
- print-outs of text messaging exchanges
- transcripts or recordings of 'live' everyday speech (for example, chats with relatives)
- questionnaire results (for example, on attitudes to talk).

ASSESSMENT FOCUS

You are researching the topic 'My talk'. Note down two sources from the list above you would choose to research if you were doing your task in this area.

Remember

- Talk – and information about it – is all around you.
- 'Capture' what is interesting and then select the source material that fits your topic.

Interviews and questionnaires

Checklist for success

- You need to find areas that interest you and which you can research in practical ways.
- You need to think carefully about your own and other people's use of language.

ACTIVITY

A short interview can be very useful in finding out about people's talk. What is the subject of this interview?

> **A:** Do you think you speak differently to pupils in class than to your own children at home?
>
> **B:** *(laughs)* I think my own kids think I talk to them like a teacher sometimes! But I try not to.
>
> **A:** Any examples?
>
> **B:** Well, it's more my tone of voice. Like at tea I'll say, 'don't all talk at once' in my loudest voice. But they still ignore me!

Notice how the interviewer (A) uses **open questions** that cannot be answered with just a 'yes' or a 'no'.

Conducting your research

Another way of finding out information about an area that interests you is to use a questionnaire. You could carry it out yourself, or give it to people to complete. For example, on the subject of 'How young people's speech has changed over the years', you could ask adults aged between 25 and 75 questions like these:

Question	Definitely not	Probably not	Probably yes	Definitely yes
Do young people today speak differently to their parents from the way that you did?				
Do young people swear more today?				

Examiner's tip ☆

It's a good idea, to allow a space on the questionnaire for respondents to note down their age and gender (no need for their names).

Focus for development:
Following up key points

You could use your questionnaire as the basis for an interview. For example, based on the questionnaire opposite you could ask respondents aged over 45:

- Can you give some examples of what was considered unacceptable to say when you were young?
- Can you give examples of times when you were told off by adults because of how you spoke? What did you say?

It may be a good idea to record the interview in case you get some long answers!

ASSESSMENT FOCUS

Having done your interviews and questionnaires, you need to decide what these tell you. Analyse your results like this:

- First, **record your results in** numbers. For example:
  4 out of 5 people questioned felt that they didn't speak with an accent.
- Then, **explain what the results tell you**. For example:
  This shows that most people think of their voices as normal even if they do have an accent.
- Finally, **include more detailed comments.** For example:
  My grandfather's way of speaking showed his local accent, for example when…

ACTIVITY

- Write a basic questionnaire to give to a friend, parent or adult you know well, with some questions about the way they speak. Try to come up with at least five questions, such as: 'Do you think you have an accent?'
- Then, develop at least two more open questions for an interview, for example: 'What sort of accent do you think you have?'

Remember

- **Use interviews and questionnaires to collect evidence for your study.**
- **Keep clear records – both of questionnaires or transcripts and of spoken (recorded) conversations.**
- **Look very carefully at your results, and explain what they tell you.**

Grade Booster

Writing up your research

Extended Assessment Task

Having selected an area of spoken language to research, and gathered your data and materials, write up what you have found out.

- Introduce the area you selected.
- Explain what you did and the research you carried out (interviews, questionnaires, source materials).
- Write about your findings:
  - What were the outcomes (the results you produced)?
  - What did these tell you about your, or other people's, language use and how it varies depending on time, place or context?
- Write a short conclusion which sums up what you found out.

Evaluation – What have you learned?

With a partner, use the grade checklist below to evaluate your work on the Extended Assessment Task.

C
- I can write up my research clearly, explaining what I did and what I found out in my spoken language study.
- I can analyse spoken language, make clear and analytical commments on spoken language data and analyse some issues which arise from the way people react to spoken language.
- I can focus clearly on the task set.

D
- I can write up my research, explaining some aspects of what I did and what it told me about the area of my spoken language study.
- I can explain how I use spoken language for particular purposes, explore elements of spoken language data and explore some issues arising from how people react to kinds of spoken language.
- I can show my awareness throughout the task that has been set.

E
- I can complete some research and write up some basic notes and ideas about the area of my spoken language study.

You may need to go back and look at the relevant pages from this section again.

The Spoken Language Study Topics

Introduction

This section of Chapter 6 helps you to

- explore the three areas of spoken language study: Social attitudes to spoken language, Spoken genres, and Multi-modal talk. Each of these will be explained clearly as you progress.

Why is learning about these three areas important?

- There will be tasks in the Controlled Assessment for each of the three areas and you will choose one area for your study, so you need to be clear about what each area involves.
- The three areas overlap. For example, social attitudes can be seen in the area of multi-modal talk – in different groups' perspectives on the language of texting.

A **Grade D** candidate will

- explore how they and others use and adapt spoken language in different situations
- explore some features from spoken language data: research, transcripts etc
- explore issues that arise from how we react to forms of spoken language but the explorations are likely to be under-developed.

D

A **Grade C** candidate will

- show some confidence in writing about spoken language
- begin to analyse how they and others use language for particular situations
- begin to analyse some features of spoken language data
- begin to analyse how we react to forms of spoken language in a sustained response focused on the task.

C

Prior learning

Before you begin this unit, think about

- what you already know about attitudes to different groups and the way they talk
- how talk can be different in everyday situations
- what you already know about types of talk influenced by technology.

Does your language change when you are with a particular group of people?

Do you use certain phrases when you take an item back to a shop or when you visit the dentist?

Do you chat on social networking sites? How does the language you use to chat change when you are texting?

Social attitudes to spoken language

What does social attitudes to spoken language mean?

Many of us use different language with different groups of people. For example, with our friends we might use nicknames or phrases that only make sense to them. This can be a barrier to outsiders. It is this type of language use that you will be exploring through this topic.

ACTIVITY

Discuss with a friend or in a group:

- When you meet someone for the first time, what do you notice most? The way they look? The way they speak? They way they dress?
- Now role-play these two extracts, before you discuss the questions below:

Speaker A

> Gosh, Jemima. I am absolutely flabbergasted that Simon Cowell complimented that quite awful singer.

Speaker B

> No way, Jem! I mean get real, Simon. She ain't no singer, innit?

What can you tell about the speaker in each case, for example about their age or their background?

Is this first impression fair? Or is it just prejudice on your part?

A student writes...

I don't like talking about this sort of thing – it makes me feel snobbish.

Answer...

Our attitudes about how people speak are very powerful but that doesn't mean they automatically make us racist, ageist or sexist. Thinking about these attitudes helps us become aware of any prejudices we might have.

Focus for development:
Other people's attitudes

Read these comments from people about the way they speak and their attitudes to other people's talk.

Employer: When I interview someone and he or she starts dropping his 't's, like 'wha' I did', or he/she says 'we was' instead of 'we were', they weaken their chance of getting the job.

Pupil in school in Cornwall: I hate it on TV when they use a west-country 'yokel' accent to show someone is slow or stupid. It's like an easy laugh, but I don't think it's funny.

Teenager: There was this funny sketch on *The Armstrong and Miller Show* where these two World War Two pilots are talking in posh accents, but using modern teenage slang.

ACTIVITY

Look at each example and make notes about the attitude displayed by the speaker. Decide

- whether the attitude is a positive one
- what we learn about their attitude to accent, dialect and non-standard English.

Think of one example when ways of speaking have been used for comic effect. Does the humour come from the accent? Or does it come from the language chosen: for example, talk that is out of place in a certain situation?

ASSESSMENT FOCUS

Write one or two paragraphs in which you

- comment on attitudes to accent, giving any examples you know of accent being used to present a stereotyped character
- explain your own attitude to any accent and why you might have it. (Be honest in your views!)

Remember

- We all have attitudes to spoken language; it may just be that we don't stop to think about them very often.
- 'Unpicking' what we feel, and explaining it in a clear way, is a key to getting a better grade.

'Yoof Slang' – what do you think?

Learning objective

- To explore attitudes to modern urban talk.

Checklist for success

- You need to find an area that interests you and which you can research in some depth.
- You need to think carefully about the language used by a particular social group or age group and what others think of this language.

ACTIVITY

Read the article below. Then discuss these questions in groups.

- What have Tesco done to make 'youth speak' more easily understood by some of the older staff?
- What examples are given of 'youth speak'?
- Which stores, in particular, is it targeting?
- What do the staff who are interviewed have to say about the idea?
- How would you describe the tone of the article? Is it negative, serious or humourous – or a bit of each?

Tesco's old timers get yoof slang pamphlet

By Lester Haines

Tesco has issued old timers working at some of its 1,500 stores with a handy guide to the kind of English guaranteed to have Middle England choking on its cocoa – that favoured by hoodies, wannabe homies, and anyone under 21 who considers the baseball cap to be the US's greatest contribution to English street culture.

The supermarket monolith has targeted outlets 'with a high proportion of employees over retirement age', *The Sun* reports. The plan is to improve communication between those who prefer 'lovely' to 'phat' and playing Bridge with their chums to hanging with the bloods.

A Tesco spokesman explained: 'This is a one-stop guide for lingo-lean staff to get word-savvy on today's "deadliest" street phrases. It aims to help bridge the generation gap and offer a guide for older members of staff looking to chat with younger colleagues and customers.'

Among the gems on offer are 'ballin'' (doing rather well), 'slammin'' (not unattractive) and the inevitable 'minging' (notably unattractive).

The idea has evidently found favour with employees at the Tesco Extra store in Eastbourne. Lionel Gardner, 70, who works in the bread and cakes section, enthused: 'It's a great idea. I love working with young people but a lot of the time I have difficulty understanding what they are trying to say.'

Ash Coley, 18, from the store's price control, offered: 'We youngsters learn a lot from the old timers. It is very interesting to talk to them – especially when they go on about the war. Hopefully, we will be able to have even better conversations with them now with the help of this guide.'

The initiative is the brainchild of Tesco PR chief Jon Church, who had the help of daughters Nicola, 15, Gemma, 14, and Hannah, 11, in putting together the aid to transgenerational understanding. He said: 'We have a very diverse workforce and customer base and in today's fast-moving world there can be a communication barrier between generations. If the leaflet is well received, we will roll it out to all UK stores.' ®

ASSESSMENT FOCUS

Write your own personal view of teenage slang. You could comment on

- particular examples you know and when and where they are used
- why you think it has become popular – if it has
- how much you use teenage slang yourself and your view of it
- what the adults you know think about it
- where it comes from (music, TV, films, friends?)

Remember

- Explain how your source material shows speakers' attitudes to different types of talk.
- Show how the language used can add richness and variety, and appeal to one group, or make it a barrier to other social groups.

Spoken genres – the media

Learning objectives

- *To learn about different 'spoken genres'.*
- *To understand that these often follow particular speech patterns and use common features or conventions.*

What are spoken genres?

Just as there are different genres or types of writing, for example ghost stories or newspaper articles, so there are also recognisable genres of talk.

Talk varies according to the **context** or situation. However, certain spoken areas of life – the media, for example – have their own patterns and **conventions** of speech.

ACTIVITY

Read these two extracts with a partner. For each, try to identify

- what the context is (where it takes place)
- who is speaking (the type/role of person)
- how you know.

Extract 1

And that's a fantastic ball to Henry… back to Ibrahimovic… he crosses… oh… here's a chance… brilliant block from Pepe… but Madrid can't clear, it's back in… corner to Barca. [pause] Graham, what do Madrid have to do to improve after half-time?

Extract 2

X: Look, I have to say, it wasn't your fault. It was a terrible song choice.

Y: Hang on a minute, I thought it…

X: Don't listen to him, it was terrible. It was like a dog had got stuck in a cat-flap.

W: I don't agree. I thought you nailed it.

Y: So did I. It was bang on the money and you made it your own. You'll be in the final, no problem.

Focus for development: Speech patterns and routines

Each extract uses a variety of different **routines** or **conventions**. For example, look at this analysis of the live TV football commentary from Extract 1.

Context	Talk	Example	Speech conventions
Studio – presenter faces camera; guests on sofa.	Presenter introduces game and studio guests; then switches to the stadium.	***Presenter****: We're live at the Nou Camp to see Barcelona take on Real Madrid. With me, I have former England player, Robbie Smith…* ***Guest****: Hi there.*	Shared understanding with audience of what 'Nou Camp' (stadium name) is. Convention of introducing the guest 'With me…'
Inside the stadium.	Introductory voiceover from presenter; then interview between reporter and manager in tunnel.	***Presenter****: Now over to Gerry who is in the tunnel…* ***Reporter****: So, Pepe, how are you feeling about today's game…?*	Typical conventions of 2-3 questions from reporter and brief answers from manager. Typical live presentation phrases: 'Now over to…'

ACTIVITY

In groups, role-play one of the two speech situations in Extract 1 or 2 on the previous page.

- Use the details from your grid to help you with the kinds of **speech conventions** used in that situation.
- One of you should watch the role play and comment afterwards on how realistic it is.

ASSESSMENT FOCUS

- Use a transcription of a short section from a radio phone-in programme to make notes on the kinds of typical speech routines or phrases for this type of talk. For example: 'And on line 1 we have…', 'Carrie, what's your view on…'
- Make a grid like the one above for your notes, if it helps to organise them.
- Write a short analysis of the transcript based on your notes.

Remember

- **Explain that all talk follows routines or has conventions, especially in different media forms.**
- **Discuss any typical words or phrases that come from the spoken genre you are writing about.**

255

The power of talk

Learning objective

- To see how and why language changes according to specific contexts.

What does the power of talk mean?

- In certain situations, one speaker will have more power or a higher status than another – for example, a manager talking to a trainee. You can get a clear sense of people's attitudes through the way people speak.

ACTIVITY

- Read this extract from a soap opera about a police-station. You may want to work in a group and each take a part to get a better idea of how it sounds.
- Once you've read it aloud, make detailed notes on the types of talk going on, for example:
  - the purpose of the different conversations
  - the language being used by each individual (register and formality)
  - any clear routines or patterns of language
  - the **status** or power of the speaker in each case.

Examiner's tip

Make sure you base your analysis on evidence from the extract and use technical terms (for example, status, speech routine, formal/informal) to show your understanding.

Glossary

'twoc': taking without owner's consent

Enquiry desk: 11.27a.m.

Desk sergeant: Yes, madam? How can I help?

Woman: I've lost Henry. We were on the high-street… well, Henry was; I'd left the back-door open, and…

Desk sergeant: Sorry, madam. Could you tell me who Henry is?

Woman: I have had him years… he's got curly hair…

Desk sergeant *(aside to colleague):* We've got a right one here. She's nuts… oops, here comes the Super…

Woman wanders off.

Superintendent: Dave. My room, five minutes. Get someone to cover you, OK?

Desk sergeant: Yes sir. *(to colleague)* You down the club tonight?

Colleague: Nah. SOCO want to see me. You know that kid I pulled up?

Desk sergeant: What, for twocking?

Colleague: Yeah, him. Well, he reckons it weren't him. An ARV was in the area and they saw an older guy driving the car earlier. Kid reckons it was his old man.

Focus for development: Spoken genres in everyday contexts

We tend to think of everyday talk as being unplanned, but many types of talk follow routines. For example, a boy chatting up a girl for the first time is likely to start by saying 'Hi', not 'Do you want to go out with me?'

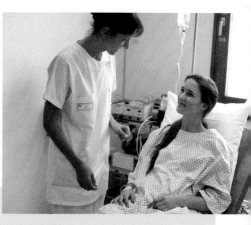

ACTIVITY

- Choose one of these everyday situations to explore: a hospital or a school.
- List the different types of talk that might happen in the situation and then make notes about each in a grid like the one for 'Talk in School' below.

Situation	Speakers	Content / Purpose	Conventions of talk in this situation
First-aid room	First aider and pupil	Find out why pupil is there Comforting sick pupil	Questions from first-aider Single word/short responses from pupil
Assembly	Head of Year	Give out information	Addressed to whole group – 'you' means the year...

ASSESSMENT FOCUS

Using your research about talk in a school or hospital, write the opening to a spoken language study. Start by introducing the range of speakers and the talk that takes place there to give a flavour of how people speak.
For example:

> A police station is a melting-pot of different dialogues, conversations and situations. In it, you will hear chatty, informal conversations between friends and colleagues, as well as highly-patterned routines such as phone enquiries.

A student writes…

Couldn't I just watch Holby City or Waterloo Road to learn about speech in these situations?

Answer…

In fact, writers of these television series are keen observers of 'talk', but they often exaggerate and, unlike in real speech, there are few hesitations or repetitions in these scripts.

Remember

- **Comment on the range of speech situations.**
- **Explain how these different situations affect the structures of talk and show the speakers' attitudes.**

Multi-modal talk

**Learning
objective**

- *To understand
  what multi-modal
  talk is and how it
  differs from other
  forms of speech.*

What is multi-modal talk?

- The term 'multi-modal' refers to the many (multi) different ways (modes) through which we can express ourselves in talk. This topic asks you to think particularly about the new modes of talk offered by recent technology, such as mobile phones and the internet.

ACTIVITY

Discuss with a partner:

- Why do we choose to call the sorts of communication that take place on social networking sites and in other digital contexts, 'talk' or 'chat'? After all, in most cases we are actually writing, not talking!
- Does this 'talk' have more in common with speech or other writing that you do?

Now look at this text message from a university student to his mother and write answers to the questions below.

> From: SAM
> Yeh got it thanx pressie is gr8
> c u 2moro luv 2 dad

- How does the content different from a letter a son might send home from university?
- How is this text more like chat than a written letter?

ACTIVITY

In pairs, role-play a conversation between a son phoning his dad to check his birthday present has arrived. Begin…

> **Son**: Hi Dad, it's Adam. Happy birthday!
> **Dad**: Thanks.
> **Son**: Did you get my pressie?

Then discuss:

- What does the spoken talk have that the 'text talk' doesn't?
- Can you 'hear' the tone of what is said in a text? What features of text talk help with this? (Think of symbols and words like 'lol.')

Focus for development: Talking the talk

Here are a few terms you might find useful when discussing 'text talk'.

Term	Meaning	Example
interactive	Where the medium or user responds to input.	'The interactive site updated itself in response to my comments.'
medium	The means or place through which communication happens.	'I used the medium of a networking site to contact friends.'
community	Group of people with shared interests.	'As a community all interested in the same band, we read and responded to his tweets after the show.'

ACTIVITY

In groups, share ideas about your use of technology. Use these questions to help you.

- Who do you talk to most using technology? What do you talk about?
- How often is the talk 'useful' (for example, arranging to meet); how often is it just to entertain each other or keep in touch?
- Are there special words and phrases that you only use when texting or messaging?

ASSESSMENT FOCUS

Write two paragraphs:

- one explaining some of the particular features of text language, including yours, and how you use it
- one discussing whether texting is closer to real talk or a written letter.

Remember

- Many terms used for written texts also apply to spoken ones, such as 'audience' 'purpose', 'content' and 'form'.
- Make sure you use the words or phrases particular to multi-modal communication where they are needed, such as 'user', 'community' and 'site'.

Online conversations

Why is learning about multi-modal and multi-voice talk important?

When several voices become involved in multi-modal speech, for example in a chat room, the talk gets more complex and can be harder to follow. Comparing different types of multi-modal talk can reveal interesting things about how you use technology to talk to one or more people.

ACTIVITY

Discuss in a group:

- Where do you use each of these forms of multi-modal talk: email, texting, msn, social network sites, chat rooms?
- Who do you use each of these forms with: individuals, groups, friends, school/work links, family?

Produce a grid like the one below to record your group's views.

Write 'yes', 'no' or 'less so' to complete columns 2–5. In column 6 choose one of the three options.

	Where used		Who with			
	More at home	More on the move	Friends	Family	School/ Work	Groups, individuals or both (please specify which)
Email						
Texting						
MSN						
Social network sites						
Chat rooms						

Why are some forms better suited to different types of talk than others?

Focus for development:
Exploring group multi-modal talk

Multi-modal talk gets more complicated when a range of voices is involved.

ACTIVITY

Look at this example of online chat sequence in response to an album release by Leona Lewis.

Aleyshaa4

Last album sold millions howcan you say that? theyre both great and this one evn better!!! BEST of luck Leona your album sounds amazin

Cally9112

STOP CRYING YOUR HEART OUT!! AMAZING

ADY5a (58 minutes ago) Show Hide

Reply   0

umm someone down said her last album has variety? O.o lol its pop tune after pop tune xD Tthis album has variety, It has rock driven songs, r&b, ballads, and uptempo. this is variety :} and it sounds really nice tbh,

MKY33(1 hour ago) Show Hide

Reply   0

No one can say she can't sing... (apart from miserable youtube pests)... Pure British diva... Goes to show, what London can do one of the Biggest talents in the world...

Pollypc67 (1 hour ago) Show Hide

Reply   0

wow love her version of stop crying your heart out . could be big as run xx

jann76 1 hour ago) Show Hide

Reply   0

Aleyshaa4

"I got you" or "Outta my head" should be her next single!!!! Like last album lots of vAriety just great songs
(1 hour ago) Show Hide

Discuss and take notes in a group:

- How is this talk different from normal/offline chat or writing?
- What is the general subject of the 'conversation'?
- How do specific contributors respond to others?
- What do you notice about the order of the conversation?
- Is it easy or hard to follow and take part in the conversation?

ASSESSMENT FOCUS

Using the notes from your discussion, write your views on

- how online chat is different from real talk
- how the technology influences the language of the conversation.

Remember

- **Find suitable research or source material for the talk area you choose to explore.**
- **Use key terms in your analysis, explaining whether examples link to 'language variation and change', 'adapting spoken language' or 'different contexts'.**

Grade Booster

Extended Assessment Task

Select a typical genre of speech from this list:

- a radio phone-in programme with an agony-aunt
- a sports coach giving a half-time team talk
- a receptionist at a hotel welcoming guests.

Write an analysis of the sort of talk that takes place, commenting in particular on

- the status (or power) of the speaker(s)
- the typical speech conventions (for example, the kinds of vocabulary, set phrases or patterns of speech which are used).

Evaluation – What have you learned?

With a partner, use the grade checklist below to evaluate your work on the Extended Assessment Task.

C
- I can make clear points about the ways people speak in my chosen context.
- I can make some reference to the attitudes shown by the speakers and the conventions of the genre.
- I can begin to analyse how speech is used for specific purposes, reflect on features found in my data and can begin to analyse issues arising from attitudes to the way people speak.

D
- I can describe some situations in which speech has patterns or conventions, and explain some of its features.
- I can explain how language is used in my chosen context and examine some features found in my data.
- I can also write about some issues arising from the way people react to varieties of spoken language.

E
- I can describe some situations in which speech has patterns or conventions.
- I can attempt to explain how language is used in certain circumstances.
- I can write about my spoken language data and attempt to comment on how the public reacts to different kinds of spoken language.

You may need to go back and look at the relevant pages from this section again.

Controlled Assessment Preparation
Spoken Language Study

Introduction

In this section you will

- find out the requirements of the Controlled Assessment task for Unit 3 Section C: Studying Spoken Language
- read, analyse and respond to three sample answers by different candidates
- plan and write your own answer to a sample question
- evaluate and assess your answer and the progress you have made.

Why is exam preparation like this important?

- If you know exactly what you need to do, you will feel more confident when you take part in the Controlled Assessment.
- Looking at sample answers by other students will help you see what you need to do to improve your own work.
- Planning and writing a full sample task response will give you a clear sense of what you have learned so far.

Key Information

Unit 3 Section C is 'Studying Spoken Language'.

- The controlled part of the task will last between **2 and 3 hours**, and is worth **20 marks**.
- It is worth **10%** of your overall English Language GCSE mark.

The Controlled Assessment task

- You have to complete **one** written task.
- Your single task will be chosen from the three topic areas:
  - Social attitudes to spoken language
  - Spoken genres
  - Multi-modal talk.
- You will write between **800 and 1000** words.
- You will choose, or be provided with, a choice of tasks to respond to from the three topic areas.
- You will then produce a piece of writing on Spoken Language that involves analysing source material and data on your chosen topic and drawing some conclusions based on your evidence.
- The task will be written up in 'controlled conditions', in the exam room or in your own classroom over a period of up to 3 hours.

Here are some example questions based on the three task areas set by the exam board.

• **Social attitudes to spoken language** Reflect on some aspects of your own personal talk (idiolect) perhaps including criticisms made of it by adults.
• **Spoken genres** Investigate a type of media talk, such as sports commentary, celebrity or news interviews, or game-show presentation.
• **Multi-modal talk** What devices do people use to be brief when messaging or texting? How does this relate to the way we speak?

The Assessment

The assessment objective for this unit (A02) states that you must be able to do the following:

- Understand variations in spoken language, explaining why language changes in relation to contexts.
- Evaluate the impact of spoken language choices in your own and others' use.

Some of the key differences between a Grade D and a Grade C are as follows:

Grade D candidates	*See example on pages 265–266*
• show some awareness of how they and others use and adapt language for different situations • show some understanding of significant features found in some spoken language data and resources (for example, transcripts) • show understanding of and explore some public attitudes to spoken language.	

Grade C candidates	*See example on pages 267+269*
• give a clear explanation of how they and others use and adapt spoken language for specific purposes • begin to analyse a range of key features found in some spoken language data or sources (for example, transcripts) • begin to analyse some of the issues arising from public attitudes to spoken language.	

Exploring Sample Responses

ACTIVITY

Read the extract below from a response to this task on social attitudes to spoken language.

> *Reflect on some aspects of your own personal talk (idiolect) perhaps including criticisms made of it by adults.*

As you read it, think about these key elements an examiner would look for:

- how well the candidate has focused on his/her own talk and that of others
- whether he/she has addressed any key features of spoken language
- how well he/she has explained attitudes and given appropriate examples.

Example 1: Social attitudes to spoken language

Me, my parents and grandparents: part one

I come from south east London so I don't have an accent. I think I get my way of speaking from my dad and mum. They were both born in London near where we live so I think I just grew up to speak like them.

Some people think that because we come from London we would use Cockney rhyming slang, like 'apples and pears' for 'stairs' but actually we don't. To be a Cockney you have to come from the East End and some people say that you must be born 'within the sound of Bow Bells' to be a Cockney. I wasn't so that's why I don't speak Cockney.

The main difference between me and my parents is my age. Me and my mates use all sorts of language like when we are chatting. This comes, probably a lot at least, from using mobiles or the net. Like we use different names for mates, such as my mate 'Danny' is called 'Dammy' cos that's what was typed into text on screen, which was probably a mistake but now we all call him that. Even my mum and dad call him 'Dammy'.

However, my mum and dad do get all upset when I speak. Sometimes I use words like 'blood' to mean 'mate'. This comes from street language like rap and urban music and stuff like that. But I *don't mean it seriously like I'm from the streets, a gangsta or something, I just mean I like using it. It's fun. But my parents don't like it. They say, 'why can't you speak properly?' but for me it's just the way I speak with my friends. They also say I speak too quick and mumble, use 'like' and 'um' all the time, but I know it's not how to speak when I am in posh serious situations, like jobs or interviews.*

My grandad says 'Crikey!' when he's cross, which I don't say and my gran uses posh words when we are laying the table for tea, but I just say 'put the stuff out'. I did an interview with them, and they talked about lots of words and phrases that aren't used anymore, like 'courting' to mean 'seeing someone'. Another thing is my mum and dad don't understand what 'got with' means (which I use) as they used to 'get off' with someone. It all means the same really!

Examiner feedback

The candidate has answered the task set and has tried to explain some particular personal uses of language and how they differ from parents and grandparents. However, some comments are made (such as the 'Dammy' example) without really explaining how this happened. There also could have been an example of the 'posh words' his grandmother uses. He does refer to some source material, the recording of his grandparents speaking, and he begins to comment on language features such as phrases that have changed over time, but without any real depth or detail.

Suggested grade: D

ACTIVITY

Read the extract opposite from a response to this task on spoken genres:

> *Investigate a type of media talk, such as sports commentary, celebrity or news interviews, or game-show presentation.*

Looking carefully at the annotations, decide how it is an improvement on Example 1.

Example 2: Spoken genres

Sports commentary: Part one, tennis match

For preparation for the task I looked at an extract from the transcript of the Federer/Roddick Wimbledon final commentary and also listened to it.

One of the things about a sports commentary is that **the vocabulary is specific and the audience know what it means**. For example, words and phrases like 'passing shot' aren't explained by the commentator or expert, they are just said right out there and then. They know because the audience are already interested in tennis that these words are understood. This means that the **context affects what is said**. For example, if I started talking to my baby brother and used terms like 'lob' or 'drop-volley' **he wouldn't understand.**

Some features of spoken language can be seen in the transcript. The first is that often the commentators don't speak in full sentences, so we have **the commentator saying, 'Wonderful smash!' (line 22),** which adds to the atmosphere. But cos this is on TV, we don't get running commentary like on radio. I mean that on radio, because listeners can't see the actual match, the commentator has to describe every shot, like:

> C: Serve down the centre, good return by Roddick but Federer down the line, back by Roddick … and ooohh Federer with a smash down the centre!

However there are other language features in the commentary. You always get the commentator asking the 'expert' what he or she thinks. These will be usually connected to the whole **category** of words for tennis. This means that there are expected things or ways of speaking we would hear in a tennis commentary, such as:

> 'He's really pumped-up now, isn't he?' (line 48)

Phrases like **'pumped-up', 'belting the ball'** (line 49) and 'stay focused' (line 50) are common to sports reports. This is how we can recognise them if we hear them.

These are **quite informal** sometimes too, but they work very well as a commentary.

Good point which is then explained

Reference to the context links to the assessment objective

Good point but actually confuses context with age and speech development

Detailed analysis of data

Not quite the right term. 'Register' or 'field' might be better

Good examples to back point up

Good point but taking discussion in a new direction; needs more

Examiner feedback

The candidate explains some of the key features of a sports commentary and supports their views with some well-chosen examples. Words like 'vocabulary' and 'audience' add to the professional sound of the response but some terms specific to spoken language would make this more analytical and focused. The candidate starts to look at difference in context, referring to a baby-brother, but the point is not developed. All in all, this extract shows a good awareness of the issues but without ever really engaging with them in detail.

Suggested grade: C

ACTIVITY

The examiner's comments draw attention to the candidate's focus on how a baby brother wouldn't understand the tennis terms.

Write two paragraphs in which you compare your language now with how a five year-old speaks.

- What is different?
- Why do you think this is?

ACTIVITY

Read the extract on the page opposite from a response to this multi-modal talk task:

> **What devices do people use to be brief when messaging or texting? How does this relate to the way we speak?**

As you read it, make notes about
- how well the candidate has addressed the focus of the task
- examples of professional language related to speech and talk
- whether there are any examples of detailed analysis
- any areas that are not fully explored.

Example 3: Multi-modal talk

Part one: text and talk, young people and old

The actual object – the mobile phone – can be said to limit what the user can do; by this I mean that you tend to type what you can see on the screen or at most two screens, because your main aim is to get in touch really quickly with friends. In the examples I researched, I noted things like abbreviations which use letters, or letters and numbers can be seen, such as 'lol' (laugh out loud) '4eva' 'forever' and 'omg' 'oh my god'.

Or even where symbols replace things, for example '?' meaning 'I don't understand', or 'why?' The funny thing is that we now use these short text letters when we are speaking sometimes, but we say 'lol' like 'loll', a word, not 'l-o-l' separate letters. Again it's because it's shorter.

However I also found out some users used hardly any shortenings. They also said (some of them) that they didn't particularly think about who they were texting when they texted, except if they were asking someone out or stuff like that, but like they texted in the same way to their gran as their friends. This might mean they also speak to their gran in the same way, but I doubt it!

Clearly, texting does reflect much of the way that teenagers talk. So, we use little short expressions like 'I went, like, hello?' instead of 'I told her she must be joking!' These are often Americanisms that come from TV, that we have imported to this country through popular programmes.

So you could say we are bad at expressing ourselves. In fact, older people may think it makes us sound stupid, even uneducated, but teenagers know that if we didn't use the right language with our groups we would be seen as outsiders. But it isn't just about that. My gran actually uses texting really well and she has learned all about how to use abbreviations – though not the rude ones! She likes using them because she can send messages quickly when she would normally take ages to type out all the words one by one.

You could say texting has had quite a big effect on how we speak but whether it has had more influence than other things is another matter. For example, TV, film, video games and music have all had a big impact, too.

Examiner feedback

This is a reasonably detailed response about a complex area. The examples are explained quite well, although the candidate only gives a small range of examples and doesn't really explore why some users use shortenings but not others. The language used is sometimes professional and there is occasional analysis, though it remains quite personal and basic without much wider comment or overview of language change – for example, with the influence of Americanisms touched on only very briefly. The end of the extract too, goes a little bit away from the task set but could open up interesting areas. Still, a lot of ground is covered in a short time.

Suggested grade: C

EXTENDED PRACTICE TASK

Social attitudes to spoken language

Reflect on some aspects of the personal talk (idiolect) of someone you are familiar with (for example your form teacher or a television presenter), commenting on

- similarities and differences in how you both speak
- attitudes to your, and your chosen person's, way of speaking.

If you only do five things…

1 Listen carefully to the different forms of spoken language used around you – from your friends to radio DJs to politicians. Try to recognise the features of how they speak. It will feed positively into what you eventually write.

2 When you are preparing for a Controlled Assessment, how successful you are will depend upon the quality of your data, so carry out any research activities carefully.

3 Plan what you are intending to write because it is almost certain to improve the quality of the mark you receive. Set down your findings logically: open with a statement of what you are examining and why, and come to a definite conclusion at the end.

4 When you are writing, always give examples, analyse or explain them and use key terminology whenever possible. Try to be as detailed in your explanation as possible. A close analysis of a slightly shorter extract or set of findings is likely to lead to a higher grade than a very general or basic examination.

5 Don't forget that
   - writing about social attitudes to spoken language means you need to show the link between what people say and how they are seen by others
   - responses to spoken genres are likely to deal in detail with the conventions of how people speak within contexts and situations
   - writing about multi-modal talk will mean having to respond analytically to the way we 'talk' to each other electronically – it will not be enough to simply pick out significant features.

ACKNOWLEDGEMENTS

The publishers gratefully acknowledge the permission granted to reproduce the copyright material in this book. While every effort has been made to trace and contact copyright holders, where this has not been possible the publishers will be pleased to make the necessary arrangements at the first opportunity.

Chapter 1 p7 'Nobody's Safe' article from *Reveal Magazine* 2009 published by Nat Mags; p8 Mykonos extract from *The Greek Islands: Eyewitness Travel Guide* published by Dorling Kindersley; p9 'After the rain, here comes The Sun' *The Sun*, 25 November, 2009 © NI Syndications. Reprinted with permission; p10 'Bolt 100m Record is beaten by a cheetah' *Metro*, 11th September, 2009. Reprinted with permission of Solo Syndication; p11 Potato Lovers Hate Waste advert. Reprinted with kind permission of WRAP www.wrap.org.uk; p12 screenshot from Club 18-30 website. Reprinted with kind permission of Thomas Cook Group PLC; p13 extract from a leaflet for Best Western Wroxton House Hotel, Banbury, Oxfordshire. Reprinted with kind permission; p15 extract from 'Roman Pavlyuchenko and Jermain Defoe leave it late to break Burnley hearts' by Henry Winter, 21 January, 2009 www.telegraph.co.uk. Reprinted with permission; p17 Dolland & Aitchison leaflet (this leaflet is out of date). Reproduced with kind permission of Boots Opticians; p18 short extracts from *Don'ts For Husbands* by Blanche Ebbutt, A & C Black 2007. Reprinted with permission; p19 article by Linda Robson from *Bella Magazine* 2009 published by Bauer; p20 'Arctic Gets Hotter' from the *Daily Mirror*, 5th September, 2009 pg 31. Reprinted with permission of Mirrorpix; p25 The Herta magazine ad is reproduced with the kind permission of Societe des Produits Nestle S. A.; p26 extract courtesy of *The Times,* 29 July 2009 © NI Syndications; p29-30 article from *Wakefield Express* 2009; p33 article by Richard White from *The Sun* Nov 2009; p34-35 extract and book cover image from *The Bookseller of Kabul* by Asne Seierstad published by Virago, part of Little Brown; p37 'Have you got money flu?' *Cosmopolitan*, January 2008. Reprinted with permission of The National Magazine Company; p39 'Shoptalk, Glamazon? I think not' *Mirror*, 25th November, 2009. Reprinted with permission; p40 cover of Leeds United Programme 2009 published by Leeds United; p41 Cover of *Sky Sports Magazine* October 2009. Reprinted with permission; p44 SPC Nature's Finest advert. Reprinted with permission of SPC Ardmona Operations Limited, Australia; p47 short extract from 'The dog that nearly drowned' from THE LONG HARD ROAD by Ron Hill, Ron Hill Sports Ltd 1981. Copyright © Ron Hill. Reprinted with kind permission of the author; p48 article from Walk on the Wild Side by James Parry from *Daily Express* 2009; p49 Rainforest SOS advert. Reprinted with permission of The Prince's Rainforests Project; **Chapter 2** p76 reproduced from charity leaflet with the permission of Save the Children UK © All rights reserved; p77 charity leaflet courtesy of Age Concern; p92 short extracts from 'To Groom or not to groom' by Kathy Lette, *Good Housekeeping*, August 2009. This was written by Kathy Lette, author of ten best-selling novels. Reprinted with permission; **Chapters 3 and 4** pp164, 171, 173, 187, 189 - extracts from *Of Mice and Men* by John Steinbeck published by Penguin Books 2000 Copyright © John Steinbeck 1937, 1965. Reprinted with permission of Penguin Books and Curtis Brown Limited; pp171, 172 extracts from *Martyn Pig* by Kevin Brooks, published by The Chicken House. Copyright © Kevin Brooks, 2002. Reprinted with permission; p174 extract from 'The River God' by Stevie Smith published by Faber & Faber; p175 'Medusa' by Carol Ann Duffy, from THE WORLD'S WIFE by Carol Ann Duffy published by Macmillan. Reprinted with permission; p177 extract from 'Mirror' by Sylvia Plath published by Faber and Faber; pp178, 179, 180, 185, 192 short extracts from 'The Darkness Out There' by Penelope Lively from A PACK OF CARDS published by Penguin. Reprinted with permission of David Higham Associates; p190 extract from *Touching the Void* by Joe Simpson published by Vintage Classics, part of Random House; p191 extract from *Lord of the Flies* by William Golding published by Faber & Faber; **Chapter 5** p207 extract from 'The Twelve Days of Christmas' by Carol Ann Duffy written for the *Radio Times*; p212 extract from Leila Aboulela 'Something Old Something New' from *Scottish Girls About Town* published by Pocket Books; **Chapter 6** p244 and 245 extracts courtesy of The British Library from www.bl.uk. Reprinted with permission; p252-253 -'Tesco's old timers get yoof slang pamphlet' by Lester Haines, 30th May, 2007. Reprinted with kind permission.

The publishers would like to thanks the following for permission to reproduce pictures in these pages:

Alamy: pp30, 60, 65, 71, 78, 93, 110, 114, 131, 143, 154tl, 154bl, 168, 238, 265; **Barcroft Media**: p10; **BBC**: pp134, 156ct, 255 (photographer Anthony Todd); **Bridgeman Art Library**: p197 'Three Witches', Fuseli, Henry (Fussli, Johann Heinrich, 1741-1825). Collection of the Royal Shakespeare Theatre / The Bridgeman Art Library; **Corbis**: p212; **Getty**: pp19, 20, 26, 48cl, 62, 116, 136, 145, 149, 163, 208, 209, 213, 221, 224, 234, 242cr, 244bl, 247; **Hat Trick Productions Ltd**: p251; **iStockphoto**: pp8c, 27, 32, 48tr, 48cr, 48br, 66, 67, 70, 72, 73, 80, 81, 84, 85, 89cl, 89br, 90, 91, 93, 94, 95, 97, 98, 99, 101, 106, 112, 123, 125, 128, 129, 135, 137, 138, 140, 152bl, 152cl, 152cr, 152r, 155, 171, 174, 177, 179, 180, 185, 190, 191, 204, 216, 218tl, 218cl, 218bl, 220l, 220c, 220r, 226, 228, 236, 240, 242cl, 244cl, 252, 258, 269; **Mirrorpix**: p39; **Movie Store Collection**: pp164, 186, 201; **North News and Pictures**: p9cl; **News Team International**: p9tr; **PA Photos**: pp9br, 120, 122, 207; **Photolibrary**: pp4, 64, 74; **Rex Features**: pp10 (Timo Jaakonaho),15 (Back Page Images), 18 (Courtesy Everett Collection), 21 (Kelly Hancock/UCF), 29 (Steve Wood), 35 (Bart Dinger), 92, 117 (NBCU PhotoBank), 126 (Steve Hill), 127 (Sipa Press), 148 (c.20thC.Fox/Everett), 151tr, 151cl (David Fisher), 151cr (Nicolas Khayat/Enigma), 156cb (Brian J. Ritchie), 161 (Image Source), 170 (Alastair Muir), 211 (Shout), 225 (Jeff Blackler), 253 (Owen Sweeney), 254 (Giuliano Bevilacqua), 257 (Burger/Phanie), 261 (Action Press), 267 (Sipa Press); **Ronald Grant Archive**: pp173, 189; **Royal Shakespeare Company**: p152 (c. Reg Wilson); **Shutterstock**: p8bl; **TalkbackThames Television**: p256 (photographer Alan Peebles).